Engaging Political Philosophy

Engaging Political Philosophy

From Hobbes to Rawls

Andrew Levine

First published 2002

2 4 6 8 10 9 7 5 3 1

Blackwell Publishers Inc
350 Main Street
Malden, Massachusetts 02148
USA

Blackwell Publishers Ltd
108 Cowley Road
Oxford OX4 1JF
UK

Library of Congress Cataloging-in-Publication Data has been applied for.

ISBN 0–631–22228–6 (hardback); 0–631–22229–4 (paperback)

British Library Cataloguing in Publication Data

A CIP catalogue record for this book is available from the British Library.

Typeset in 10.5 on 12.5 pt Sabon
by Ace Filmsetting Ltd, Frome, Somerset
Printed in Great Britain by MPG Books Ltd, Bodmin, Cornwall

This book is printed on acid-free paper.

Contents

Acknowledgments

These essays have grown out of years of working in, writing about, and teaching political philosophy. For their help in making what I have to say about the authors discussed here accessible to students encountering this material for the first time, I would like especially to thank Robin Andreasen, David Estlund, Thomas Hedemann, Sarah Marchand, Laura Osinski, Lori Saxe, and Paul Warren. I am grateful to David Estlund for his careful and penetrating criticisms of the Rawls chapter (chapter 5). Harry Brighouse gave me useful advice on that chapter as well. My views about modern political philosophy owe a great deal to my first encounters with it as a student of Professor Robert Paul Wolff, Jr. at Columbia University in the 1960s. Readers who know Wolff's work will recognize his influence in the pages that follow – especially in the chapters on Rousseau (chapter 2) and Mill (chapter 4), and on the portion of the Marx chapter (chapter 6) devoted to Marx's early work. From Wolff, too, I learned that an introduction to social and political philosophy can be a serious intervention into that discipline, and that an historically focused introduction is perhaps the soundest route to the heart of the subject.

Introduction

The essays that follow engage aspects of the political philosophies of Thomas Hobbes, Jean-Jacques Rousseau, John Locke, John Stuart Mill, John Rawls, and Karl Marx. They are intended both for readers who are encountering the work of these philosophers for the first time, and for readers who have read them before, perhaps many times. Some of the positions I defend differ from and even conflict with standard accounts of these authors' views. But I do endeavor to convey a sense of what the usual understandings are, even as I advance contentious claims of my own. This book can therefore serve as an introduction to modern political philosophy. It can be read on its own, but it is better read in conjunction with the texts it discusses. This recommendation applies especially to readers who are new to the field. At the end of this chapter, I provide a list of those texts.

These essays do not provide anything like a comprehensive history of modern political philosophy, or even a partial history, refracted through the work of six of its master thinkers. They offer, instead, philosophical investigations of some of these thinkers' ideas; with special attention paid to views of theirs that reveal the scope and limits of the philosophical tradition they did so much to forge. I will, however, advance a few very general historical claims – in this Introduction and also at a number of points in the chapters that follow. I do so in order to provide a framework for discussing some of the ideas that will be our principal concern. From an historical point of view, the story I tell is too abstract to pass muster. Even so, I would submit that it is generally sound. My aim, however, is not so much to defend it as to use it to shed light on positions our authors take.

The ensuing discussions meander through a variety of topics and themes, propelled along by the texts they discuss. The later essays also engage issues raised in the essays that precede them. Wherever possible, I have endeavored to compare and contrast the positions in play. Doing so, helps to underscore what is at stake in holding these views. However, there is an obvious danger in treating our six philosophers as if they were participants in a single, unfolding "conversation." Philosophers, like everyone else, are creatures of their time and place. It can be misleading, therefore, to ignore the context within which philosophical positions arise. On the other hand, there is no doubt that our authors knew a great deal about the history of political philosophy, and that whatever else was of concern to them, they were intent on intervening into discussions shaped, in part, by the interventions of their predecessors. In at least some instances, therefore, it is not only instructive but also fair, from an historical point of view, to present the views of the later authors on our list as if they were indeed engaging in a dialogue with those who came before them. In doing so, however, care must be taken not to distort positions or arguments for the sake of some philosophical or pedagogical point. In comparing and contrasting the positions our authors advance, I have tried to observe this caution.

Because the connections between the essays that follow are more thematic than historical, I have found it appropriate, in two instances, to discuss the figures in question out of chronological order. Thus Locke (1632–1704) follows Rousseau (1712–78), and Marx (1818–83) follows not only his contemporary, Mill (1806–73), but also Rawls (1921–). As will emerge, the figure whose work provides the point of departure for modern political philosophy is Hobbes. The reader should understand, though, that Hobbes's preeminence has do with conceptual affinities joining his innovations in political thought to subsequent work. I make no claims about the extent to which our other five authors or political philosophers generally concerned themselves directly with Hobbes's views. In any case, only the Hobbes essay, chapter 1, is entirely free-standing; the others refer back to the essays that precede them. Even so, each essay can be read without having read the others. This is especially true of the essays on Marx (chapter 6) and Rawls (chapter 5). Whoever does read these essays out of turn, however, may miss something of the point(s) being made. This disadvantage can be mitigated by also reading chapter 1. The Hobbes essay is the main point of reference for all the others.

What is Political Philosophy?

In ordinary speech and also in some more formal contexts, the term "philosophy" designates a comprehensive set of beliefs about ourselves, our relations with others, our being in the world, and any of a number of other, less general, concerns. However, this usage invites misunderstanding, especially when dealing with philosophers like our six. Let us say, then, that a philosophy is better viewed as the product of something one *does,* philosophizing, than as a collection of beliefs. To do philosophy is to try to make sense of aspects of human experience by identifying puzzlements, formulating them in ways that make their resolution tractable, and then, but only then, arriving at positions that address the questions philosophizing leads us to ask.

Puzzlements that give rise to activity of this sort are mainly *conceptual* in nature. When we already know what sort of discovery would lay our puzzlement to rest, there is seldom any need for philosophical activity. But there is philosophizing to be done when the conceptual resources available to us seem inadequate, when we are unclear about what would count as an answer to questions we are not quite sure how to formulate. In these circumstances, new information will not help. What is required instead is more fundamental – a rethinking of our conceptual moorings, a reconceptualization of our concerns.

Some philosophical questions appear to have a timeless quality. The puzzlement they articulate seems so universal and the obstacles in the way of dissipating that puzzlement seem so intractable that they may always be with us. Introductory philosophy courses are typically organized around questions of this kind. They investigate *problems* – the existence of God, the relation between minds and bodies, the problem of free will, the nature of the good, and so on. Perhaps these questions really are timeless. But however this may be, in political philosophy, few, if any, problems even appear to have a timeless character. The concerns of political philosophers are too connected to transitory real world social and political phenomena to assume such an aspect. Sometimes, however, political philosophers ignore this fact – a consequence, I would venture, of the habits of mind they have internalized, the "professional deformations" of the philosophy profession. When they do, misunderstandings inevitably follow. In dealing with our six authors, therefore, it is important not to lose sight of how their views are historically situated. To fail to do so is to risk misconstruing their positions and the rationales that support them.

The fact that the problems of political philosophy are ineluctably historical invites the construction of an historical narrative that is sufficiently rich to make sense of the emergence and subsequent career of these problems. As I have said, I will largely resist this invitation. But some attention must be paid to the rise and subsidence of the puzzlements to which the philosophical activity of our six authors responds. Real world political and social transformations have played a crucial role in shaping their work, and indeed in the making of modern political philosophy generally. Thus I would maintain that the rise of the nation state in the seventeenth and eighteenth centuries made problems pertaining to political authority and political obligation central to political philosophy, and that the consolidation of this historically particular kind of political entity in the nineteenth and twentieth centuries caused attention to these issues to wane. I would contend too that, in the eighteenth and nineteenth centuries, as the state form of political organization came to seem less puzzling, questions pertaining to the rightful limits, if any, of political authority became Topic A. And I would suggest, finally, that the struggles of the working class and others for their rightful place in the social order throughout the nineteenth and twentieth centuries made the problem of justice a central philosophical concern.

In general, conceptual puzzlements of the sort that call for philosophical responses arise in consequence of changes that upset received ways of thinking – not, of course, in everyone's mind but in the minds of the comparatively few far-sighted thinkers who recognize the implications of these changes. Thus one would expect that there would not be much philosophical activity in societies in which events seldom, if ever, threaten traditional understandings, societies in which conceptual moorings are effectively (though, perhaps, irrationally) secure. Societies of this kind, "traditional" societies, have been the norm throughout human history. As expected, they have fostered very little philosophical activity. Members of traditional societies do, of course, have philosophies in the ordinary sense of the term. They have beliefs that help them make sense of lived experience. But traditional societies have few, if any philosophers in the sense in question here; few people who do philosophy.

My concern, in any case, is with Western philosophy, and indeed with only a fragment of its long past. In the West, the most important changes that have generated conceptual puzzlement and therefore philosophical activity have had to do with new knowledge and new ways of knowing. The development of Greek mathematics nearly twenty-five hundred years ago gave rise to a conceptual crisis out of which classical Greek philosophy – the philosophy of the pre-Socratics, Socrates, Plato and Aristotle –

emerged. This was the moment of the birth of Western philosophy. The rise of the new sciences of nature in the seventeenth century posed another great challenge to received ways of thinking. What is conventionally called "modern" philosophy, the philosophical movement that is conventionally said to have begun with Descartes and that continues to this day, was, in part, induced by this new way of apprehending nature. It is not surprising, therefore, that questions about what we can know and about what there is, epistemological and metaphysical questions, have been the principal concerns of Western philosophy throughout its history. Typically, issues pertaining to society and politics have played a more peripheral role, even when they arise in response to puzzlements generated by social and political transformations of momentous importance. This is why epistemology and metaphysics, not social and political philosophy, constitute Western philosophy's core. In this respect, Hobbes's example is illustrative. Even as he philosophized about politics and society, he was concerned to make his views accord with the vision and practice of the new sciences of nature, as he understood them. Hobbes wanted a theory of the state that would be systematically integrated into a more general, materialist account of being, a metaphysical stance that he thought the new sciences of nature made rationally compelling.

But Hobbes and other seventeenth- and eighteenth-century political thinkers were also responding to far-reaching transformations in European social and political life. This is not the place to dwell on the causes of these transformations. Evidently, technological development, what Marx would call the development of "productive forces," and the emerging capitalist organization of European society, a phenomenon Marx linked to the growth of productive forces, had much to do with the great transformations that brought modern political philosophy into being (see chapter 6). So too, as Rawls would insist, did the Protestant Reformation and the wars of religion that followed in its aftermath (see chapter 5). These larger historical themes will be broached, as necessary, in the pages that follow. For now, I would only call attention to two important historical phenomena that effectively transformed European civilization at the dawn of the modern age. They bear special mention at this point, before I undertake to discuss particular philosophers' views, because they have shaped the agenda of modern political philosophy decisively.

Great Transformations

The first of these phenomena is the rise of the modern state. Political authority itself, the right to compel compliance through the use or threat of force, is undoubtedly a universal of human social life. Few, if any, human groupings have persisted for very long without authority relations of some kind, relations that are properly political in the sense that they are ultimately coercive in nature. What was new in early modern Europe was the concentration of political authority into a single institutional nexus. In feudal Europe, authority relations were scattered and diffuse. This was the norm nearly everywhere else as well. To be sure, in the premodern period, empires of various sorts existed. Typically, they were large, sometimes very large. Where empires existed, hierarchically organized bureaucracies maintained a semblance of control over subject populations, aided by military garrisons loyal to the central authorities. This form of political organization was more common in Asia than in Europe – though, following the Roman example, Europe too had empires from time to time, even if, like the Holy Roman Empire, they existed more often in theory than in practice. But it was only with the rise of the state form of political organization that the right to compel compliance became fixed in a single, centrally controlled mechanism of administration and coercion.[1] Thus *sovereignty* in its distinctively modern sense, supreme authority over a given territory or population, emerged. Sovereignty was, at first, "incarnated" in individuals – indeed, in monarchs, as Hobbes supposed. After the English revolutions of the seventeenth century, parliamentary institutions assumed this role to some extent, at least in England; a fact registered in Locke's political philosophy. By Rousseau's time, a full-fledged notion of popular sovereignty, of the people themselves as sovereign, was widely intimated. Rousseau gave this idea theoretical expression. It would therefore be only slightly glib to say that the principal concern of each of these authors was to get sovereignty

[1]   Empires continued to exist, however, even in the less developed areas of Europe, though their political institutions came increasingly to resemble those of modern states. Even so, the Ottoman and Hapsburg Empires did not fall until after the First World War. That war and the Revolution it helped to foster also caused the demise of the Russian Empire – though it was immediately reborn, some would say, when the Soviet Union consolidated its hold over the non-Russian peoples whom the Czars had formerly ruled. But the Soviet Union was hardly an Empire in the traditional sense; it was, for all effective purposes, a modern state. In any case, by the last decade of the twentieth century, it too no longer existed.

right and then to justify it. Each of these political philosophers sought to develop a theory of this emerging authority relation. I will go on to suggest that none of them fully succeeded. But, as noted, the issue has waned as the state form of political organization, having become the norm, has come to seem less puzzling.

The second of the great transformations to which modern political philosophy was a response was more social than political. With the dissolution of feudal solidarities, the wearing away of the communal bonds that joined people together in premodern times – or, what comes to the same thing, with the emergence of economies organized mainly through exchange relations – the individual was born. Here too, Hobbes's example is telling. Hobbes's account of sovereignty takes for granted the *atomization* of social relations that resulted from feudal disintegration. His point of departure was what might be called *the atomic individual*. This use of "atomic" is, of course, metaphorical. But the description is apt. As remarked, a goal of Hobbes's was to develop a political philosophy joined systematically to a metaphysics that reflects the findings of modern science. Hobbes thought that the new sciences of nature implied a metaphysics relevantly similar to that of ancient Greek and Roman atomism. For the atomists, atoms, indivisible units of matter, were both the fundamental constituents of material things and also radically independent entities. The second atomist tenet was as important to Hobbes as the first. Everything that is essential to a particular atom is, in the atomist's view, in the atom itself. What an atom essentially is therefore has nothing to do with its relations with other atoms; it could be alone in the universe and still be the atom that it is. Of course, atoms do not, in fact, stand alone; they exist in multitudes and enter into a host of relations with other atoms. But these relations are always *external*; they never affect what philosophers would call the atom's "identity conditions." This was how Hobbes viewed human societies. For him, individuals, conceived apart from their relations with other individuals, provide the proper starting-point for thinking about social and political arrangements. These individuals are the radically independent, fundamental constituents of political life. In this respect, as in many others, Hobbes dramatized starkly what each of our authors, with the partial exception of Marx, assumed. Modern political philosophy, following Hobbes's lead, accords paramount importance to individuals and their interests, often to the exclusion of everything else.

Thus a necessary condition for the political philosophies of our six authors, including even Marx's, was the emergence of the individual. Needless to say, everyone everywhere has always recognized that human beings have distinct bodies and minds. But, until the modern period, this fact did not impinge on theories of social and political institutions in the way that it has after Hobbes. The fundamental constituents of premodern societies – families, clans, tribes and, in European feudal societies, relations based on ecclesiastical status and on fealty and other forms of *personal* loyalty – no longer serve as a basis for thinking about political arrangements. Their place has been taken over by the individual. Thus it has become part of the common sense of our intellectual culture that, for virtually all normative and explanatory purposes, individuals precede society. This way of thinking would have seemed strange, if not incomprehensible, to people in other times and places. But it is a core component of the underlying conceptual framework, the deep structure, of modern political thought.

The idea that political institutions are justified to the degree that they accord with individuals' interests is an assumption that all strains of modern political philosophy share. It plays a role in the thought of each of our authors – including Marx, who was more a critic of modern political philosophy than a practitioner of it, but whose reflections on politics nevertheless developed themes implicit in the work of several of the other philosophers discussed in this volume. Because it is so pervasive and because its implications are so far-reaching, it will be useful to think of this idea as a fixed point in modern political philosophy, an orientation that philosophers unconsciously assume. The idea that what matters exclusively are individuals and their interests has become so deeply entrenched that it is seldom expressly endorsed or even acknowledged. It functions instead as a guiding metaphor, a piece of imagery that different philosophers adapt in their own characteristic ways.

Since his use of this imagery was particularly striking, it is instructive, again, to remark on Hobbes's case. Hobbes was not only an atomic individualist. He was a Galilean atomist, intent on incorporating Galileo's notion of "inertia" into the atomist picture, along with Galileo's understanding of absolute space. Because atomic individuals, for Hobbes, are inertial entities, they remain (metaphorically) in motion until they are interfered with by the motion of other atomic individuals. Because they inhabit an absolute space, a space whose coordinates are determined prior to and apart from the entities that occupy it, the "position" of each atomic individuals is (metaphorically) independent of the positions of all other atomic individuals. For Hobbes, then, individuals are beings who pursue their ends independently and unrelentingly in a fixed but also confined area. Therefore, other individuals are, for them, either means for realizing their ends or obstacles in the way of pursuing them. What other individuals do matters to everyone. But other individuals are of no intrinsic importance to anyone. In this sense, atomic individuals, like the atoms of Hobbes's metaphysics, are radically on their own. However, because they coexist in the same space, they will frequently "collide" with one another as they proceed along their various paths. These collisions are impediments to natural motion. Less metaphorically, since Hobbes identified individuals' ends with their desires, they are impediments to desire satisfaction. Individuals therefore all want, as it were, to regulate these collisions and to dissipate their ill-effects. They all have an interest in coordinating their behaviors. In Hobbes's view, as we will see, this fact motivates the institution of sovereignty. We will find too that, for all their many differences, each of our other five philosophers, like nearly everyone else who has thought philosophically about politics after Hobbes, was, in this crucial respect, a Hobbesian.

There are, of course, a variety of ways that individuals' interests can matter. Some of these ways, all the important ones, will be encountered in the chapters that follow. We will find that our authors disagree about how to accord individuals' interests their due. They agree, however, that individuals' interests matter preeminently. This is, I submit, a distinctively modern thought. It is very different, for example, from supposing, as even the most astute political philosophers once did, that what matters preeminently for political philosophy is God's will, authoritatively revealed and interpreted. It is also different from supposing that what matters most is "natural law" or any other ideal order that is independent, logically, of individuals' interests.

This assumption is actually a composite of two distinct background positions – the individualism I have remarked upon, and the idea that political philosophy is, so to speak, interest-driven. In principle, there could be interest-driven accounts of political arrangements that are not individualistic in Hobbes' sense. At the present time, we seem to be witnessing the emergence of just such understandings, especially in multinational states without clear constitutional settlements. Thus it is sometimes said nowadays that, for some purposes, what matters fundamentally is the interests of particular communities within states rather than the interests of individuals within these communities. This thought is most commonly raised in debates around constitutional matters and is therefore typically expressed in terms of rights – as when it is claimed, for example, that (some) linguistic communities have language rights. Claims of this sort are not reducible to claims about individuals' rights. To say, for example, that the francophone community in Quebec has (or ought to have) a right to have the French language protected within Quebec and throughout Canada is not the same thing as to say that individual Quebeckers or Canadians ought to have the right to speak French. The latter, individualistic right is assured so long as neither Quebec nor Canada proscribe the speaking of French. On the other hand, the former right, for its implementation, requires the active intervention of some agency, the state presumably, to assure that French will be the dominant language in Quebec and an official language in the rest of Canada. Thus the francophone community in Quebec might be thought to have an interest that is irreducible to the interests of the individuals who comprise it. Similar claims have lately been made with respect to national self-determination, and to such diffuse interests as peace, economic development, and environmental integrity. Even more radical positions have been advanced by some environmentalists, again in the form of rights claims. Thus it has been said that plants and animals, individually or in groups, and even landscapes and other parts of nature have rights. In these instances, too, rights talk usually articulates claims about interests. But the interests are not those of Hobbesian individuals. They are not even interests of human beings. Political philosophies that acknowledge contentions of these kinds and that accord them normative force are appropriately described as interest-driven. But they are not individualistic in the Hobbesian sense.

It is conceivable and even likely that, in the future, these and other departures from the prevailing orthodoxy will become commonplace. Perhaps too, contemporary uses of the concept of rights and other devices of interest-driven normative political philosophies will someday seem more problematic than is now the case. If so, the deep structure that has shaped political philosophy for more than three hundred years will have changed profoundly. But political philosophy is not at that point yet. The possibility is nevertheless worth noting because it focuses attention on aspects of our authors' thinking that might otherwise seem too obvious to bear mention. With the exception again only of Marx, each of the philosophers considered here is of the old school. Each continues the tradition Hobbes began – softening the impact of his imagery, but never abandoning it or even modifying it enough to move political philosophy into a qualitatively less individualistic, less interest-driven space.

Neither are our authors ready to think about abandoning the state form of political organization; though Rawls's later work does finally take issue with traditional understandings of sovereignty. It is conceivable, however, that real world circumstances will, in time, render states too increasingly problematic – in practice and therefore, eventually, in theory as well. Then sub-state and super-state political arrangements will assume a more prominent place on the philosophical agenda. This is a likely prospect. The state was not always with us; there is no reason to think that it will permanently endure. I will return to this speculation in the chapter on Marx, and again in the Conclusion to this volume. But it should be noted, at the outset, that there is very little sense of this possibility in the work we will consider here. Even Marx's political theory, as it applies to the foreseeable future, is resolutely statist.

Continuities

I have so far emphasized how *discontinuities* in knowledge and in lived experience give rise to philosophical activity. But, in the political domain, there are important *continuities* too. The conviction that politics is a positive good for human beings and the competing view of politics as, at best, a necessary evil are both longstanding. They predate and also survive the epochal social transformations that gave rise to modern political philosophy. The idea that politics is an indispensable component of a fully human life and therefore a positive good was a conviction of Aristotle's and indeed of ancient Greek political thought generally. It will be convenient to call it the *classical* view. The idea that politics is a necessary evil dates back at least to the rise of Christian political theory in the fourth century AD, when Christianity became an official religion of the Roman Empire. I will therefore call it the *Christian* view. Hobbes was a Christian in this sense and so was Locke, though to a less extreme degree. Rousseau was not. By the nineteenth century, the difference between these very different conceptions of political life had become blurred. Thus one finds elements of both classical and Christian political theory in Mill's work and also in Rawls's. Marx, however, like Rousseau, stands in the classical tradition. It is fair to say that, on the whole, modern political philosophy has been more Christian than classical.

On the Christian view, in its pre-Hobbesian form, human beings are so corrupted by Original Sin that they are incapable, by their own efforts, of doing good for themselves or for each other; incapable of achieving the earthly excellence classical writers extolled. Rather, the good for humankind lies outside this world, in the world to come; and access to it depends entirely on unmerited grace. Were human beings left to their own devices, their lives would degenerate into a devastating "war of all against all." But this condition is contrary to God's will, as St. Augustine, the greatest of the Christian political philosophers, maintained.[2] It threatens to upset Providential design. God therefore established political institutions to save human beings from themselves. Fallen humanity cannot attain excellence through them. But, through their workings, God insures that order will prevail, thereby allowing providential design to unfold. To this end, repressive political institutions, mechanisms of coercion, are indispensable. Unless persons are made unfree to do what they want, the evil that lurks within them would engulf human society, undoing any semblance of peace.

It is instructive to think of the modern theory of the state as a secular variant of this ancient teaching. Needless to say, none of our authors is committed literally to the doctrine of Original Sin. But insofar as they are Hobbesians, they do think that human nature is such that its free expression would lead to a devastating war of all against all. This is a fate to be avoided if at all possible – not because it is contrary to what Providence requires, as in the original Christian conception, but because it is radically detrimental to individuals' interests. For a modern, however, no *deus ex machina* can save humankind. The secular version of Christian political theory has no place for divinely established institutional arrangements. If individuals want their interests served, they have only their own resources to deploy to this end. They themselves, not God, must concoct a remedy.

Hobbes, Rousseau, and Locke emphatically agree that individuals' interests are at risk when individuals are entirely free to act on their own desires. The problem for them, therefore, is to conceive a way in which individuals can make themselves unfree to do so, as their interests require. Rousseau put this thought to use ingeniously – in behalf of the classical conviction that political institutions are indispensable components of the good life for human beings. But Hobbes and, to a lesser degree, Locke and the liberals that followed them, including even Mill and Rawls, regard it as unfortunate, and therefore regard its "solution," the state, as an imposition upon humankind, an evil – albeit a necessary evil, in the sense that its absence would be even worse than its presence is. For St. Augustine, political institutions were simultaneously a punishment for Original Sin, but also, because they prevent a war of all against all, a (partial) remedy for its consequences. Modern political philosophers, because they are Hobbesian statists, share this conviction, whether they realize it or not. Even Rousseau, by endorsing a Hobbesian rationale for

---

[2]   St. Augustine's masterwork, containing the core of his political philosophy, was *The City of God* (New York: Random House, 1950).

sovereignty, participates in the consensus view. Thus a Christian sensibility pervades modern political philosophy, extending even into the thinking of its most classical exponent.

If there is a moral to be extracted from the chapters that follow, it is that political philosophers would do well to free themselves from the grip of Hobbesian statism, and to take a more classical turn. This is why Rousseau and Marx and also the later-day liberals, Mill and Rawls, to the (limited) extent that their thinking too is classical, emerge as the heroes of the story that runs through these pages. Hobbes and Locke are not exactly its villains. But they do seem to have led modern political philosophy into a kind of cul de sac. It is fruitless to speculate about the shape of things to come. Political philosophy's future, like its past, depends too much on what happens in the world at large. But it is not idle to hope that the secularized but still Christian intuitions that have shaped modern political philosophy so decisively will wane in importance, and that the political philosophy of the future will take greater sustenance in its classical roots.

The principal subject of the essays on Hobbes and Rousseau is the state and, more generally, political authority and political obligation. The essays on Locke and Mill focus mainly on liberalism, on authority's rightful limits. All of these issues are resumed in the essay on Rawls, where the main topic is justice, but where political legitimacy is also a prime concern. The chapter on Marx stands somewhat apart from this unfolding story. It does address many of the issues raised in the essays that precede it, though in the context of a "moment" in German intellectual and political history that will seem exotic to contemporary readers, but that must be grasped in order to convey Marx's ideas. This chapter also addresses the implications for political philosophy of some extra-philosophical theories of Marx's pertaining to social classes, the state, and history. This side of Marx's thought is eminently relevant to modern political philosophy. But it is not exactly of a piece with it. It is therefore appropriate that the essay on Marx should stand apart from the rest, and that it should come after the liberals have had their say.

The following texts are discussed directly or indirectly in the essays that follow. This is a bare-bones list. Bibliographical references are provided only for works not in the public domain.

Chapter 1: Thomas Hobbes, *Leviathan*, chapters 1–6, and 13–20.
Chapter 2: Jean-Jacques Rousseau, *The Discourse on the Origin of*

Inequality Among Men or, as it is also called, *The Second Discourse*; and *The Social Contract*, Book I, Book II, chapters 1–7, Book III, chapter 1, Book IV, chapters 1–2.

Chapter 3: John Locke, *Second Treatise of Government*.

Chapter 4: John Stuart Mill, *Utilitarianism;* and *On Liberty*. The essay discussed in the Appendix to chapter 4 is Herbert Marcuse's, "Repressive Tolerance," in Robert Paul Wolff, Jr., Barrington Moore, and Herbert Marcuse, *A Critique of Pure Tolerance* (Boston: Beacon Press, 1965).

Chapter 5: John Rawls, *A Theory of Justice* (Cambridge, Mass.: Harvard University Press, 1971), chaps. 1–3; *Political Liberalism* (New York: Columbia University Press, 1993), lecture 1; and "The Idea of Public Reason Revisited" in *The Law of Peoples: with The Idea of Public Reason Revisited* (Cambridge, Mass.: Harvard University Press, 1999).

Chapter 6: Karl Marx, "Toward a Critique of Hegel's Philosophy of Right: Introduction"; the section on "Alienated Labor" from the (1844) *Paris Manuscripts;* "On the Jewish Question"; the "Theses on Feuerbach"; *The German Ideology* (co-authored with Friedrich Engels), part 1 ("Feuerbach"); the *Communist Manifesto* (co-authored with Friedrich Engels), and the (1859) "Preface" to *The Critique of Political Economy*.

1

Hobbes

Thomas Hobbes (1588–1679) was, above all, an anti-revolutionary, writing in the midst of the revolutionary upheavals gripping seventeenth-century England. This political orientation was an important motivation for his political philosophy, perhaps the most important of all the factors affecting it. It would even be fair to say that the principal aim of *The Leviathan* (1651), Hobbes's masterpiece, was to establish the claim that it is never justified to rebel against existing authorities. In pressing this case, Hobbes considered a host of pro-revolutionary positions with a view to showing, in each instance, how the deeper theoretical convictions of those who propose these views, properly understood and developed, actually support anti-revolutionary positions Since most seventeenth-century English revolutionaries were militant Christians, intent on justifying rebellion theologically, most of *The Leviathan* is concerned with the political implications of theological doctrines prominent in Hobbes's time. I will not address this side of Hobbes's case against revolution at all. It belongs to a very different world from that of modern political philosophy. I mention it only because those thoroughly secular positions of Hobbes's that *can* be mined for insights of contemporary relevance arose in the course of his employment of a similar argumentative strategy – with respect to emerging political ideas of a distinctly modern cast. In the portion of *The Leviathan* I will consider, chapters 1–6 and then especially chapters 13–20, Hobbes took the thinking of some of the more radical English revolutionaries as his starting-point, developed it in ways that only a genius of Hobbes's order could, and then, ironically, turned it to anti-revolutionary ends.

We must credit the most advanced of the English revolutionaries for introducing a political vocabulary that plays a prominent role in political theory and practice to this day. Among their innovations was a certain understanding of *freedom* or *liberty,* words which I will use interchangeably. Essentially, their idea was that what matters is freedom *from* (coercive) restraint or, as Hobbes put it, "the absence of External Impediments" (*Leviathan*, hereafter *L*, chap. 13). These English revolutionaries accorded value to freedom in this sense; they valued *negative* liberty. The more of it, the better, other things being equal. This conviction remains in force today. From the time these revolutionaries raised the idea and Hobbes gave it theoretical expression, a presumption for negative liberty has been almost universally acknowledged.

Another concept that some of the English revolutionaries broached and that Hobbes developed is the notion of *moral rights.* Rights claims are always addressed to others. To assert a right is to claim that others have a duty to do or forbear from doing certain things that affect the right bearer's interests. Thus a Robinson Crusoe, alone on his island, would have no rights, because rights claims make sense only when there are others to whom they are directed. Rights can only exist within communities. In the Western tradition, rights had a place in political discourse long before the seventeenth-century English revolutions. From the time of ancient Rome, they were invoked in legal contexts. Individuals had rights and corresponding duties in consequence of the laws under which they lived. More generally, as the original usage implies, rights follow from "the rules of the games" we play; as when, for example, in playing chess, players have the right to move their bishops diagonally, when it is their turn to play, but not to move their opponents' bishops or to play out of turn or to move bishops as though they were knights. Before the seventeenth century, the term was reserved, in the main, for "games" that had some juridical basis. The English revolutionaries extended the range of application of rights talk beyond this institutional context – to the entire political community. They took over the legal notion and used it to articulate their demands. Thus, the notion of moral rights came into being. A moral right, then, is a claim on others to do or forbear from doing certain things in virtue of their moral status, irrespective of the legal standing of the claim being made. Hobbes took over this notion too and developed it perspicuously. Partly in consequence of his work, the idea survives to this day. In fact, it has never flourished so much as in our time. Ours is a political culture that expresses itself munificently in this idiom.

Both negative liberty and moral rights are individualistic notions; they follow naturally, if not inexorably, from the image of the atomic individual. Atoms follow their own inertial motions; their "natural condition" is to move without restraint. Hobbes was officially opposed to Aristotelian science and therefore, one would have thought, to the Aristotelian identification of the natural with the good. But he was still enough of an Aristotelian to succumb to this understanding at an intuitive level. The "absence of External Impediments" is good because it is a natural condition which, other things being equal, ought to be enjoyed. Similarly, atomic individuals have interests that they seek to further and protect. Rights talk is a convenient way to press this concern. To assert a moral right is, in effect, to claim that one has an interest that others ought to accommodate. Thus rights are devices that atomic individuals can bring to bear to promote their interests in circumstances in which they and other atomic individuals are obliged to interact.

As remarked in the Introduction, Hobbes set out to think about society and politics in a way that was joined systematically to the picture of reality that he believed the new sciences of nature implied. Hobbes also wanted to apply what he took to be scientific standards of explanation. In his view, to explain something is to show how it came to be, to discover what Aristoteleans would call its "efficient cause."[1] To this end, Hobbes thought it necessary to break phenomena down in such a way that their constituent parts stand revealed and then to tell a causal story that explains how these fundamental constituents came to be put together in just the way that they are. This view of explanation very much affected how Hobbes set out to account for political authority. He began with "the natural condition of mankind," the state of nature, and then told a causal story about how its fundamental constituents, atomic individuals, concocted political arrangements of the kind he set out to explain.

---

[1] Hobbes expressly upheld the notion of efficient causality, the ancestor of modern understandings of causality, while rejecting the other three kinds of causes recognized in Aristotelian science and metaphysics: material, formal and final causes. A material cause is the substratum or stuff of which a thing is made – the bronze of a statue, for example. The formal cause is the thing's form – the statue's shape. Final causes are ends or purposes – that for the sake of which the statue was made. Efficient causes are whatever suffice to bring changes about. Hobbes inveighed against Aristotelean understandings of causality most famously in *De Corpore*: 15:3.

The State of Nature

In doing so, Hobbes developed a methodology that philosophers today call *contractarian* because the idea of a "social contract" is central to its application. Contractarianism is actually a collection of (related) methods; the version Hobbes invented is only one very influential variation on this theme. We will find that Locke's contractarianism is not quite the same as Hobbes's, and that the contractarianism of Rousseau and Rawls differ even more radically. But all contractarian methodologies share some common features. The basic idea is to abstract away everything pertaining to what is to be justified and then to show how rational (atomic) individuals, given their interests, would "contract" into just the set of institutional arrangements that the contractarian wants to defend. In seventeenth- and eighteenth-century applications of this methodology, there was some confusion about the historicity of the causal story contractarians told. Thus Hobbes seemed to say, and may actually have believed, that once upon a time people really did live in a state of nature, and then somehow got together to establish a sovereign power. Understood this way, contractarianism is plainly false. There is no reason to think that anything like a state of nature ever existed or that there ever was a social contract. The plain recognition of this fact partly explains why, in the nineteenth century, contractarianism fell into disrepute. But it has become clear by now that contractarianism, properly understood, is not in any way committed to false historical explanations. We can think of the state of nature as an element in a *thought experiment* in which we imagine what life would be like in the absence of, say, political arrangements – without in any way supposing that there ever was a time in which people actually lived without political arrangements of any kind. Similarly, we can think of the social contract not as an actual (presumably unwritten) document, produced at a particular time and place, but as an implicit reconstruction of the principles that individuals in a hypothetical state of nature would choose to organize, say, their political affairs. This understanding follows from the prior resolve to take atomic individuals and their interests as points of departure for thinking about political arrangements. Atomic individuals have interests that they seek to advance. For a contractarian, the right way to think about advancing individuals' interests is, as it were, to let individuals fend for themselves; in other words, to imagine what rational, self-interested individuals would do in the counterfactual circumstances they call a state of nature.

Thus whatever Hobbes may have believed, the state of nature is an idealization, a *model*. Accordingly, in identifying its salient features, Hobbes did not describe literally everything that would be the case in the absence of political arrangements, but only those things that matter for explaining political authority. What Hobbes did was to identify features of human nature and the human condition that are universal, that in no way depend upon political authority relations, and that are relevant to explaining political authority causally. The fact, for example, that human beings need food and water and air to survive meets the first two conditions, but not the third. It therefore plays no role in the model Hobbes constructed.

What plays a decisive role in Hobbes's account of the state of nature is the *relative equality* of atomic individuals. It is important to realize that when Hobbes spoke of equality (see *L*, chap. 13), he did not mean equality in a moralized sense – as when, for example, in the US *Declaration of Independence*, it is declared that "all men are created equal." What Hobbes had in mind is the distribution of physical and mental endowments. His claim was that these endowments are distributed by nature among human beings in such a way that even the weakest, slowest and dumbest among them can kill the strongest, fastest and smartest. All human beings are, in other words, vulnerable to mortal assault at the hands of all others. Needless to say, this claim too is false. The very young, the very old and the very infirm generally pose no mortal threat to able-bodied persons in the prime of life. But, again, Hobbes's aim was not to describe what is literally the case. It was to model what is explanatory, according to his own understanding of what a proper explanatory practice requires. Were it pressed on him that normal adult human beings face no threat from infants, he could reply, anachronistically but correctly, that, if his idealization is on track, this fact is just so much "noise" to be abstracted away. He could insist, in other words, that what is pertinent for explaining sovereignty is the range of variation he models, not the range of variation that exists in fact. This would be a fair rejoinder. If Hobbes's state of nature is a bad idealization, it will be for reasons much deeper than the observation that there are categories of human beings who comprise exceptions to what Hobbes claims about the relative equality of persons. We will go on to see that Locke endeavored to invoke reasons of sufficient depth to dislodge Hobbes's account; and that, in a very different fashion, Rousseau did as well. But whatever we finally conclude about their rival views, the crucial point, for now, is that relative equality plays a crucial role in the explanation of political authority. Were the range of variation of natural endowments among human beings greater than it actually is, the problems atomic individuals confront in a state of nature would be very different from those Hobbes described. If natural endowments were distributed among atomic individuals in the way that they are, say, between healthy adult human beings and house-flies – if, in other words, mutual vulnerability to mortal assault was not a universal fact of the human condition – we might be able to dispense with a social contract altogether. But this is not the case, and therefore, in Hobbes's view, a social contract is indispensable for our interests to be served.

What Hobbes had to say about human nature is similarly trans-historical. If a disposition is ascribed to "natural man," it must also hold, if not quite in any imaginable circumstance, then at least in a state of nature – that is, in the absence of political arrangements and their effects. This is how we should understand Hobbes's claim that human beings are "diffident" – in other words, prone to fear – and that the thing they fear most is violent death (*L*, chap. 13). Hobbes's claim is that diffidence obtains irrespective of the conditions under which persons live; that it can be more or less acute, depending on circumstances, but that it is "hardwired" into the human psyche and therefore always capable of governing social relations among human beings. In the absence of politi-cal arrangements of any kind, this omnipresent fact of human nature takes on an enormous significance.

Knowing that human beings are relatively equal and diffident, we can be confident that, in the absence of countervailing factors, a state of na-ture will be "a war of all against all." For when these conditions obtain, atomic individuals are nothing but threats to other atomic individuals. Everyone therefore has an interest in killing everyone else preemptively, whenever possible. Insofar as individuals are capable of knowing their interests and of adapting means to ends, as Hobbes assumed they were, and insofar as nothing holds them back, they would then act as their interests dictate. In a Hobbesian state of nature, nothing does hold them back, not even unenforceable rules, for in a state of nature there are, by hypothesis, no rules of any kind. Therefore even "moral" injunctions to do or forbear from doing certain things – for example, not to kill – have no effect in a state of nature. Like other systems of rules, morality has no place in the pre-political world Hobbes imagined.

This is an especially dramatic way of making the point that the rules under which people live, moral and otherwise, are ultimately human con-trivances. They are neither God-given nor in any other way *out there*, awaiting discovery in the way that the mysteries of nature are. Rather, they are concocted by those whose behaviors they regulate. In this sense, they are *prescribed*, not *detected*. Again, Hobbes was not committed to the view that there was a time in the actual past when moral and other rules governing human behavior were expressly contrived or formally declared. Contractarians are in the business of providing rational reconstructions, not historical fictions. But, with this understanding in mind, it is fair to say that, for Hobbes, morality too is a human contrivance. As such, it obtains when and insofar as it is advantageous to its makers. Hobbes will argue that, in general, morality always is advantageous to individuals living *within* political communities, where order obtains, but that it is not advantageous to anyone in a state of nature. The reason is plain: in state of nature conditions, to act in accordance with moral rules is to put oneself at greater risk than one would otherwise be in an unrelenting war of all against all.

"Diffidence" is only one aspect of universal human nature. Hobbes claimed a similar status for "competition" and "glory" (*L*, chap. 13). By "competition," Hobbes meant what we might today call acquisitiveness. This idea plays a central role in moral, social and political philosophy after Hobbes. But it was not much emphasized by Hobbes himself. Nor did Hobbes do much to clarify what he had in mind. He suggested, but could not possibly have meant, that everybody always wants more and more of everything. Such a claim is plainly mistaken. The problem is not that universal acquisitiveness is false in the benign way that all idealizations are. The fact that people sometimes exhibit generosity or sometimes renounce the things of this world need no more embarrass the claim that individuals are moved by competition than the fact that people are in varying degrees reckless need embarrass the claim that they are diffident. Generosity and voluntary poverty, like recklessness, may just be "noise" to be abstracted away. The problem, instead, is that people almost never desire more and more of any particular thing. Indeed, satiation is as much a fact of universal human nature as acquisitiveness is. Still, Hobbes's position can be corrected in a way that accommodates the intuition that motivated it.

The concept of diminishing marginal utility, an idea anticipated in the eighteenth century by Daniel Bernoui and then developed in the nineteenth and twentieth centuries by leading economic theorists such as W. S. Jevons, Alfred Marshall and A. C. Pigou, provides some help in this regard. The general idea is that, in nearly all circumstances, the more of some item one has, the less benefit there is in acquiring more of it. The benefit may even diminish to a vanishing point. But it is never the case, when this concept applies, that there is a negative benefit from an additional increment. Perhaps Hobbes ought to have claimed something like this, instead of maintaining, implicitly, that individuals' wants are not affected by what they already possess. But, of course, this revised claim is false too; there are circumstances in which individuals want less, not more (no matter how little), of particular things. But it may not be false in a way that damages Hobbes's account of the state of nature. If, instead of thinking of particular objects of desire, we reformulate the claim in the way that economists do, to apply to things in general or, what comes to the same thing, to money, where money is a universal measure of exchange, then Hobbes's contention may be on track. For it can be claimed, with considerable plausibility, that everyone desires more of this universal equivalent, albeit in diminishing degrees, the more of it they already have, because everyone always wants more of *something*, even if they do not always want more of *everything*. No doubt, this claim too is literally false; some people, some of the time, may not want more of *anything*. But it could be argued that, to the degree that it is false, it errs only in the way that any idealization that excludes a few imaginable real world counter-examples does.

By "glory" (or "vainglory") Hobbes meant the desire to best others. Hobbes focused on "esteem," but the idea can be generalized. Insofar as individuals are vainglorious, they seek not only to increase their own distributive shares, but also to do better than others – to increase the *difference* between their shares and the shares of everyone else. Glory is the most historically particular of the purportedly universal motivations Hobbes attributed to atomic individuals. The extent to which it governs behavior is almost certainly dependent upon the norms of the society in which individuals live, norms that vary across societies and historical periods. Nevertheless, it is unlikely that glory, as Hobbes conceived it, is ever entirely absent from (most) human beings' natures. But even if it is, and Hobbes therefore failed to model trans-historical human nature correctly, this flaw would hardly undermine the idea that he wanted to express.

The reason it would not is that the conclusion Hobbes drew – that the state of nature is a universal war of all against all – is *overdetermined*. There are at least three distinct grounds, each of them sufficient, for sustaining this description. We have already seen how a state of war follows from diffidence and relative equality alone. It also follows from the claim that atomic individuals are by nature competitive, in conjunction with the fact that most of the things they desire are scarce. *Relative scarcity* is another of Hobbes's universal and pertinent facts of the human condition. It obtains whenever the things people want are sufficiently scarce such that not everyone can have everything they want, but not so scarce that individuals cannot benefit from cooperation. Most of the things people want are, in fact, relatively scarce. Whatever is not is either *abundant* or *absolutely scarce.* A good is abundant if everyone can have all of it that they want without diminishing anyone else's share, except in negligible ways. Thus air is abundant in most circumstances. A good is absolutely scare if it is in such limited supply that, in general, there is no reason to cooperate with others for its acquisition. Water on a lifeboat that is sufficient for the survival of only one of several passengers is an example. A struggle among the lifeboat's occupants to acquire this water would be a "zero-sum game." There would be only winners (in this case, one winner) and losers, and the winners would benefit at everyone else's expense. Nearly everything people want is scarce, either relatively or absolutely. Therefore, competitive atomic individuals are in competition with everyone for (almost) everything. So long as no countervailing factors obtain, they would therefore find themselves in a war of all against all. Thus, as Hobbes maintained, competition is an independent "cause for quarrel." Glory is another independent cause. It motivates everyone to seek to dominate everyone else, and therefore to wage war against them in order to best them and not be bested by them. To be sure, this putative fact of universal human nature differs from the other two inasmuch as it only motivates war to the point of submission – not, as the others do, to the point of death. It does suffice, however, even in the absence of the other causes, to turn a state of nature into a condition in which everyone is at war with everyone else.

There is another fact of the human condition that Hobbes does not expressly acknowledge, though it is a feature of the imagery that underlies his model. I will call this condition *geographical proximity*, the fact that atomic individuals are obliged to interact in the same "space." If geographical proximity did not obtain, a state of war would be avoidable, even if everything else is as Hobbes maintained. For then, atomic individuals could exit from situations that would otherwise lead to conflict. Inhabitants of territories that have no contact with one another have no basis for quarrel – even allowing that they are relatively equal in natural endowments, that they live in a milieu of (relative) scarcity and that they are diffident, competitive, and vainglorious by nature. If geographical proximity did not obtain, individuals in a state of nature could enjoy peace for a similar reason. They could withdraw from the war of all against all. But this is not their fate. According to Hobbes's model, people inhabit the same (bounded) space and are therefore obliged to interact. Exit is not an option.

As Hobbes explained, a state of war "consisteth not" in overt battle, but "in a general disposition thereto" (*L*, chap. 13). Hobbes's claim, then, is that in the absence of suitable political arrangements, individuals find themselves in a situation in which they could not but evince a disposition to wage war against everyone else. But this state of affairs is at odds with their interests, a point Hobbes made graphically clear in his celebrated description of the state of war: ". . . In such condition, there is no place for industry; because the fruit thereof is uncertain; and consequently no culture of the earth; no navigation; nor use of the commodities that may be imported by sea; no commodious building; no instruments of moving, and removing, such things as require much force; no knowledge of the face of the earth; no account of time; no arts; no letters; no society; and which is worst of all, continual fear and danger of violent death; and the life of man, solitary, poor, nasty, brutish and short" (*L*, chap. 13). Each individual therefore has an overriding interest in terminating this unhappy situation. In principle, of course, they could always put the war of all against all to rest by changing their natures or their condition or both. But this way out is, by hypothesis, unavailable inasmuch as human nature and the human condition are assumed to be timeless and unchangeable. The problem, therefore, cannot be conjured away. There is no choice but to confront it directly and, if possible, to negotiate a solution.

The Problem

It is in each individual's interest to end the state of nature by instituting a regime in which individuals' behaviors are coordinated; in which rulelessness is replaced by *order*. To this end, Hobbes thought that individuals must address the main source of the problem they confront, the relative equality of persons. Since they cannot abolish this fact of the human condition, they must contrive a way to overcome its effects. Given the fact of relative equality, no one is in a position to impose order. No one is even able to enter into negotiations with greater bargaining power than anyone else. But since no one will agree to a negotiated outcome unless it is in their interest to do so, the outcome of the (hypothetical) negotiating process into which atomic individuals enter will have to be advantageous to everyone. What is sought, then, is a *mutually advantageous* solution to the problem individuals in a state of nature confront.

Put differently, individuals have only their own resources to depend upon when they set out to put the state of war to rest. Neither God nor any other superior power can come to their aid; no solution can be imposed from without. But as long as relative equality obtains, it seems that it also cannot be imposed from within. In a society of relatively equal atomic individuals, no one is sufficiently powerful to transform "the natural condition of mankind"; no one is able to issue enforceable commands. But if relative equality were overcome, fear of overwhelming force would end the war of all against all. Therefore the task atomic individuals in a Hobbesian state of nature confront is to concoct such a power, a force so mighty that whoever wields it is able permanently to establish peace.

Thus the fundamental problem of political life, as Hobbes conceived it, is to create "a common power to hold . . . [individuals] in awe." Ironically, this power will take advantage of diffidence to overcome the problems diffidence along with competition and vainglory create. Order, for Hobbes, is based on fear ("awe"); above all, the fear of violent death. What individuals in a state of nature must therefore do is put their diffident natures to work in behalf of civil order. In the face of their own relative equality, they must create an overwhelming power to fear.

Rational Agency

It is useful to distinguish Hobbes's implicit but enormously influential theory of practical reason, of reason in its application to human action, from his explicit account of human nature and human interests. Hobbes claimed that individuals are everywhere and always diffident, competitive and vainglorious. From this, it follows, given the human condition, that there are certain universal human interests – in peace or order, in acquiring resources, in esteem. But if these interests are to be of use in explaining sovereignty or any other institutional arrangement, human beings must be capable in general of acting on them. In elaborating on this idea, Hobbes pioneered a fruitful explanatory strategy, rational choice theory. Implicitly, he also invented a new account of practical reason or rational agency.

Before Hobbes, rationality was a standard for assessing ends. What Hobbes maintained instead was that practical reason is *instrumental*, not *substantive*; that it concerns the adoption of means to ends, not ends themselves. Ends are neither rational nor irrational; they just are what they are, thanks, in part, to the way human nature and the human condition happen to be. Were the facts different from the way Hobbes thought they were, were it the case, say, that human beings are by nature reckless even to the point of welcoming situations that increase the likelihood of their own violent death, it would not be rational to will peace, as Hobbes thought it was (*L*, chap. 14). Peace is a rational end for the inhabitants of the state of nature and for us, inasmuch as they are us, because our psychological constitution requires it. Reason itself is strictly neutral on this and all other matters.

This is not to say that, so far as reason is concerned, the ends individuals hold are beyond reproach. Individuals may act *imprudently*; they may fail to act in accord with their own best interests, not because they improperly adopt means to ends, but because they misconstrue what their ends are. From within a broadly Hobbesian perspective, it is fair to say that individuals act imprudently whenever they fail to act on the ends they *would* have acted on, had they had full or at least sufficient knowledge of the consequences of their actions, had they adequately reflected on this knowledge, and perhaps also had they actually done what they knew to be best.[2] Also, *consistency*, a property of a set of agents' ends, rather than of the ends themselves, is a requirement of Hobbesian rational agency. An individual who, for example, chooses A over B, B over C, and C over A, chooses inconsistently. Inconsistent choices are irrational, in the Hobbesian view, because reason requires us to do what is individually best, given our interests as represented by our preferences for alternatives in contention. Individuals who choose inconsistently do not and cannot do what is individually best because their preferences and therefore their choices cycle. For them, there is no choice that is best, and therefore no rational way to act.

Hobbes claimed *both* that human beings are instrumentally rational and that they have the interests he ascribed to them. This is why it would be irrational for an individual in a state of nature not to seek peace. Seeking peace is neither rational nor irrational in itself. But it is irrational for such beings as we are, beings with psychological dispositions and therefore interests and therefore preferences like our own, not "to endeavor peace, as far as . . . [they] have hope of obtaining it" (*L*, chap. 14).

A Prisoners' Dilemma

It will be instructive to reconstruct what Hobbes had in mind by making use of conceptual tools borrowed from the theory of games, that branch of twentieth-century mathematics that models rational choice in situations in which, as in many games, how well individuals do depends, in

---

[2] Socrates famously maintained that people cannot fail to do what they know to be best, but most philosophers after him, including Hobbes, have thought otherwise. This is the phenomenon Aristotle called *akrasia*, weakness of will.

part, on what other players do. As a good first approximation, a Hobbesian state of nature can be thought of as a generalized Prisoners' Dilemma game. In a Prisoners' Dilemma, the *unintended* consequence of
doing what is individually best is an outcome that is worse for each player
than need be – not according to some external standard of better or worse,
but according to the very interests that motivate players to do what is
individually best. This is the case in a Hobbesian state of nature. It is
because individuals, in the absence of a "common power" to hold them
in "awe," act rationally, because they do what is individually best, that
they find themselves in a war of all against all – a situation worse, indeed
much worse, than the peace they all desire.

The Prisoners' Dilemma is so named because of the story with which it
has come to be associated. Suppose that two prisoners, Smith and Jones,
have been arrested for some crime – say, armed robbery. Suppose too
that the prosecuting attorney has only enough evidence to convict them
of a lesser crime – say, breaking and entering – unless one or the other
confesses. The prosecutor therefore offers each prisoner a deal. She tells
them that if one confesses and the other does not, the one who confesses
can go free, while the other one must spend 20 years in prison. If both
confess, she promises that they will each get no more than 10-year prison
sentences. But if neither prisoner confesses, she concedes that the most
she can do is convict them both for breaking and entering, for which they
will each be confined in prison for 3 years. We can think of this story as
a game in which there are two players, Smith and Jones, and two moves,
confess or don't confess. If, as is customary, we represent these outcomes
in a payoff matrix, with the payoffs to Jones on the left and the payoffs
to Smith on the right, then, pictorially:

Smith

		confess	don't confess
	confess	−10, −10	0, −20
Jones			
	don't confess	−20, 0	−3, −3

If we assume that Smith and Jones are self-interested, rational agents
intent only on minimizing their own years in jail, it is clear what would
happen. They would each confess. The reason is straightforward: the
payoff to each "player" depends on what the other player does. The

opposing player can either confess or not confess. As is apparent from the payoff schedule, in either case, both players are better off confessing. Both will therefore confess. As a result, both Smith and Jones will get 10-year sentences. But, given their interests, there is a better outcome for both of them – the one in which they each get 3-year sentences. However, to get to that point, both Smith and Jones would have to not confess. They would have to forbear from doing what is individually best. If, as is customary, we define an *optimal* outcome to be one in which no player can do better without another doing worse, we can say that the unintended consequence of each player doing what is individually best in a Prisoners' Dilemma is *sub-optimal*. There is an alternative outcome that is better for each player. But self-interested, rational players cannot reach it.

Notice that, in this case, there is no need for Smith and Jones to employ sophisticated strategies for rational choice in conditions of uncertainty – strategies that would depend, in part, on their attitudes towards risk. There is no reason, in other words, for them to employ a *maximin* strategy, where they seek to maximize the minimal payoff, as risk averse players might, or to adopt a *maximax* strategy, where they try to maximize the maximal payoff, as players who are prone to incur high risks for the sake of high gains would. Strategizing is unnecessary in this case, because, in the circumstances described, there are no relevant uncertainties: *whatever* the other player does, each player is better off confessing.

Of course, if Smith and Jones could trust each other not to confess, they could arrive at the optimal outcome. But, in the story just told, there is no rational basis for trust. To underscore this point, let us assume that Smith and Jones have no longstanding relationship, criminal or otherwise. Past experience therefore provides them with no basis for trust. Let us suppose too, as is commonly emphasized in the telling of the Prisoners' Dilemma story, that Smith and Jones are unable to communicate and therefore to collude together when the prosecuting attorney offers her deal. These addenda to the basic story change nothing of substance, but they do underscore the force of the conclusion: that, in Prisoners' Dilemma conditions, doing what is individually best makes individuals worse off than they could otherwise be.

Hobbes's state of nature is a Prisoners' Dilemma in both of these respects. In a war of all against all, doing what is individually best leads to sub-optimal outcomes. And, in the absence of a "common power" to hold individuals "in awe," there is no basis for anyone to trust anyone else. Thus it is in each individual's interest "to seek, and use, all helps, and advantages of war" (*L*, chap. 14), and in so doing, unintentionally but inevitably, to render everyone's life, including their own, *unnecessar-*

ily "solitary, poor, nasty, brutish and short." Individuals would be better off if they could interact with one another in peace. But they cannot achieve this result, except by adding to their own vulnerability to mortal assault. Disarmament in the international arena is difficult to achieve for the same reason. Even if all sides would be better off agreeing to disarm, in the absence of good reasons to trust one another, there is no way, consistent with self-interest, for any of the parties actually to do so.

In principle, the optimal outcome could be achieved if individuals co-operated; if they voluntarily deferred from doing what is individually best in order to advance their common ends. But in a Hobbesian state of nature, cooperation, though desirable, is irrational and therefore impossible for rational agents. In general, players cannot cooperate their way out of Prisoners' Dilemmas![3] This is why Hobbes thought political authority necessary. The only way out of a state of nature, in his view, is to alter the payoff structure individuals confront by making activities that constitute war more costly than activities that constitute peace – thereby changing what rational agents will find to be individually best. But as long as relative equality governs human life, no one is in a position to force a move away from a Prisoners' Dilemma payoff structure. Therefore, peace, cannot arise from the self-constraint of rational agents. This, then, is Hobbes's problem: to show how self-interested and rational atomic individuals can turn a Prisoners' Dilemma payoff structure into one in which acting rationally actually improves individuals' situations – despite relative equality, despite human nature and the human condition, and despite the fact that individuals can rely on no powers other than their own.

A Monitoring Problem

What keeps individuals mired in Prisoners' Dilemma situations is not an inability to *agree* to cooperate. Smith and Jones could agree not to

[3] Strictly speaking, this claim is false – when Prisoners' Dilemma games are played indefinitely many times. Since Robert Axelrod's seminal study, *The Evolution of Cooperation* (New York: Basic Books, 1984), it has been widely recognized that in iterated Prisoners' Dilemma games, cooperation can *evolve* – through a process akin to natural selection. But cooperation *is* impossible in one-play Prisoners' Dilemmas, and it is at least arguable that, in a war of all against all, individuals would indeed interact with one another only once, or at least so infrequently that a one-play Prisoners' Dilemma game is a more apt representation than an iterated Prisoners' Dilemma game is.

confess because they can each see that not confessing would improve the outcome for each of them. The problem is that it would be irrational for either of them to *abide by* this agreement. Not to confess is to invite disaster. Similarly, cooperators in a Hobbesian state of nature render themselves more vulnerable to mortal assault than they would otherwise be when they disavow some of the "advantages of war" without adequate assurance that, in so doing, their security will be protected. In the state of nature, as Hobbes described it, no assurance of this kind is forthcoming. How to change this state of affairs? We know that we cannot alter human nature or the human condition, and that we cannot rely on any external force, on a conquering army or a God, to save us from ourselves. What we must therefore try to do is to turn ourselves into the functional equivalent of a conquering army or a God, into a force capable of imposing order on self-interested and rational atomic individuals.

The objective, in short, is to nullify the consequences of relative equality. To see how key this goal is, it will be helpful to contrast a Hobbesian state of nature with a Hobbesian view of real world *inter*-state relations, relations between established political entities. Because there are no global or regional institutions that have the power to force nation states to comply with their commands, there is no sovereign power at the international level, just as there is none in a state of nature. A Hobbesian could then go on to hold that, in the same way that individuals are free to do anything at all to one another in a state of nature, states may do anything at all other states in the international arena. But even those who think of international relations this way would have to concede that states are generally not in a state of war. The reason why is that relative equality does not obtain. At the international level, the distribution of forces is so unequal that major powers are not in danger of mortal assault from lesser powers. They are therefore able, with varying degrees of efficacy, to establish "balances of power" sufficient to secure peace among themselves, and to issue enforceable commands to weaker countries. Thus they can satisfy their interests in peace without recourse to the institution of sovereignty. In a genuine state of nature, however, the relative equality of persons renders this path to peace unreachable.

In a state of nature, everyone is absolutely free, but people are generally unable to realize their interests as free beings. Indeed, it is the absolute freedom of the state of nature that generates sub-optimal outcomes. To optimize freedom, it is necessary to restrict it. Similarly, in a state of nature everyone has an unlimited right to everything. The result is that no one has any particular rights to anything, and therefore that no one is able to benefit from a system of universally acknowledged rights claims.

For there to be particular rights, individuals must "lay down" some of the (unlimited) rights they enjoy in the state of nature. This is tantamount to forfeiting liberties, inasmuch as rights claim, when acknowledged, limit the liberty of those to whom they are addressed. To claim a right to X is to claim that others have a duty to do or forbear from doing certain things. A's right to free speech, for example, limits everyone else's freedom to interfere with A's speech; and B's property right in W renders W off-limits to everyone other than B, except those to whom B allows access. Similarly C's right to vote entails not only that others not interfere with the exercise of this right, but also that the state do whatever is necessary to insure that C is able to vote – that it conduct proper elections, provide security, and so on. C's right to vote therefore renders particular others, state officials, unfree not to do the things that C's right to vote entails. The resulting loss of liberty will sometimes be trivial, sometimes significant. Of course, any diminution of liberty is something to regret, inasmuch as liberty ("the absence of External Impediments") is a positive good and restrictions on liberty are therefore always *prima facie* bads. But restricting liberty is the price of peace; and peace matters most of all. It is therefore a *law of nature*, according to Hobbes, "that a man be willing, when others are so too, as far-forth, as for peace, and defence of himself he shall think it necessary, to lay down this right to all things; and be contended with so much liberty against other men, as he would allow other men against himself" (*L*, chap. 14).

By a "law of nature," Hobbes meant a general precept of reason, not a regularity that admits of no exceptions. Since reason does not rule on the content of our ends, we must know something about the nature of rational agents to know what general precepts apply to them. The laws of nature Hobbes identified pertain only to beings like ourselves; to beings who are diffident, competitive and vainglorious, and for whom the relative equality, relative scarcity and geographical proximity conditions apply. It is in this sense that "seek peace and follow it . . ." is a law of nature. It is in this sense too that Hobbes went on to say that it is a law of nature that individuals be willing to do whatever is necessary for peace, but only insofar as, in seeking peace, they do not render themselves more vulnerable than they would otherwise be in the war of all against all. Thus any laying down of rights or restricting of liberties that rational agents undertake in pursuit of peace will have to be conditional on others doing so too.

But how can rational agents who are prepared to take whatever measures are necessary for peace be confident that others will do their part? If they cannot, they will remain in a state of nature forever. Hobbes

reasoned that this unhappy outcome is not inevitable; that, with sufficient ingenuity, it is possible to establish the requisite degree of confidence. This is what Hobbes's account of the social contract purports to
demonstrate. We have already seen how the problem of political authority, as Hobbes conceived it, devolved into a problem of enforceability in
the face of relative equality. We can now see that the enforceability problem is ultimately a *monitoring* problem. Individuals must be in a position
to know that other individuals are doing what they must for it to become
rational for them to renounce "the helps, and advantages of war." The
social contract solves this problem.

The Social Contract

Because Hobbes imported the idea of a contract into political philosophy
from the law, and because the legal concept has remained essentially
unchanged from Hobbes's time to our own, the Hobbesian contract is
less problematic and more understandable than some of the rather different social contracts we will encounter in later chapters. It consists of
nothing more than exchanges between independent parties, each motivated by self-interest. Thus the Hobbesian contract has the same structure as contracts with which everyone is familiar – landlord/tenant leases,
for example. Landlords and tenants exchange living quarters for rents.
Each are better off in consequence. The reason why is clear: if we exclude
force and fraud, either of which normally render agreements void, contracts are entered into voluntarily. Assuming the self-interest and rationality of the contracting parties, the well-being of each party is enhanced
whenever individuals do what they freely choose to do. Contracts therefore ratify agreements that are mutually advantageous. Rational individuals will enter into them, therefore, whenever it is possible for them to
do so, whenever doing so advances their interests.

We can think of the Hobbesian contract as a solution to a vexing but
not intractable bargaining problem. Because bargaining has a Prisoners' Dilemma structure, the optimal outcome is every bargainer's second-best choice in the sense that there is a better possible outcome, for
each individual, than the bargaining solution. The best outcome for
each individual will always be the one in which others do what the
bargain requires, but one does not do so oneself. Each bargainer's third
choice is that bargaining fails; that no exchange takes place, the analogue of a state of nature. What each bargainer wants least is to do
what the bargain requires while others do not; the analogue of unilat-

eral disarmament in war. Thus if Brown wants to sell his car to Green, what Brown wants most is that Green turn over the money to Brown without Brown turning over the car to Green, and what Green wants most is Brown's car for free. The second-best option for each of them is that a deal be struck. This is the bargaining solution. It is unanimously preferred to no deal at all, which is preferable, in turn, from Brown's point of view, to the case in which Brown turns over his car without getting Green's money or, from Green's point of view, to the case in which Green pays Brown but gets no car in return. As this example makes clear, bargains are possible (rational) if and only if the interests of the bargainers overlap. Then there is an "area" within which a deal can be struck because each of the negotiating parties prefers that a deal be struck *anywhere* within that area than that no deal be strike at all. Where within that area a deal actually is struck will depend on many factors – including market conditions, access to information about opponents' positions and strengths, and the various parties' bargaining skills. In the Hobbesian case, the bargainers are atomic individuals living in a state of nature – similarly situated, similarly motivated and similarly rational. There are therefore no significant differences in "market positions"; everyone knows everyone else's situation, and individuals are equally able to attend to their own interests. Therefore, a Hobbesian social contract, unlike most real world contracts, including the majority of landlord/tenant leases, will be equally demanding on all the parties to it. It will reflect the equality among persons that makes it both necessary and possible.

How, then, can diffident, competitive and vainglorious rational individuals, living in a state of nature, negotiate its end? They cannot lay down their rights to each other because doing so would increase their vulnerability in the war of all against all, a prospect they must avoid at all costs. A social contract that individuals in a state of nature can accept will therefore have to oblige no one to lay down rights that others do not lay down too. Insofar as it disadvantages its adherents in the war of all against all, it must disadvantage them equally. In addition, this social contract will have to be susceptible to monitoring, so that the contracting parties will know that the conditions under which they lay down their rights actually obtain. These parties can only be individuals because, in a state of nature, only individuals exist. There is no already established political community or "people" and, of course, no "sovereign." Hence neither the people nor the sovereign can be parties to a social contract. But, then, since individuals cannot lay down their rights to one another, how possibly can they lay down their unlimited right to everything, as their interests require? And to whom can they lay their rights down?

Since there are only atomic individuals, the social contract can only be between atomic individuals. These individuals cannot contract with one another to become rulers and subjects. But they can agree, conditional on others agreeing too, to enforce the commands of a third party against each other. To be that third party, the one whose commands others enforce, is to be a *sovereign*; for sovereignty, as Hobbes conceived it, just is the capacity to issue enforceable commands. Thus even though individuals cannot lay down their rights to one another, they can, by contracting with each other, concoct a sovereign. When they do so, they neither agree to obey one another, nor do they enter into a covenant with the sovereign they thereby establish. Indeed, the sovereign is not a party to the social contract at all. Here, Hobbes's virtuosity in combining theoretical exigencies with anti-revolutionary politics is especially evident. Because a sovereign cannot be a party to a social contract, a sovereign's failure to live up to the terms of the social contract cannot possibly trigger a right of revolution – contrary, for example, to what Thomas Jefferson claimed in the US *Declaration of Independence*. In that document, George III's treatment of the English colonies in North America is described as a breach of contract; a breach that, in the view of the *Declaration's* signers, justifies rebellion. Had Jefferson been a Hobbesian, he could never have drawn this conclusion.

In a state of nature, it is irrational to agree to become subservient to anyone else. Hobbes's social contract respects this requirement. But, by means of this contract, individuals do, by indirection, succeed in making themselves the sovereign's subjects. For if a sufficient number of individuals agree to enforce the sovereign's commands against others, relative equality, the condition that turns the state of nature into a war of all against all, ceases to obtain. The individual who is sovereign is still, of course, relatively equal to others in natural endowments. But, as a public person, the sovereign is vastly more powerful than any of his subjects because the sovereign has the combined strength of all the contracting parties at his disposal. With these enforcers at the ready, he can issue enforceable commands. Thus, despite relative equality, the sovereign *can* establish order by force.

The social contract therefore changes the payoff structure individuals confront. Once a sovereign is in place, individuals no longer face a generalized Prisoners' Dilemma. They find themselves instead in circumstances in which defection from mutually beneficial rules or, what comes to the same thing, disobedience of the sovereign's commands is more costly and therefore less desirable than conformity or obedience is. For where there is a sovereign, there is also a "police," a force capable of imposing sanctions that no one can reasonably expect to resist. In a state of nature, everyone wants everyone else to conform to rules, while they themselves remain free to do as they please. Everyone wants to be a lone disobedient. But as long as they act on this preference, a state of war remains in force. In pursuing what they most prefer, lone disobedience, rational individuals find themselves unintentionally generating the outcome they prefer least, the state of nature. The only way out is to establish a sovereign, for wherever sovereignty exists, fear of the sovereign's police will cause everyone to prefer conformity to the sovereign's commands over lone disobedience. Then when rational individuals act as their preferences require, peace will result – for universal conformity to rules (in this case, to the only rules there are, the rules that follow from the sovereign's commands) *is* peace.

In establishing a sovereign, individuals effectively organize themselves into an overwhelming force, capable and ready to enforce the sovereign's commands. The sovereign, then, is not the victor in the war of all against all. In that war, there are only losers. To be sure, some individuals will do better than others, and it is likely that the sovereign will be chosen from among those who have fared comparatively well. But no individual can become a sovereign by triumphing over other individuals in the state of war. Sovereignty is a "gift" of the people themselves (*L*, chap. 14). Therefore any individual *could* in principle assume the sovereign's powers. Sovereignty resides in the people, and it is ultimately up to them to determine in whom it is "incarnated."

It is plain, then, that Hobbes's social contract is not really *a* contract at all, except in a manner of speaking. It is many contracts. Everyone contracts with everyone else to become the enforcer of the sovereign's commands against others. No one, however, agrees directly to obey the sovereign; no one agrees directly to become his subject. Although it is in everyone's interest that everyone be the sovereign's subject or, more prosaically, that everyone be obligated to do what the sovereign commands, no one in a state of nature can agree to take this step, except on pain of irrationality. But when individuals contract with each other in the way Hobbes described, what was otherwise impossible becomes unavoidable. Thus political obligations are by-products of the social contract. Only individuals can bind themselves, and rational individuals who are diffident, competitive and vainglorious and who live without "a common power to hold . . . [them] in awe" cannot bind themselves directly. But, by contracting with each other to enforce commands issued by a noncontracting party *against others,* they create a situation in which it is generally irrational, given their interests, not to do what that third party, the sovereign, commands. In these conditions, obeying the commands of that individual will almost always be prudent. In Hobbes's view, this is all that political obligation is.

Contracts entered into out of fear are generally invalid; like fraud, force (or the threat of force) delegitimates agreements. Thus when Green agrees to turn over a sum of money to White in consequence of White's threat to cause Green bodily harm, Green's agreement, however prudent, has no normative force. The transaction is not legitimate. But, as Hobbes insisted (*L*, chap. 14), the fact that fear – specifically, fear of violent death – leads individuals to make a social contract in no way undoes the contract's legitimacy. This is because in a war of all against all, notions of legitimacy and normative force have no place. These and other moral requirements make sense only in circumstances in which abiding by agreements is generally advantageous; circumstances that cannot exist until *after* the state of nature is laid to rest. Thus there is a sense in which, for Hobbes, might makes right. Might creates the conditions for the possibility of a world in which notions of right and of morality generally, of what Hobbes called *justice,* have a place.

Hobbesian Justice

For Plato, "justice" encompassed most of what philosophers today understand by "right," as that term applies both to actions and to public institutions. Aristotle understood justice more narrowly, and it is Aristotle's understanding that modern political philosophy has taken to heart. Following Aristotle, theories of justice address two distinct kinds of social practices: there are, first of all, theories of *distributive justice,* which deal with the distribution of benefits and burdens across individuals or groups; and then there are theories of *retributive justice,* which deal with the nature and justification of punishment. The guiding idea, in both cases, is that "like cases be treated alike." This is a formal principle; it says nothing about what counts as a like case or what counts as equal treatment. But it is susceptible to supplementation by substantive principles that give it content. "To each according to merit" or "to each according to need" are examples. The consensus view, again following Aristotle, is that different substantive principles apply in different domains. Merit may rightfully govern, say, the distribution of grades in an examination, and need the distribution of resources necessary for health care. But, in all domains, the formal principle that "like cases be treated alike" obtains. Intuitively, then, the core idea is fairness; fairness *is* treating like cases alike.

It is possible for both the formal principle of justice and for any of the substantive principles that give it content to apply to some human beings and not others. Aristotle, for instance, would have rejected notions of fairness that cut across the difference between free citizens and slaves or between men and women. Modern understandings of justice reflect what might be called a universal humanism, the idea that, presumptively, what is fair for one human being is fair for another. More generally, modern understandings reflect the moral point of view: the idea, anticipated in the Golden Rule, that, in at least some deliberative contexts, what matters is what persons have in common, not what distinguishes them from one another. This is what it means "to do unto others as you would have others do unto you." The idea is that whatever distinguishes *you* from *others* ought not to count in your deliberations; that, in deliberating, you should regard *yourself* and *others* in the same way. The Golden Rule therefore implies that, where moral deliberation is called for, agents ought to assume an impartial or agent-neutral perspective, according to which facts about the identities of particular moral agents, including oneself, play no role. What links universal humanism with the moral point of view is the conviction, pervasive in modern moral and political thought, that all human beings are moral agents.

These ideas figure only implicitly in Hobbes's own discussion of justice. What Hobbes maintained is that individuals act justly when they abide by agreements they have entered into freely and therefore that "injustice is the non-performance of covenants made" (*L*, chap. 15). This is an idiosyncratic usage. Its connections with Platonic or Aristotelian understandings of justice are unclear, as are its affinities with universal humanism or the moral point of view. But Hobbes's remarks do underscore how, in his view, justice is a human contrivance. It is a standard adopted, as every other human contrivance is, out of self-interest. So conceived, justice is not beneficial in all imaginable circumstances. Because it can never be beneficial to relinquish liberty in a war of all against all, it can never be beneficial to place oneself under the requirements of justice as long as a state of war obtains. This is why justice comes into its own only *after* the social contract is in place. Without the assurance of order that sovereignty provides, it is irrational to perform covenants made.

Here, again, Hobbes's ingenuity in combining political philosophy with anti-revolutionary politics is evident. If injustice is the non-performance of covenants made and if the sovereign is not a party to the social contract, the sovereign cannot even in principle act unjustly. Therefore the claim that the sovereign is unjust can never justify rebellion. Indeed, it is logically impossible for a sovereign to be unjust. A sovereign is like an atomic individual in a state of nature for whom considerations of justice do not apply.

For justice to be advantageous, rational agents must have reason to believe that the terms of the agreements they enter into will be fulfilled. Some cooperation is possible, of course, even in a state of nature. It is rational to trust others when we can be sure that they will do what they say they will do, and this condition can sometimes be satisfied without the benefit of the sovereign's police. Thus Hobbes conceded the possibility of (temporary) "confederacies" arising even in a war of all against all. To insure compliance in these cases, individuals must be able to monitor what other individuals do or at least be able to make confident predictions about what they are likely to do, given what is known about their interests and situations. The problem in a state of nature is that no one can have stable or enduring expectations of this kind. But some agreements are effectively self-enforcing; exchanges that take place on the spot, for example. It is plainly rational to enter into mutually advantageous self-enforcing agreements, whether or not there is a generally reliable enforcement mechanism in place for agreements that are more difficult to monitor or that rational individuals in a state of nature cannot be expected to honor. This is why a Hobbesian social contract is possible – the covenant that ends the state of nature is, to some degree, self-enforcing. Individuals can see that its terms are fulfilled when they observe that others actually do act as enforcers of the sovereign's commands.[4]

Cooperation is overwhelmingly advantageous for individuals in or out of a state of nature. But in a state of nature it is almost never possible for individuals to cooperate. Once the state of nature is ended, however, the situation changes radically, and the prospects for rational cooperation expand enormously. This is why Hobbes maintained that it is a "law of nature," a general precept of reason, to comply with covenants made (*L*,

---

[4] The following, quasi-Hobbesian scenario for getting out of a state of nature is also imaginable. Suppose that there exist a number of unconditional cooperators, individuals disposed to cooperate even when they have no assurance that others will cooperate too. Then if they can combine together and withstand the assaults of "defectors," they will, in time, come to prevail – for, in coming together, they effectively create a power sufficiently "awesome" to overcome the consequences of relative equality. In Hobbes's account of the state of nature, however, there are no unconditional cooperators. Therefore, this "solution" to the problem individuals in a state of nature confront is unavailable in his model.

chap. 15). Wherever there is a confident expectation of compliance, cooperation is rational; and, wherever sovereignty exists, confidence in the compliance of others is warranted. The social contract therefore changes the background conditions underlying individuals' interactions – from a Prisoners' Dilemma to an Assurance Game. In an Assurance Game, mutual cooperation is each player's first choice. But it is conditional cooperation that everyone wants most; no one wants to cooperate while others defect. Pictorially,

	C	D
C	1st, 1st	4th, 2nd
D	2nd, 4th	3rd, 3rd

or:

	C	D
C	1st, 1st	4th 3rd
D	3rd, 4th	2nd, 2nd

In situations with these payoff structures, unlike in a Prisoners' Dilemma, there is no collective action problem. Cooperation will occur whenever conditions permit players to act on their preferences; in other words, whenever they can be confident that others will "abide by covenants made."

It is well to bear in mind, though, that the social contract leaves individuals' interests and rational capacities just as they were in the state of nature. It only changes the context in which individuals interact. Thus there is a sense in which everyone would still like to be a lone disobedient even after sovereignty is established. Everyone would like the sovereign's police to regulate everyone's behavior except their own. It might be otherwise if individuals believed that their own cooperation was essential for the security that the sovereign's police provide. But because sovereign power typically extends over large populations and territories, a lone disobedient would hardly be expected to put civil order in jeopardy. Thus Prisoners' Dilemma preferences persist, even when the "game" individuals play is no longer a Prisoners' Dilemma. This fact poses a danger to civil order, as we will see.

However, the danger is not as acute as may at first appear. For, if

Hobbes was right, in addition to the sovereign's police, there is another very powerful factor promoting order that comes into being once individuals live together in a "commonwealth." After the sovereign establishes order, individuals are finally able to act on the realization that they will be better off, in the long run, if they suppress their desires to be lone disobedients. Thus what would otherwise be a debilitating collective action problem, lurking just beneath the fragile surface of a Hobbesian state, awaiting only the relaxation of fear of the sovereign's police to swell up, is at least partly transformed into an intra-individual, interest-balancing problem. Individuals must balance their long-term interests against their short-term interests. Each individual's short-term interest is to benefit from defection whenever possible; each individual's long-term interest is to cooperate with others in order to be thought of as a trustworthy cooperator, the better to benefit from future, mutually beneficial agreements. In a commonwealth, individuals' long-term interests can and generally will prevail over their short-term interests. In a state of nature, where stable expectations are out of the question, short-term interests will always govern individuals' lives. But no matter how advantageous a good reputation can be after sovereignty is established, the fact remains that individuals are permanently disposed to free ride on the contributions of others to the extent that they can. Everyone wants the benefits of living in a world in which others conform to rules, but no one wants to pay the costs of conforming to those rules themselves.

Nevertheless, with sovereignty in place, it becomes a general precept of reason to abide by covenants made. *Fairness* matters. In the state of nature, it did not matter at all. In those conditions, individuals might be able to empathize with others when they complain, for example, about the size or composition of their distributive shares. They might realize that, were they themselves in a similar situation, they too would have similar complaints. But no one was rationally compelled to acknowledge the legitimacy of the complaints others expressed because there were no circumstances in which anyone owed anything to anyone else. Therefore, no one could claim that they had not gotten their fair share, their due. But once mutually advantageous agreements become possible, individuals can complain on precisely these grounds, whenever others fail to uphold their part of the agreements they have made. In short, once it becomes rational for individuals to enter into agreements with others, *fairness* – or, at least, that aspect of fairness that the idea of *reciprocity* captures – becomes an urgent concern. Failing to do one's fair share becomes reprehensible.

To generalize this claim: in collective endeavors, it is unfair that some individuals reap the benefits of the contributions others make without contributing themselves to their production. If individuals are to benefit from the sacrifices of others, from their not doing what is individually best, then they too should sacrifice – ideally, to a comparable degree. This is the rationale for Hobbes's superficially implausible contention that the law of nature, *that men perform their covenants made*, is equivalent to the Golden Rule (*L*, chap. 15) or, as we might say today, to the idea that, in appropriate circumstances, individuals ought to act as impartial or agent-neutral deliberations dictate. Hobbes is for fairness, but not for its own sake. He is for fairness when and insofar as it is mutually advantageous. Thus justice or fairness is *not* a bedrock principle for Hobbes. It comes into its own only when and insofar as self-interest prescribes it; in other words, only after the social contract establishes peace. Hobbes's laconic and very idiosyncratic account of what justice is, properly understood, therefore implies an answer to a perennial question of moral philosophy – Why be moral? For Hobbes, morality is indeed something to do and not merely to contemplate. But morality is something to do for the same reason that anything else rational agents do is – because it is in their self-interest. What Hobbes had to say about what morality is is in line with what most moral philosophers after him would maintain. What is moral is what is underwritten by Golden Rule deliberations or, more generally, by impartial or agent-neutral rules. But what Hobbes said about moral motivation is controversial. Mainstream moral philosophy, especially those forms of it influenced by Immanuel Kant (1724–1804), is, as philosophers today would say, *internalist*; it maintains – sometimes implicitly, usually explicitly – that the fact that an action accords with what morality requires is itself a reason, typically a compelling reason, to perform that action. Hobbes's position on moral motivation is very different. For Hobbes, everything, even morality, is interest-driven; rational agents do only what self-interest prescribes. It is Hobbes's contention, however, that, in conditions of peace, acting morally *is* what self-interest prescribes. The reason to be moral is that, in the right circumstances, it is a wise policy for self-interested rational agents to follow.

It may seem that this conclusion is too hasty even for Hobbes to draw, given his commitment to self-interest. Why follow moral rules rather than deliberate in a self-interested way on a case-by-case basis? Why submit to *any* rules that may, in particular applications, make oneself worse off? Contemporary moral philosophers, sympathetic to Hobbes's position, might defend following rules on the grounds that, in general, doing so saves information gathering and processing "costs," rendering individuals better off than they would be if they considered each case on its merits. But, as indicated, Hobbes defended following rules in a different way. He focused on *reputation*. Consider promise-keeping, a requirement of morality that is linked conceptually to justice itself as Hobbes understood the term. It is very much in individuals' interests that the institution of promise-making exist; when individuals are able to make promises to one another, everyone is better off. It is also the case that particular individuals will benefit from promise-making to the degree that they have good reputations for keeping promises. Individuals therefore have interests in cultivating their reputations as promise-keepers. But to succeed in this endeavor, they must actually keep promises. They must do what morality requires. It was Hobbes's idea, at least implicitly, that what holds in this case holds in general. Thus prudence underwrites morality. To act morally is to act as one's own best, long-term interests require.

"The fool hath said in his heart, there is no such thing as justice; and sometimes also with his tongue; seriously alleging, that every man's conservation, and contentment, being committed to his own care, there could be no reason, why every man, might not do what he thought conduced there unto; and therefore also to make, or not make, keep, or not keep, covenants, was not against reason, when it conduced to one's benefit" (*L*, chap. 15). The "fool" Hobbes had in mind is evidently the fool of Psalm XIV, the one whom St. Anselm invoked, centuries earlier, in proposing what philosophers today call the "ontological argument" for the existence of God. Anselm's contention was that whoever denies that God exists is guilty of a conceptual error. "God," Anselm maintained, "cannot be conceived so as not to exist."[5] Hobbes's fool, however, makes a rather different mistake. For there is nothing self-contradictory in entering into an agreement that one does not intend to keep. Indeed, as Hobbes himself had implied, in a state of nature, this "folly" is warranted, even

---

[5]   As an argument-type, the ontological argument's first appearance was in the second chapter of St. Anselm of Canterbury's (1033–1109) *Proslogion*, where Anselm identified atheists with "fools" and diagnosed their folly as conceptual in nature. In subsequent years, the ontological argument has been asserted in a variety of ingenious ways by rationalist philosophers. In brief, the ontological argument is a deductive, *a priori* argument that purports to establish God's existence by analysis of the concept "God." Its general contention is that God's existence is provable in the way that it is provable, say, that triangles have three sides. We know *a priori* that a plane figure with any number of sides other than three would not count as a triangle. Thus one could maintain that "a triangle cannot be conceived so as not to be three-sided" or, as some philosophers might say, that "being a three-sided (plane) figure" is *included* in the concept "triangle." Proponents of the ontological argument believe similarly that God's existence is somehow included in the concept "God."

rationally required. Thus, despite what Hobbes's language suggests, Hobbes's fool is not guilty of self-contradiction. But, if Hobbes was right, the fool does reason incorrectly. Shorn of rhetorical excess, Hobbes's point is just that after the social contract has established sovereignty, after it has become possible to establish a reputation as a follower of moral rules, individuals who fail to do so act in reckless disregard of their own interests. This, Hobbes seems to have thought, is a sin against reason, as reprehensible as falling into a logical contradiction. But it is not strictly the same mistake.

The Sovereign

Because Hobbes's England was an absolute monarchy and Hobbes an anti-revolutionary, and because Hobbes stood only on the threshold of the modern era and could not yet envision the transformations in political forms that would come in time, Hobbes identified the sovereign with an individual, and the institution of sovereignty with absolute monarchy. But, in key respects, Hobbes's account of the nature of sovereignty transcended these limitations. For one thing, the sovereign Hobbes described – the office, not the individual – is an *artificial* person, the *representative* of the individuals who constitute it (*L*, chap. 16). It only happens, then, that sovereignty is embodied in a natural person, a living, breathing human being. Thus Hobbes opened the way to supporting very different institutional arrangements from the ones that he defended. As we will go on to see, a Hobbesian, unlike Hobbes himself, need be neither a monarchist nor a proponent of absolutism.

Hobbes's account of the nature of sovereignty, like his support for absolute monarchy, effectively straddled late medieval and early modern political theory. On the one hand, it looks back to the medieval doctrine of "the king's two bodies," itself an adaptation of the Christian doctrine of transubstantiation, according to which the monarch is simultaneously a natural person and a public person (*res publica*), the physical embodiment of the state. This is why it is fair to say, as I did earlier, that, in Hobbes's view, sovereignty is "incarnated" in a particular individual, one who is chosen arbitrarily. On the other hand, because the sovereign's existence *qua* sovereign depends entirely on the "free gift" of the people, Hobbes's account of sovereignty looks forward to the notion of full-fledged popular sovereignty that would emerge a century later. Still, for Hobbes himself, the sovereign is not quite identical to the individuals whose contracts among themselves bring him into being. Rather, as

Hobbes would have it, these individuals *authorize* the sovereign to act on their behalf, to serve as their *representative*, in roughly the way that, in the law, one individual is able to invest "power of attorney" in another. The difference is that, in establishing sovereignty by means of a social contract, the only means available to them, individuals authorize the sovereign to represent them on *all* matters that the sovereign deems important, and to act on their behalf in perpetuity. Thus, unlike other grants of power of attorney, Hobbesian sovereignty, once conferred, is unlimited and irrevocable. Here, then, is another instance in which Hobbes's political theory and his political convictions ingeniously coincide. In depicting the sovereign as he did, Hobbes provided yet another reason why it is wrong to rebel. In rebelling against their sovereign, individuals rebel against themselves or, more precisely, against their absolute and *eternal* representative.

In the end, of course, political authority and political obligation exist only insofar as it is in each individual's interest that they do. Paradoxically, therefore, an individual's obligation to obey the sovereign is limited in a way that the sovereign's authority is not. In Hobbes's view, it is almost always in an individual's interest that there be a sovereign. It is therefore almost always in an individual's interest to obey the sovereign, inasmuch as general obedience to the sovereign's commands is, according to the third law of nature, a condition for the possibility of sovereignty itself. An individual's obligation to obey the sovereign is therefore very nearly absolute. But in extreme and unlikely circumstances – when, for example, a sovereign seeks to take an individual's life or to put that individual's life in extreme jeopardy – the advantages of living under the sovereign's protection disappear and the individual is no better off than in a state of war. Then the individual has no reason to obey the sovereign's commands and consequently no obligation to do so. In that event, the sovereign may still rightfully take his subjects' lives or do anything else that he pleases. There are never any restrictions on what the sovereign can rightfully do. But the individual is under no obligation to obey.

With respect to his subjects, the sovereign is still, as it were, in a state of nature. But he is not in a state of war! For the situation the sovereign confronts is not relevantly similar to the one that individuals confronted before the social contract. The social contract establishes peace between all of the parties to it. But it also establishes peace between these individuals and the sovereign, a third party who is not contractually bound to the rest. After the social contract, these individuals are the subjects, not the enemies, of the individual who assumes sovereign power. In virtue of the social contract, then, that individual obtains what, by hypothesis, all individuals always want – security, wealth, and power and esteem.

Moreover, the individual who becomes the sovereign receives these benefits without giving up anything in return, without laying down any of his own rights. For that (fortunate) individual, sovereignty is a "free gift." Because this gift is motivated ultimately by self-interest, the sovereign has nothing to fear from his subjects. Insofar as they are rational, the sovereign is secure in his office.

Not so his subjects, however. They do have something to fear from the sovereign, inasmuch as he owes them nothing contractually and is therefore in a state of nature with respect to them. But this peril is mitigated somewhat by two related considerations, one that Hobbes expressly adduced, the other that is implicit in his approach to the problem. The sovereign, Hobbes says, owes his subjects gratitude (*L*, chap. 15). "As justice dependeth on antecedent covenant; so does *gratitude* depend on antecedent grace; that is to say, antecedent free gift; and is the fourth law of nature; which may be conceived in this form, *that a man which receiveth benefit from another of mere grace, endeavour that he which giveth it, have no reasonable cause to repent him of his good will.*" In other words, the sovereign is duty bound to do well by his subjects in the way that, say, children are duty bound to do well by their parents. This protection is plainly less secure than a contractual constraint undergirded by self-interest and backed by overwhelming force. But it is no trivial consideration because it is grounded in human nature. A Hobbesian sovereign cannot be reproached for acting unjustly, but he can be accused of ingratitude, and this prospect provides some check on his behavior. Perhaps a more powerful constraint, though, is the sovereign's own self-interest. In most imaginable circumstances, it would be irrational for a sovereign to act in the way that an ingrate would, because the sovereign is the beneficiary of his subjects' free gift. He therefore has ever reason to cultivate his subjects' good will, and no reason to move adversely against any of them – unless, of course, he has reason to fear that their irrationality is a threat to his power. But if we assume full compliance with the demands of reason on the part of the sovereign's subjects and on the part of the sovereign himself, then subjects have good reason to expect that their sovereign will rule them well. Both gratitude and self-interest conspire together to this end.

A political message is implicit in this conclusion too. Rebellion, in Hobbes's view, is a consequence of irrationality on the part of the sovereigns' subjects, of just the kind of irrationality that would cause a rational and otherwise grateful sovereign to govern repressively. Thus there is, in Hobbes's account of the constraints that regulate the sovereign's behavior towards his subjects, a claim for the existence of a virtuous circle with anti-revolutionary implications. The more obedient subjects are, the more likely their sovereign is to rule them gently, and therefore the less likely that repression will unleash the kind of irrationality that makes for disobedience and ultimately for revolution. It is important to realize, though, that this consideration speaks only to the question of how subjects ought to act towards their sovereign, not to the rationale for sovereignty itself. Hobbes's case for sovereignty obtains irrespective of how beneficent or malign a sovereign may be, and has nothing to do with factors that might impel a sovereign to govern either gently or with brutal force. However gentle or harsh a sovereign may be, it is never rational and therefore never right to rebel.

Hobbes and Liberalism

Because *liberalism* will figure prominently in the chapters that follow, it will be instructive to turn from Hobbes' account of sovereignty itself, to the question of the relation of Hobbes's view to liberal political philosophy. For liberals, there are principled limitations on the use of public coercive force; restrictions on what sovereigns may rightfully do. Hobbes was plainly not a liberal in this sense. Indeed, it is a tenet of his theory of sovereignty that the sovereign's power is necessarily unrestricted, that a sovereign can rightfully do anything. Nevertheless, it is fair to depict Hobbes as a forerunner of liberal political thought. If nothing else, the core liberal value, *liberty*, understood in roughly the way that Hobbes conceived it, as "the absence of External Impediments," was a core value for Hobbes. Hobbes was arguably the first political philosopher, certainly the first political philosopher of major importance, to conceive liberty this way, and the first to accord it preeminent normative force. Hobbes demonstrated that a maximal level of freedom, unrestricted freedom, is sub-optimal. Where unrestricted freedom exists, individuals' interests as free beings are poorly served. Hobbes's central claim, then, was that unrestricted political authority is necessary for individuals to attain optimal levels of freedom; that, paradoxically, the way to optimize freedom is to restrict it by concocting a sovereign whose authority is in principle absolute. Hobbes and the liberals part ways on this crucial issue. But they were of one mind on the value of liberty itself.

I would venture that their differences in this regard follow, at least in part, from the different intensities of their respective commitments to a generally Christian view of political life. As remarked (in the Introduction), both Hobbes and the liberals stand in the tradition of those political philosophers who take Sin or its secular analogue, the darker side of human nature, seriously. For Hobbes, only the sovereign's police can save individuals from themselves and from each other. Without quite disagreeing, liberals have a more sanguine view of the human prospect. They stand to Hobbes in much the way that the mainstream Protestant clergy of today stand to the fire and brimstone preachers of old. But they each agree on the core point – that sovereignty goes against nature, and is therefore an evil in its own right. It is a necessary evil, of course, inasmuch as a state of nature is even worse than a state is. Nevertheless, the price free beings must pay for the order necessary for them to pursue their interests as free beings is a certain diminution of their liberty. The idea, then, is to retrieve as much as possible of the freedom of the state of nature without remaining in it; to provide as much liberty to individuals as they can enjoy without undermining their basic interests. This was Hobbes's goal, and it is also the goal of political philosophers who stand unambiguously in the liberal tradition, as it has unfolded in the wake of Hobbes's groundbreaking work.

Hobbes's Conservatism

Hobbes's political philosophy and his anti-revolutionary political convictions are inextricably joined. But Hobbes's opposition to rebellion is only a special case of a more encompassing *conservatism* that shaped his view of political life. This conservatism both motivates and follows from Hobbes's account of the origin and nature of sovereignty. If only to put his position in perspective therefore, it warrants attention here.

Hobbes's conservatism is Christian. It is a conservatism that takes seriously the psychology of "fallen" humankind. Among modern conservatisms, it is therefore closer in spirit to the strain of conservative theory and practice that predominates in authoritarian, especially Catholic, political cultures, than to the kind of conservatism familiar to citizens of more liberal regimes. The latter, non-Hobbesian form of conservative political philosophy emerged in reaction to the French Revolution – in the writings of generally liberal political thinkers who opposed events in revolutionary France. Edmund Burke's reflections on the French Revolution exemplify this tendency; so too do Alexis de Tocqueville's.[6] This

---

[6] See Edmund Burke, *Reflections on the Revolution in France*, Connor Cruise O'Brien, ed. (London: Penguin, 1968) and Alexis de Tocqueville, *The Old Regime and the Revolution* (François Furet and Françoise Mélonio, eds.), Chicago: University of Chicago Press, 1998.

kinder, gentler strain of conservative theory is indifferent to Original Sin or its modern equivalent, that side of human nature that, left unchecked, would bring the human race to ruin. It is based instead on a view of the nature of politics and governance. Its core idea is that governing a state is an activity that more nearly resembles cooking or carpentry than geometry.[7] These are skills in which a reservoir of accumulated wisdom and good sense, built up over generations and materialized in techniques, implements and traditions matter more than rational insight or deductive acuity. The French Revolutionaries, on the other hand, were moved by a rationalist spirit. They overthrew the old regime in order to build a new world on rational foundations, in much the way that philosophical rationalists like René Descartes sought to overthrow existing knowledge claims in order to start over from the beginning, on sound, rationally compelling foundations. For conservatives like Burke and Tocqueville, the French ought instead to have been moved by a finely-tuned sensibility to existing traditions and received ways of doing things. Had they been so moved, great misfortunes might have been averted and everything worthwhile that the revolutionaries accomplished would have come about in time anyway. For these conservatives, then, it is wise governance, not the fear of uncontrolled human nature, that motivates aversion to abrupt or fundamental change, and that advises caution in tampering, even slightly, with the institutional arrangements of the status quo.

The influential strain of conservative theory exemplified by Burke and Tocqueville therefore defends gradualism in politics for reasons foreign to Hobbes's way of thinking. His conservatism was motivated mainly by the idea that human beings are incapable of doing well for themselves, incapable even of maintaining civil order, in the absence of powerful *political* – that is, coercive – authority relations and other institutional constraints, such as those provided by the family and the church. These institutions save human beings from their own depraved natures. Hobbes's conservatism rests, in short, on the conviction that human nature is so utterly insufficient for realizing human beings' true ends that its free expression must be suppressed before it can wreak devastating effects.

Freedom must therefore be restricted for order to exist; it must be restricted by a sovereign power. But because sovereignty is an artifice opposed to nature, it is easily undone. A wise politics will take this fact into account. It will therefore eschew not only rebellion, but change in

---

[7]   No conservative thinker has articulated this view more cogently than Michael Oakeshott. See, especially, "Political Education" in Michael Oakeshott, *Rationalism and Politics* (London: Methuen, 1962).

general, because changes are almost always destabilizing. The more far-reaching a change is, the more threatening it is to order, and the more it therefore ought to be opposed. It is a consequence of Hobbes's theory of sovereignty, then, that the political superstructure that holds human nature in check is forever prone to ruin by forces that it can only barely control. Putting these delicate arrangements in jeopardy is always inordinately risky. It hardly matters, then, what the prevailing order is; what matters is just that it *is* an order. Given human nature and the human condition, and taking *better* and *worse,* as Hobbes did, to mean more or less in line with individuals' desires, then even the worst commonwealth is better by far than a state of nature. But inasmuch as all political orders go against nature by restricting liberty, even the best commonwealths envisioned by revolutionaries and reformers are not much better than the worst regimes. Weighing the likely benefits against the costs, it therefore follows that it is almost always unwise to resist the authorities in place. The possible gains are too slight to justify the very great likelihood of falling back into a condition so dreadful that anything, even tyranny, is preferable to it.

To be sure, it is neither necessary nor possible to remain forever frozen in time. But it follows from Hobbes's rationale for sovereignty and his account of its nature that it is always best that political changes be initiated and directed by existing authorities, and that subjects never attempt to exceed the wishes of their leaders. Thus Hobbes's conservatism, unlike the conservatism of Burke or Tocqueville, implies unflinching support for existing authority, whatever it may be. It is worth recalling that both Burke and Tocqueville defended the American Revolution, even as they opposed the French. It would be hard to imagine anyone with Hobbes's sensibilities doing likewise. For in the Hobbesian view, sovereignty is such a fragile but indispensable concoction that it must, on no account, be put at risk, lest the human race degenerate back into the condition that only sovereignty can remedy.

From this vantage-point, then, the most enduring threat to individuals' well-being is not outright rebellion, since revolutions come onto the historical agenda only in extraordinary times. Nor is it even the spirit of reform, though reform is a constant temptation. The main problem is that individuals will forget the state of nature and its perils, that they will become less than ardent enforcers of the sovereign's commands. The danger, in short, is not so much that sovereignty will be overthrown as that it will lapse. This is a danger fed as much by complacency as by social upheavals and therefore, ironically, by peace itself. Rebellion and reform are dangers too, of course; and in particular historical conjunctures, such as the one Hobbes lived through, the threat they pose is especially salient. But laxity is the greatest threat of all, for it continually puts sovereignty at risk.

Rational individuals, having established sovereignty, cannot seek to overthrow it or even to change it fundamentally. To do so would be to act against their own best interests. But they can, in time, become less vigilant in maintaining the institution they have contrived. Sovereignty, after all, is nothing other than the organized force of the individuals whom the sovereign represents. Its strength and ultimately its very existence therefore depends on their commitment to it. The social contract that establishes sovereignty is indeed irreversible, but only in the sense that, given what Hobbes assumed about individuals' interests, individuals cannot alter it fundamentally or withdraw the authority they have invested in it without acting irrationally. In the real world of politics, however, sovereignty can, as it were, *wither away,* as the reason for its existence becomes increasingly remote to the individuals who benefit from it. A politics true to the spirit of Hobbes's political philosophy must therefore, above all, militate against this eventuality.

For a Hobbesian, then, establishing sovereignty is only the first step in "solving" the problem individuals in a state of nature confront. The social contract must be actively and continually renewed. In short, the Hobbesian social contract is not so much a founding *event* as an ever-present reality underlying the permanently insecure edifice individuals concoct because it is in the interest of each of them that it exist. But because tampering with that structure is inordinately risky, it is in their interest too that there be active support for the leadership the sovereign provides and therefore support for whoever the sovereign happens to be. Thus the same consideration that justifies sovereignty in general suggests *respect* for the particular sovereign under whom one lives. This, then, is where Hobbes's conservatism leads. Unlike Burke's or Tocqueville's, it underwrites not only gradualism and sensitivity to traditional practices and styles of governance, but also support for the incumbents of existing offices, for those individuals who actually exercise authority. At the limit, Hobbes's conservatism shades off into the kind of authoritarian politics that so many twentieth-century regimes tragically exemplified.[8]

---

[8] I hesitate to use the word "totalitarian" to describe this political tendency because, during the early Cold War period, that term became fraught with misleading implications in the writings of anti-Communist ideologues intent on identifying Communism, which enjoyed a comparatively good reputation in the West during and immediately after Second World War, with Naziism, which was universally discred-

Yet, at the same time, because freedom is a value of paramount importance, self-interest also requires a *minimal* state, a state that restricts liberty no more than it must. There is, then, a tension in Hobbes's thought. Hobbesian political philosophy has authoritarian implications. But it has a liberal or, rather, libertarian aspect as well. Happily, in the making of modern political philosophy, the libertarian side of Hobbes's thinking has been more influential.

Hobbesian Statism

In any case, for Hobbes himself and for all of Hobbes's successors, liberal or authoritarian, the state is indispensable for liberty and order and indeed for all other values political institutions are called upon to advance. In the centuries after Hobbes, this conviction has become the most deeply entrenched tenet of modern political thought. It is *the* modern orthodoxy, and it was largely Hobbes's invention. However, Hobbes articulated this idea in a way that belongs to a very different world from our own. He was prone, moreover, to exaggerate the considerations that motivated his conclusions, and to paint a far bleaker picture of human nature and the human condition than seems appropriate. It will therefore be well to conclude by restating exactly what Hobbesian statism involves, apart from Hobbes's own account of it.

The Hobbesian idea, in short, is that individuals cannot in general cooperate sufficiently to coordinate their behaviors in the way(s) that their interests require, at least not outside of groups much smaller than

---

ited after the war. The effect, which lingers to this day, was to obfuscate crucial differences between regimes of the Left and the Right. This ideological operation was so successful that, by the 1980s, the term "totalitarian" was commonly used only in reference to Communist countries, prompting some later day Cold War ideologues to distinguish "totalitarianism" from "authoritarianism," the latter term being used to denote repressive regimes friendly to the United States. It was said, in those days, that authoritarian regimes were bound to evolve in democratic and liberal directions, while Communist (totalitarian) regimes would never change, except by war. Inasmuch as this purported difference was proved false almost from the moment of its assertion, the distinction has fallen into disuse. In any case, it should be clear to the reader that my use of "authoritarian" is innocent of the ideological uses to which the term has recently been put. What I have in mind by it is roughly what the term "totalitarian" commonly, though imprecisely and tendentiously, is widely understood to suggest, now that the political impetus behind earlier uses of that troubled notion have faded from the political consciousness of most people.

political communities must be. Thus individuals face the prospect of a generalized Prisoners' Dilemma, in which their doing what is individually best leads them to outcomes that are worse, given their interests, than need be. These individuals will therefore, if possible, make themselves unfree to do what is individually best, when and insofar as this constraint on their freedom is necessary for advancing their interests. They will establish a coercive mechanism, the state, that forces them to refrain from acting in ways detrimental to their own well-being. They cannot achieve this result directly, thanks to human nature and the human condition. But they can achieve it indirectly, by investing an authority of their own creation with sufficient power to compel compliance to its commands.

To make this point even more clear, it will be useful to take advantage of yet another contemporary notion – the idea of a *public good*. Like many other entries in the economist's lexicon, the term is encumbered with imprecisions and ambiguities that affect even its strictest applications. For our purposes, however, we can think of a public good as a good that requires the contributions of many for its production (*jointness in production*), and that has benefits that spill over to individuals largely irrespective of their contributions towards its production (*jointness in supply*). Defense of the national territory is a textbook example; it is a benefit that requires the contributions of many to produce, and that, once supplied is available to all – inasmuch as it would be difficult, if not impossible, to defend some inhabitants of the national territory while leaving others unprotected.

There is a further condition that must be satisfied before we are entitled to speak of a good as a public good; it must be something that is generally desired within the population for which it is public. Of course, for Hobbes, this was not a problem. In his idealized account of the state of nature, everyone, by hypothesis, wants the same thing(s). With respect to public goods provision in general after a commonwealth is established, it is also not a problem. If Hobbes was right in holding that rational individuals living in commonwealths will pursue a Hobbesian conservative politics, the public will generally desire whatever the sovereign commands, just in virtue of the fact that the sovereign commands it. Then if, as Hobbes believed, the sovereign is always a particular individual, there will be no problem in ascertaining his will. However, this will not be the case once the medieval side of Hobbes's theory of sovereignty is discarded. If sovereignty is not incarnated in a living human being, but rather in "the people" themselves, there is no avoiding the problem of ascertaining their desires. But *the people* is comprised of individuals, and individuals want different things. I will address this problem in later chapters. For now, it will suffice to say that a public good is any good for which the jointness in production and jointness in supply conditions obtain, and that is, in fact, generally desired.

Jointness in production and jointness in supply make public goods provision problematic. For when these conditions hold, self-interested individuals will prefer free riding on the contributions of others to contributing themselves towards the production of the goods they desire. After all, public goods are available to everyone, whether they contribute or not towards their production, and why pay for what one can get for free? But, of course, if enough individuals act on their free-riding preferences, the good will not be produced and everyone will be worse off than they might otherwise be. Therefore, to obtain the public goods that they want, individuals must make themselves unfree to free ride. They must contrive means that make it impossible or, at least, inordinately costly to do what would otherwise be individually best. If only for this pragmatic or practical reason, the state is indispensable. If public goods are to be provided, productive contributions must be coerced. But only states can coerce the requisite contributions reliably. They must therefore be employed for this purpose.

The possibility of individuals free riding on the contributions of others also raises a moral problem that the state solves. The moral, as opposed to pragmatic or practical, problem with free riding is the one that Hobbes identified in his discussion of justice. It is that it is unfair to enjoy benefits without contributing towards their production, to take without also giving back. To the degree that this principle is acknowledged, there is a normatively compelling reason to proscribe free riding, in addition to the pragmatic or practical reason just noted. Free riding offends the idea of reciprocity. According to the now prevailing orthodoxy, this is reason enough for states to exist, whether or not a concern with reciprocity properly extends all the way back into the state of nature, as Hobbes denied, or whether, as Hobbes believed, reciprocity matters only after the state of nature is ended for pragmatic reasons. In either case, it is morally urgent that free riding not be allowed. This task falls to the one institution that can coerce contributions justifiably, the state.

Nowadays, it has become commonplace, especially in libertarian circles (but not only there), to laud markets, systems of voluntary exchange, as mechanisms for coordinating individuals' activities; and to deride state interferences with individuals' lives and behaviors, especially in the economic sphere. But market incentives are generally inadequate for insuring that public goods will be provided. This why even the most ardent proponents of market relations today believe that public goods provision is a legitimate state function. The most ardent of them believe, in fact, that it is the *only* legitimate state function. In this respect, even they, despite their vaunted hostility towards states, are Hobbesian statists. For Hobbes's case for sovereignty is a special case of the more general claim that states are justified because they are indispensable for providing public goods. Hobbes's focus, again, was on security. It should now be plain that security is a public good; it is jointly produced and its benefits spill over indifferently to everyone, contributor and non-contributor alike. Moreover, it is urgently desired by all individuals. According to Hobbes's story, it is to obtain this good that individuals leave the state of nature to form commonwealths, for it is only when they succeed in establishing sovereignty that their security is assured. In Hobbes's view, there is no other way to obtain this good, which all individuals are rationally compelled to seek; no system of voluntary exchange can possibly provide it. In the more general case, there is no other way to obtain any public good that individuals might, for any reason, desire.

Political philosophers after Hobbes would go on to disregard the more flamboyant claims Hobbes made in pressing this case. But the idea that states are indispensable for providing public goods, and that the state is justifiable on this account, has become a constant of modern political thought, denied only by the anarchists. In this respect, even Marx, who shared certain of the anarchists' convictions, can be grouped, albeit uneasily, with the rest. Therefore despite the fact that no political philosopher today would want to identify with Hobbes's views on institutional arrangements, and despite the fact that his brand of conservatism nowadays finds few adherents, even among thinkers of a generally conservative disposition, modern political philosophy, in virtue of its fundamental commitment to Hobbesian statism, is Hobbesian to its core. From its inception in Hobbes's own work, Hobbes has been its foundational thinker.

2

Rousseau

Jean-Jacques Rousseau's (1712–78) declared aim in *The Social Contract* was to give an account of rightful or legitimate political authority, authority *de jure*. This was not and could not have been Hobbes's aim. For Hobbes, because morality compels action only when and insofar as it is in individuals' interests that it do so, questions about the legitimacy of political authorities cannot arise in the way that they do for Rousseau. For Hobbes, *de jure* authority is of no concern in a state of nature. The task there is only to establish authority *de facto*, in fact. So long as authority claims are acknowledged, there is no gainsaying their legitimacy. What is decisive is might, the power to issue enforceable commands. We saw (in chapter 1) how Hobbes ultimately made a place for a notion of right – how, in his view, morality becomes advantageous for individuals and therefore germane to their lives *after* sovereignty is established. For Rousseau, in contrast, the world of might and the world of right are, from the very beginning, independent dimensions of human experience. It is the task of descriptive political science to investigate the former domain. It falls to the political philosopher to deal with questions of right – with "men as they are and laws as they might be" (*Social Contract*, henceforth *SC*, Introductory Note).

As this formulation suggests, a theory of *de jure* authority, of "laws as they might be," must be consistent with human nature, with "men as they are." But "men as they are" is an equivocal concept. At the very beginning of *The Social Contract*, Rousseau contrasted how human beings are really (ideally) with how they actually are. "Man is born free but is everywhere in chains" (*SC*, I, 1). With respect to being free, then, how human beings actually are is the opposite of how they are really and therefore how they ought to be. This inversion of appearance and reality is of central concern to Rousseau's political philosophy and ultimately, as we will see, to his politics as well. For now, it will suffice to infer from this formulation, read in light of others that follow it, that, for Rousseau, freedom is central to being human – not at the level of appearance but at the level of the real, of what ought to be. What is *essential* to being human, to "men as they are," is the (purported) fact that they are "born free."

Hobbes, of course, valued freedom too. But he never maintained anything like what Rousseau's declaration implies. For one thing, freedom or liberty, I will again use the terms interchangeably, mattered less to Hobbes than to Rousseau. The difference is not just that, for Hobbes, freedom is only one value among many – including order, the value that is the condition for the possibility of the rest. It is that Hobbes and Rousseau understood freedom differently. For Rousseau, freedom is not "the absence of External Impediments" or coercive restraints. It is *autonomy* – self-governance or self-direction. One is free to the degree that one obeys only oneself. This notion is foreign to Hobbes's way of thinking. But it is precisely the possibility of being free in this sense, of being an autonomous agent, that constrains what Rousseau will say about "laws as they might be." For Rousseau, rightful institutional arrangements must respect human beings' essential autonomy.

Hobbes insisted, as fervently as Rousseau did, that institutional arrangements accord with human nature. But Hobbes understood human nature psychologically, just as he understood authority empirically. Rousseau moralized both ideas. In his political philosophy, what matters is authority in right, not in fact; and what matters about human nature are not facts of human psychology but a metaphysical fact about human beings – that they are essentially free (autonomous) agents. We will find that Rousseau's views about human psychology play an important role in his account of the just state, and even that Rousseau and Hobbes were of one mind on the psychological dispositions of individuals in a state of nature immediately prior to the adoption of the social contract. But, for Rousseau, psychological factors do not constrain institutional arrangements in anything like the way that they do for Hobbes. Ultimately, Rousseau's and Hobbes's differences on this issue have more to do with metaphysics than psychology. In the place of Hobbes's all-encompassing materialism, Rousseau situated philosophical reflections on politics in the non-material reality of the moral world order that Kant, following Rousseau's lead, investigated decades later.[1]

[1] In *The Phenomenology of Mind*, in the section called "Spirit certain of itself: Morality," Hegel famously named this discovery of Rousseau's "the moral vision of the world," arguing that Rousseau discovered this aspect of the real, but that it fell to

...e one that leaves individuals free; that respects their essential au-
...ny. This is why pacts of slavery cannot model legitimate political
...iations; why, in addition to respecting the equality of persons, a
...mate social contract must also respect the autonomy of each and
...associate.
...e implications of this conclusion for political authority are set forth
...ok I, Chapter 6, where the basic argument of *The Social Contract* is
...out. Book I, Chapter 6 is the central text for Rousseau's theory of
...ical authority. It would be only a slight exaggeration to say that
...thing else in *The Social Contract* and in Rousseau's many other
...ical writings either anticipate it or comment upon it. But before set-
...forth the heart of his case, Rousseau had one additional point to
...e. In Book I, Chapter 5, he distinguished what the political theory of
...ay called *pacts of government,* "the act by which a people selects a
...," from *pacts of association,* "the act by which a people becomes a
...le." Rousseau's social contract is a pact of association. It constitutes
...political community. Rousseau's contract therefore contrasts with
...ocial contract that, according to the US *Declaration of Independ-*
..., the British monarch, George III, had and then broke with his colo-
...in North America. The dissolution of that contract, in consequence
...e king's alleged misdeeds, triggered a supposed right of revolution.
...it did not dissolve the political communities that had contracted with
...king. Thus Rousseau expressly distinguished sovereignty from gov-
...ment. Sovereignty is the issue of a pact of association; government is
...t follows from a pact of government. Book III of *The Social Contract*
...bout government. I will have almost nothing to say about it here.
...k I and most of Book II, especially its first six chapters, address issues
...aining to sovereignty.

A Digression

...ore turning to Book I, Chapter 6 of *The Social Contract,* it will be
...ructive to set that work aside in order to insert another line of argu-
...nt, taken from Rousseau's *Discourse on the Origin of Inequality*
...ong Men,* the so-called *Second Discourse,* into the account of *de jure*
...itical authority that has unfolded to this point. These texts were never
...nded to be read as one. It is, therefore, unusual, to say the least, to
...them together in the way that I will. But it is worth doing, especially
...anyone who would read Rousseau after Hobbes. The *Second Dis-*
...rse* recounts a story, set in the distant past, that is replete with insights

It is fair to say, then, that what Rousseau sought to provide in *The Social Contract* was a *deduction* of the concept of *de jure* political authority. I use "deduction" here not in the sense that is commonplace in modern (and ancient) logic, according to which conclusions are deduced from premises, but in the sense that Kant developed in his critical philosophy, again making explicit an idea that Rousseau had earlier intimated. For Kant, to deduce a concept was, first, to demonstrate its internal coherence and then to establish its possible applicability. This is what Rousseau set out to do in *The Social Contract*: to show how the concept of a just state can be conceived without contradiction and how it is applicable to persons as they *really* are. One could therefore say that, in doing political philosophy, Rousseau placed himself in the tradition Plato began. His aim was to show that the *idea* of a just state, of *de jure* political authority, is real. Allowing for the fact that Rousseau never subscribed overtly to Plato's metaphysics, one might even say that the domain Rousseau investigated in *The Social Contract* was the realm of Platonic ideas or forms – in contrast to the world of appearance, where *de facto* legitimate states exist.

It is therefore possible that the concept of a just state can be satisfactorily "deduced," but that all existing states and therefore all *de facto* authority claims fall so far short of what is required for *de jure* legitimacy that all existing states are all, as a matter of fact, illegitimate. I would venture that this conclusion actually is implicit in the argument of *The Social Contract*. Rousseau does say that "taking men as they are and laws as they might be" he can demonstrate the existence of "some legitimate and sure rule of administration in the civil order" (*SC*, I, 1). But this claim is consistent with there being no actually existing legitimate states – past, present or future. It is one thing to deduce a concept and quite another to advance the hypothesis that it applies in one or another case. Rousseau's objective was the former. On the question of the actuality or

Kant to elaborate its nature. See G. W. F. Hegel (James Baillie, trans.), *The Phenomenology of Mind* (London: George Allen and Unwin, 1910), pp. 615–27. This is, in fact, a main task of Kant's practical philosophy, evident particularly in such works as *The Groundwork of the Metaphysics of Morals* and *The Critique of Practical Reason.* In more recent time, the idea that Rousseau "discovered" a conceptual universe that Kant later explored was vigorously promoted by Ernst Cassirer. See *The Question of Jean-Jacques Rousseau* (Bloomington: Indiana University Press, 1954) and especially *Rousseau, Kant, Goethe* (Princeton: Princeton University Press, 1945). For an extensive defense of these claims, see my *The Politics of Autonomy: A Kantian Reading of Rousseau's "Social Contract"* (Amherst, Mass.: University of Massachusetts Press, 1976).

even the historical feasibility of *de jure* legitimate states, *The Social Contract* is tactfully discreet.

States coordinate individuals' activities through the use or threat of force. But no state could make do with force alone. There are not enough police; and who, finally, would police the police! Thus, for states to exist at all, some of the people all of the time and all of the people some of the time must effectively acknowledge the legitimacy of the institutions under which they live; they must do as the authorities command because they believe that the authorities command rightfully. All existing political communities are therefore to some degree *de facto* legitimate. But this fact is irrelevant to Rousseau's question, except insofar as beliefs about legitimacy occasion philosophical investigations of its possibility *de jure*. Whether or not authority exists in right is logically independent of beliefs about existing authority claims in just the way that beliefs about the existence of God have no bearing on the question of whether or not God really exists. Rousseau's concern, again, is with the *justification* of political authority, not with the nature of people's beliefs about the legitimacy of the political arrangements under which they live. The question is whether and under what conditions some members of political communities can *rightfully* command others, and when, if at all, these others are *rightfully* obligated to obey.

Rousseau's Contractarianism

Hobbes's use of a contractarian methodology was an innovation. By Rousseau's time, contractarianism had become standard. Rousseau's investigation of the rightfulness of political authority and political obligation respected this practice. Thus, like Hobbes, he set out to investigate what mutual advantage prescribes. In this vein, in the opening chapters of *The Social Contract*, Rousseau considered and rejected a number of imaginable social contract types, implicitly challenging much of the political theory of his day in the process. In Chapter Two, he dismissed social contracts that assume that sovereignty can be modeled in the way that patriarchal authority can, drawing the lesson that a legitimate social contract cannot countenance natural dependencies or other inequalities but must instead assume the equality of all the relevant contracting parties. In Chapter Four, Rousseau heaped scorn on what he called "pacts of slavery." Rousseau's use of the term is idiosyncratic. For him, "slavery" does not denote what it usually does: a property relation, according to which some individuals are owned by others. Rather, by "slavery,"

Rousseau meant the subordination of an individ[ual to] another. So understood, slavery contrasts with [self-rule,] obeying only oneself. Slavery in this sense is there[fore what Kant would] later call *heteronomy*, obedience to a law legislat[ed by another. Follow-]ing a longstanding convention among political the[orists ... in using] "slavery" in the usual way, Rousseau distinguish[ed pacts of voluntary] slavery from pacts of involuntary slavery. In the fo[rmer, individuals] exchange liberty for some other good – for [security or ... In] Rousseau's terminology, then, Hobbes's social co[ntract is an instance] of voluntary slavery. In the case of involuntary sla[very, the alternative to] becoming a slave is death. In faulting pacts o[f involuntary slavery,] Rousseau took aim at views derived from Roma[n law that support] the alleged right of conquest. He faulted the idea [that conquest estab-]lishes authority *de jure*. But the heart of the argum[ent of Chapter] 4 is implicit in the case Rousseau made there aga[inst voluntary] slavery. Rousseau's contention is that self-interested [individuals cannot] "alienate" their liberty (autonomy). "To alienate," [he wrote, "is to give] or to sell" (*SC*, I, 4). Obviously, it can never be in [anyone's interest] to give autonomy away. But neither, Rousseau insis[ted, is there anything] for which liberty can be advantageously exchange[d – not ... sub-]sistence or security or anything else. The reason w[hy is that autonomy is] *priceless*. It has what Kant would later call "dignit[y." Its value] is absolute or, as Kant would say, "categorical." Thi[s claim, for now,] is asserted, not demonstrated. But, as we will see, it [is fundamental] to his account of political authority and political ob[ligation. For now, it] will suffice to observe how it explains why even [pacts of voluntary] slavery are illegitimate. If autonomy cannot be advan[tageously exchanged,] it cannot be exchanged even for life itself.

In asserting this claim, Rousseau expressly identi[fied liberty with] moral agency, effectively clarifying the contention, imp[licit in the declara-]tion that "man is born free," that it is autonomy [that makes human] beings truly human. "Renouncing one's liberty," R[ousseau wrote,] "is renouncing one's dignity as a man, the rights of [humanity and even] its duties. There is no possible compensation for any[one who renounces] everything. Such a renunciation is incompatible wit[h man's nature] ..." (*SC*, I, 4). With these words, Rousseau declared [in effect that] autonomy is *the essential* property of being human, [and therefore that] it is the source of all human value. To renounce lib[erty is to renounce] what one essentially is and therefore, for reasons R[ousseau never ex-]plored but that Kant would later elaborate, the cond[ition of the possi-]bility of value as such. It therefore follows that a legiti[mate ...]

about political life and much else as well. In this brief digression, I can hardly do justice to all that can be teased out of this masterpiece. I will focus instead only on those aspects of it that bear on what Rousseau does in Book I, Chapter 6 of *The Social Contract*; specifically, on what fills in the gap between the first five chapters of Book I and Chapter 6.

Although it is ostensibly about life in primitive times, *The Second Discourse* does not purport to provide a factual account of the lives of the first human beings. It is not a history in the contemporary sense; in fact, it is remarkably free of evidence of any kind. At its outset, Rousseau even declared that he would deal with the facts "by setting them aside," and he remained true to his word. In short, *The Second Discourse* is a philosophical fable, not a speculative history. It is a tale contrived to explore philosophical positions. As such, it takes atomic individualism seriously, more seriously even than Hobbes did. It describes the first human beings living in almost complete isolation from one another, without any settled social institutions, without language and without any recognizable culture. In this original state of nature, human beings could not have been in a state of war if only because the geographical proximity condition, so crucial to Hobbes's account, fails to obtain. As one might expect of beings that are regarded as atoms, the first men and women led lives that were radically independent of one another. They came together to mate, and infants stayed with their mothers until they were able to fend for themselves. But beyond what was necessary for reproducing the human race, social interactions were accidental, of short duration, and rarely more than incidental to individuals' short-term aims.

For our purposes, the most salient feature of this original state of nature is the fact that in it people cannot be said to have had *wills* of any kind. Their cognitive capacities were too undeveloped. Thus they could not even begin to act strategically; to take one step back in order to take two steps forward. Rather, their desires were limited to what they immediately perceived. As Rousseau put it, they would set out to hunt a deer that they saw, and become distracted by the first rabbit that crossed their path, the instant the deer darted into the woods and out of sight. The inhabitants of the original state of nature had impulses that propelled them to act. But they did not have genuine volitions – plans of action with determinate characteristics, shaped by practical reason and susceptible to rational criticism. It therefore follows that the interests that Hobbes imputed to individuals in a state of nature, those that follow from their diffident, competitive and vainglorious natures, were beyond the capacities of the first men and women. In their natural condition, human beings had desires in roughly the way that higher animals do; they were incapable of anything more. These ancestors of ours were therefore as unable to deliberate in a self-interested way as they were to deliberate in an agent-neutral or impartial way. They were not capable of deliberation at all. Thus there is nothing "natural" about being self-interested. This general disposition can no more to be taken for granted than morality can. The contrast with Hobbes is plain. In Hobbes's view, self-interest was unproblematic and morality was derived from it. For Rousseau, both must be derived – from the dispositions and capacities of the individual "atoms" who populated the original state of nature.

As is well known, Rousseau maintained that the first men and women were generally content. Hence the idea of "the noble savage" and also the contention, dear to Rousseau's heart, that civilization corrupts. This last claim follows from the observation that people nowadays, unlike their ancestors, are anything but happy. It is important, however, to be clear about just how Rousseau understood the contentment of the first men and women. They were content because, given their cognitive and volitional deficiencies, they were incapable of entertaining desires that their environment was unable to satisfy, no matter how impoverished their environment might be. They lacked the requisite imagination. But the original state of nature was no Garden of Eden where goods of all kinds fell to earth like manna from heaven. Indeed, Rousseau thought that very few resources actually were available to the first men and women, far fewer than would become available later. But, in the original state of nature, scarcity was not a fact of the human condition in the way that it was for Hobbes. For scarcity to matter in the way that Hobbes thought it did, individuals must apprehend its reality, they must understand, at the very least, that nature supplies them with less than they desire. The inhabitants of the original state of nature were far from any such apprehension. They lived in a world bereft of resources, but this fact hardly impinged on their consciousness. Viewed from our point of view, scarcity was pervasive. But, from their point of view, it did not exist at all.

Rousseau speculated too that, as with other animal populations, the size of the human race in those early days was roughly in equilibrium with environmental conditions. Barring natural calamities or other external events that might temporarily disrupt the usual balance between the supply of resources and the demand for them, the ratio of births to deaths would keep the human population at just the right level to allow human beings, like other animals, to thrive to the best of their very limited capacities. Even illness was not a problem in the state of nature, Rousseau reasoned, because, again like other animals, human beings who became ill would, in short order, either recover or die. Infirmities of old age were rare; those who could not survive on their own would mercifully expire. The inhabitants of the original state of nature were therefore generally healthy and robust. In principle, then, this primitive condition could have lasted forever; no internal pressures threatened it – not a growing population, not the demands of vulnerable and dependent persons, not anything at all.

Although the benefits, such as they are, of civilization were unavailable to the first men and women, the original state of nature was anything but a condition that its inhabitants would have wanted to end, even had they been capable of forming the intention. Everyone in a Hobbesian state of nature has an interest in terminating "the natural condition of mankind"; no one in Rousseau's state of nature does. The contrast is as plain as could be. Rousseau's individuals are neither diffident, competitive nor vainglorious. Neither do they live in a world of scarcity, no matter how few resources they have available. Even the unstated geographical proximity condition, so important to Hobbes's argument, fails to obtain. Individuals are, of course, still relatively equal in Hobbes's sense. But, in Rousseau's original state of nature, this fact of the human condition is benign. Vulnerability to mortal assault is not a concern. This is not to say that the original state of nature was unchangeable. Obviously it was because it did come to an end. But when it changed, it did so for reasons that were extrinsic to its own internal organization.

The psychological dispositions that Rousseau imputed to the inhabitants of the original state of nature were few. Like other animals, the first men and women were moved by self-love (*amour de soi*); they sought to advance their own well-being, as best they were able to ascertain what it was. And, again like many other creatures, they were capable of pity (*pitié*) or empathy towards others of their own species. Otherwise, Rousseau had little to say about human nature in Hobbes's sense of the term. Implicitly, though, it is plain that he thought that human beings are capable of being moved by a variety of dispositions, depending on circumstances and therefore ultimately on the historical conditions that shape their lives. Human beings are susceptible to taking on the dispositions of the inhabitants of Hobbes's state of nature, as the first paragraph of Book I, Chapter 6 of *The Social Contract* effectively claims. But they are also capable of being moved by moral considerations or, as Rousseau would have it, by a general will. Moreover, as circumstances change, individuals's dispositions change. Social orders and the dispositions they engender can be transformed. Indeed, circumstances can be changed deliberately, by individuals contracting together. Hobbes thought so too in a sense. He thought that self-interested, rational individuals could contrive to overcome relative equality, thereby turning an otherwise in-tractable Prisoners' Dilemma game into an Assurance Game, as individu-als' interests require. Rousseau envisioned a far more radical change of circumstances. For him, the social contract transforms the very terms of the problem it is contrived to solve. It changes human nature. Therefore, even if it is sometimes fair to model human beings as diffident, competi-tive and vainglorious beings, individuals themselves can, so to speak, transform the model. This idea is utterly foreign to Hobbes's way of thinking.

What turned human nature Hobbesian, in Rousseau's story, also trans-formed the human condition, making it too more Hobbesian. It was the successful introduction of private property in land. In Part Two of *The Second Discourse*, Rousseau declared that the first person ever to mark off a parcel of land and to call it his own, and then to get others to believe him, was "the true founder of civil society." Rousseau attributed his suc-cess to the "simplicity" of those who accepted his claim. There is there-fore nothing natural about private property, in Rousseau's view. It is an arbitrary social invention. Land, of course, was the principal means of production for individuals in primitive times and also in Rousseau's day. It is therefore fair to say that what holds for land holds for productive property generally. It is private property as such that wrenched human-kind away from its original contentment. Its introduction unleashed an inexorable, internally necessitated, process that culminated, eventually, in a war of all against all.

The revolution in social relations inaugurated by the introduction of private property liberated technologies in agriculture and metallurgy. There is no need to recount here how Rousseau accounted for techno-logical innovations in the original state of nature. Suffice it to say that he attributed an innate intelligence to the first men and women, unknown elsewhere in the animal kingdom, and that, in the fullness of time, hu-man intelligence bore fruit. Of course, much that was invented had to be reinvented countless times, for there was no reliable way to pass along news of new instruments and new techniques. But sometimes technologi-cal innovations took hold, becoming part of the legacy transmitted from one generation to the next. The emergence of language is crucial to Rousseau's account of how this happened, and so too is the rise of the patriarchal family, the first form of social organization. I will pass over what Rousseau had to say about these matters, however, to point out that the "true founder of civil society" was the first to be able to utilize agricultural technology on a significant scale. With his property rights acknowledged, he was able, for the first time in human history, to reap what he had sown. Without private property, his crops, like everything else, would simply be there for anyone to take; with private property, they were his alone. Others followed his example, at first voluntarily, because it made their lives easier and therefore better. Eventually, others were obliged to follow his lead from necessity, as the number of imitators grew. For as settled agriculture took up more and more of what used to be common land, the original form of economic life – hunting and gathering – became increasingly untenable. In time, the remaining non-agricultural land became insufficient to support the hunters and gatherers who had roamed about freely in the past. At that point, no one had any choice but to adopt the new social relations and the new technologies.

Settled agriculture vastly increased productivity in the sense that more food was produced per unit of land than had been the case before. But, paradoxically, this increase in productivity established scarcity as a fact of the human condition. It did so by upsetting the original equilibrium between population size and land capacity. With more food available, population rose. But once the transition from hunting and gathering to agricultural production occurred, the productivity of the land remained roughly constant. Agriculture's ability to expand productivity was exhausted almost as soon as it was introduced.[2] Family plots, however, were divided among increasingly numerous male heirs. Thus the number of family plots rose at the same time that their size diminished. Eventually, there was less food per household and therefore per person than there had been before.

A new equilibrium might have established itself but for the sort of phenomenon that has come to be called a *tragedy of the commons*.[3] Imagine a group of farmers, sharing a common grazing land for their privately owned cattle. Each farmer has an interest in adding one more cow to his stock. Up to a certain point, the addition of a cow does not affect the amount of food available for other cows to eat. But once the land's carrying capacity is exceeded, each additional cow diminishes the food supply for all the cows that graze on the commons. Eventually, because their cows have less to eat, all the farmers are worse off in the sense that the amount of beef that they are able to produce altogether is less than it

[2] It was only in the twentieth century, thanks to mechanization and then to technological advancements in agronomy, that the productivity of agricultural land has improved substantially over levels established centuries and even millennia ago.
[3] See Garrett Hardin, "The Tragedy of the Commons," *Science*, vol. 162 (December 1968), pp. 1243–8.

had been. They are therefore less well-off in terms of the very interests that motivated them to add cows to the commons. But, even so, self-interest requires that individual farmers continue to add cows, so long as the net investment yield on an additional cow is positive. Thus, as in a standard Prisoners' Dilemma, by doing what is individually best, these farmers make themselves worse off than they could otherwise be. They improve themselves to ruin. Similarly, Rousseau's peasant farmers each have interests in adding children to their families. In settled agricultural societies, children are sources of labor and supports in old-age. But as they do so, they cause overall well-being to decline, and they transform the human condition for the worse. For even if the amount of food available overall remained constant or even rose slightly, food scarcity – the fear of its possibility, as much as its actuality – became an increasingly salient fact of human life.

This change in circumstances necessitated the actualization of human beings' cognitive and volitional capacities. Where persons were once moved by impulse only, they soon became the fully volitional creatures people are today, capable of strategizing and otherwise acting with a view to advancing their long-term interests. At the same time, circumstances shaped the nature of individuals' wills. Finding themselves in circumstances in which scarcity was becoming an increasingly important factor in their lives, individuals had no choice but to be mindful of their futures. They therefore had to become rational accumulators. Human beings never lacked the ability to become calculative and self-interested. In the original state of nature, however, the requisite capacities were undeveloped. It took the social revolution brought on by the introduction of private property in productive assets to trigger their actualization. But once the human race set itself on this course, human nature evolved into what Hobbes claimed it always was. People became "competitive."

Rousseau also recounted how self-love, *amour de soi,* developed into *amour propre.* In Rousseau's usage, the term can mean "rational egoism." But it also suggests what Hobbes meant by "glory." In the new world order shaped by scarcity, individuals come to seek "recognition." They therefore came to value standing high in the esteem of others, and to abhor signs of disrespect. This development too helped to transform Rousseau' state of nature into Hobbes's. In time, therefore, thanks to a process that unfolded according to the internal "logic" that the second part of *The Second Discourse* describes, humankind came to find itself in a condition very much like a Hobbesian war of all against all. The contented and peaceful inhabitants of the original state of nature became competitive and vainglorious individuals, living in a world of relative scarcity from which exit was no longer a feasible option. To be sure, relative equality and diffidence, the main factors in Hobbes's account of the state of nature, hardly figure in the story of *The Second Discourse*. But what Hobbes had to say about their joint effect is entirely consistent with Rousseau's speculative reconstruction of human life in the aftermath of the transformations the introduction of private property wrought. In any case, Hobbes's claim was that the warlike character of the state of nature was overdeter-mined; that there are a number of grounds, each of them sufficient, for bringing about this result. Some of them – competition in conjunc-tion with relative scarcity, glory, and geographical proximity – appear more or less directly at the end of Rousseau's story; others – diffidence and relative equality – apply, if at all, only implicitly. But the conclusion remains: the condition that precedes the adoption of the social contract is a war of all against all. For Hobbes, this condition is a timeless fact with which political philosophy must contend, no matter what institutional arrangements prevail or what system of property rights is in place. For Rousseau, it is an historically situated fact. Moreover, it is a contingent circumstance in the sense that the root cause of the problem, private property in productive assets, need never have appeared. But, given that what might not have happened actually did occur, a state of war became a stage through which humankind must pass on the way to the ultimate restoration of the primordial happiness of the first men and women – at a higher level in a *de jure* state.

Before turning back to *The Social Contract*, one other claim advanced in *The Second Discourse* should be noted. Rousseau's official topic in that text was, of course, the development of inequality, and so there is a great deal of discussion there of the rise of inequalities of status and wealth. In this connection, Rousseau discussed the rise of *de facto* states. He was not kindly disposed to existing political forms. Indeed, he described the state as a trick foisted on the poor by the rich. States make laws, and laws, Rousseau observed, apply to everyone universally. Universality is, in fact, intrinsic to the very idea of law, a point Rousseau would make again, with great effect, in Book II, Chapter 6 of *The Social Contract*. Thus states protect the property of the rich and the poor equally. But in actually existing states, thanks to inequalities of wealth, it is the well-off who benefit most from this protection. So long as there are institutions in place that allow their interests as rational accumulators to be served, the rich are much better off after a state is established than they were before. They do lose the right to take anything they can obtain. But this is the price they must pay for state protection for all that they have acquired. Taking the costs and benefits into account, the rich are far better off than they would otherwise be. Whether it is also beneficial for the poor to have the protection of *de facto* authorities is much less clear. But, in Rousseau's view, there is no doubt that these authorities, along with the rich for whom they do so much, have an interest in encouraging the poor to believe that it is.

The Social Contract

In Book I, Chapter 6 of *The Social Contract,* Rousseau formulated and "solved," at least to his own satisfaction, what he called "the fundamental problem of political life." That problem is occasioned by the fact that, in private property regimes, social life, in the absence of *de jure* authority, increasingly takes on the aspect of a war of all against all. In a sense, then, Rousseau's "fundamental problem" and Hobbes's are similar. But Rousseau described this condition in a way that is importantly different from Hobbes's account. For Hobbes, the war of all against all is a consequence of an eternal antagonism afflicting the wills of rational, self-interested, and radically independent entities, atomic individuals, living in conditions that cannot be fundamentally changed. Here is Rousseau's description: "I suppose that men have reached the point where obstacles that are harmful to their maintenance in the state of nature gain the upper hand by their resistance to the forces that each individual can bring to bear to maintain himself in that state" (*SC*, I, 6). What stands in opposition, then, are "obstacles" and "forces"; not radically independent entities, but different aspects of the same entity, the social relations that obtain between individuals in an ever-developing state of nature. Thus the situation Rousseau described is not a condition in which discrete entities, atomic individuals, stand in timeless opposition to one another. Rousseau described an internally developing contradiction. Thus Rousseau not only anticipated Kant, but Hegel too. His account of the relation between individuals' "forces" and the "obstacles" they confront illustrates precisely what Hegel would later intend by his own use of the term "contradiction." A unitary entity – in this case, human social relations – developing according to its own internal dynamic, becomes increasingly structurally unstable. Eventually, it "[reaches] a point" at which "the human race would perish unless it changed its mode of existence" (*SC*, I, 6). Thus the "obstacles" each individual confronts are other individuals' "forces," and their opposition is a consequence of the "mode of existence" under which this internally developing contradiction matures. It is important to realize too, as the third paragraph of Book I, Chapter 6 makes clear, that the "forces" available to individuals include liberty (autonomy) in addition to the physical and mental endowments that individuals can use against one another in a state of war.

Both in his understanding of liberty and in his inclusion of it among individuals' forces, Rousseau differed from Hobbes. However, Rousseau's claim that a solution to the problem individuals in a state of nature confront lies not in the introduction of new "forces," but in a change in those individuals' "mode of existence, " a redeployment of forces, is a Hobbesian idea. So too is Rousseau's contention that individuals, finding themselves in a war of all against all, can only redeploy their forces by forming an "association" directed "by a single will" (*SC*, I, 6). But Rousseau's understanding of what such an association would look like was not at all the same as Hobbes's. For Rousseau, the people themselves are sovereign; for Hobbes, the sovereign is only the peoples' authorized "representative." Rousseau's view of what would happen should individuals in a state of nature fail to change their mode of existence, his claim that "the human race would perish" is non-Hobbesian too. Hobbes thought that an unchecked war of all against all would lead, in time, to the annihilation of the human race. But, although Rousseau does say that "the human race would perish," it was evidently not physical annihilation that he had in mind. After all, as Rousseau made clear in his discussion of pacts of involuntary slavery, life itself is of no value if essential humanity is lost. What the ever-developing antagonisms of the state of nature threaten, then, is not human life but humanity's essence, autonomy. Essentially, human beings are "born free"; they are morally autonomous agents. In regimes of private property, they become unfree, as the imperatives of rational accumulation, not rational volition, increasingly govern what they do. To say that the human race would perish is to say that this loss of freedom would, at some (rapidly approaching) point, become irreversible.

The fundamental problem, as Rousseau conceived it, is to constitute a political authority – by combining the wills of many, much in the way that Hobbes envisioned, but, contrary to Hobbes, *without sacrificing any individual's autonomy.* The problem, in other words, is to reconcile authority and autonomy: "To find a form of association which defends and protects with all common forces the person and goods of each associate, and by means of which, each one, while uniting with all, nevertheless obeys only himself and remains as free as before" (*SC*, I, 6). The social contract "solves" this problem.

This solution, Rousseau maintained, consists in "the total alienation by each associate of all his rights to the whole community" (*SC*, I, 6). But how can individuals alienate everything to "the whole community" when the point of the social contract is precisely to constitute themselves as a community? Recall that the social contract is an act by which a people becomes a people, a pact of association. Prior to it, there are only atomic individuals. Thus there is no "whole community" to which individuals could alienate everything! And how can individuals enter into a contract of "total alienation?" Rousseau had already established that individuals cannot alienate liberty. But since liberty is part of each individual's endowment in the state of nature, would it not follow that a contract of total alienation is impossible? Liberty (autonomy) is inalienable because there is nothing in principle for which it can be advantageously exchanged or, what comes to the same thing, because the renunciation of liberty is tantamount to the renunciation of essential humanity itself. A contract of "total alienation" would therefore seem to be, in Rousseau's earlier words, "vain and contradictory" (*SC*, I, 4). Thus it appears that Rousseau's "solution," a social contract of "total alienation" between individuals and "the whole community," is inconsistent with the main claims Rousseau had established prior to formulating "the fundamental problem" that this contract is supposed to solve.

I would therefore suggest that the idea of a social contract is actually not suitable for expressing the thought that Rousseau was trying to convey, despite his thoroughgoing adherence to a contractarian idiom. Rousseau indicated an awareness of this possibility when he pointed out, in an almost self-conscious equivocation, that, in entering into the social contract, each individual "contracts, as it were, with himself" (*SC*, I,7). Needless to say, one cannot literally contract with oneself, a point that Hobbes had made emphatically clear. A contract is an agreement between at least two independent parties. Hobbes addressed this problem in his own way, but at the cost of forcing all individuals, except one, into what Rousseau would call a pact of slavery. Rousseau must therefore address it differently. But how?

Setting this question temporarily aside, it should be observed that Rousseau thought that the social contract did indeed work to the advantage of each of its adherents, as any genuine contract should. He even described its benefits in the language of double-entry bookkeeping, adding up the "credits and debits" (*SC*, I, 8). In part, what Rousseau concluded recalls the reckoning made in *The Second Discourse* for *de facto* states. In entering into the social contract, individuals lose the natural liberty of the state of nature but gain "civil liberty" – the freedom, protected by law, to do whatever the law does not proscribe. Individuals lose the unlimited right to everything, a right that was theirs in a state of nature, but gain property rights, and therefore protection for what they have acquired. Whether, in this case too, the result is accurately described as a trick foisted on the poor by the rich will depend on the degree of wealth inequality in the society the just state superintends, an issue that does not arise at the level of abstraction at which Book I of *The Social Contract* is pitched. But whatever we ultimately conclude about the consequences of private property rights for different segments of the population, what matters preeminently in a *de jure* state is that in it, in contrast to the states Rousseau excoriated in *The Second Discourse*, individuals gain autonomy – they are able, finally, to become the free beings they always potentially were. It should be noted, finally, that, on the first two of the purported advantages of the social contract, the two the *de jure* state shares with *de facto* states, Hobbes and Rousseau were of one mind. However, of the last and by far the most important advantage, the realization of essential autonomy, Hobbes had no inkling.

As if to underscore how much the social contract is in each individual's interest, Rousseau went on to proclaim that entry into the political community ennobles humankind, turning "stupid, limited animals" into "intelligent beings and men" (*SC*, I, 8). In this respect too, Rousseau and Hobbes stand opposed. For Hobbes, the establishment of sovereignty changes nothing in human nature. It only alters the payoff structure individuals confront. For Rousseau, "the passage from the state of nature to the civil state produces quite a remarkable change in man, for it substitutes justice for instinct in his behavior and gives his actions a moral quality they previously lacked. Only then, when the voice of duty replaces physical impulse and right replaces appetite, does man, who had hitherto taken only himself into account, find himself forced to act upon other principles and to consult his reason before listening to his inclinations" (*SC*, I, 8). Only then, in other words, does a form of volition radically different from the kind whose history Rousseau recounted in *The Second Discourse* enter political life.

Like Hobbes's social contract, Rousseau's is "equal for all" (*SC*, I, 6). But unlike Hobbes's contract, Rousseau's does not have the indirect consequence of subordinating individuals to anyone, not even to a sovereign. For the sovereign is the people themselves in the "mode of existence" that the social contract makes possible. The sovereign is therefore not exactly the peoples' "representative," as Hobbes had maintained; the sovereign and the people are one. What makes this reconceptualization of sovereignty possible are those "other principles" that the social contract "forces" individuals to act upon. These principles follow from the generality or universality of rational deliberation. It is in this context, then, that Rousseau introduced his most important contribution to modern moral and political thought, the idea of a *general will*.

This notion is inscribed in the social contract itself: "If we eliminate from the social contract whatever is not essential to it," Rousseau wrote, "we find that it is reducible to the following terms: *Each of us places his person and all his power in common under the supreme direction of the general will; and as one we receive each member as an indivisible part of the whole*" (SC, I, 6).

The General Will

The general will is distinguished from private or particular wills. Private wills aim at private interests – at what is best for persons viewed atomistically. The general will aims at general interests – at what is best for persons viewed as integral parts of collective entities. In principle, individuals have private interests in all matters, at least once human societies have passed through the stages recounted in *The Second Discourse*. However, individuals may fail to discover what their private interests are, or may know what their private interests are and still not act on them. Therefore, private interests may not always govern individuals' actions, even in a Hobbesian state of nature. But individuals still have private interests, whether or not they make them their own. Similarly, if Rousseau was right, individuals living in just states have general interests, interests as indivisible members of "the whole community." But they too may fail to discover what that interest is and, even knowing what it is, may fail to make it the object of their volition.

We will see that, in Rousseau's view, after the social contract, there is an eternal struggle for supremacy *within each individual* between the private and the general will, a struggle that can only be addressed, finally, at the institutional level. But at the level of abstraction from institutional arrangements sustained in Book I, Chapter 6, Rousseau's claim is only that each of these wills is at all times a permanent possibility for persons who find themselves in the situation he described. Each individual's private will aims at what is best for that individual viewed apart from the community the social contract creates. Each individual's general will aims at what is best for the individual viewed as an *indivisible* part of the collective entity established by the social contract.

Thus Rousseau's claim is not nearly so odd or contentious as may at first appear. He did not claim that the general will is the will of a mysterious supra-individual entity, "the whole community," with volitional capacities similar to those of individuals with private wills. Individuals are the bearers of both private and general wills. These wills differ in their objects, in the nature of the interests towards which they aim. But there is no difference in the kinds of beings whose wills they are. Both are wills of human beings, and of human beings alone.

To obtain a better purchase on what Rousseau had in mind, it will be well to reflect on groups much smaller than whole communities. Think, for example, of John and Mary, husband and wife. Suppose that Mary is deliberating about where to live. She could ask herself what is best for herself, all things considered – that is, taking all relevant factors into consideration, including the impact of her place of residence on John and on her marriage with John, insofar as these factors bear on her own well-being. If she deliberates in this way, she would be engaging in what might be called private will deliberation. Alternatively, she could ask herself what is best for the couple John–Mary, viewed as an *indivisible* whole. She could reflect, in other words, on what would be best for the "community" constituted by her marriage to John. Then she would be engaging in a general will deliberation. Rousseau's claim is that there is a John–Mary interest writ large, a John–Mary interest encompassing everyone within the political community. Rousseau also held that, in political contexts, this interest ought to govern individuals' deliberations.

Philosophers committed to one or another individualistic doctrine might cavil at the very thought of a John–Mary interest. I would venture, though, that most people, including most philosophers, would, on reflection, find the idea perfectly intelligible. However, the claim that there exists a John–Mary interest writ large in the way that Rousseau believed, that "the whole community" can be relevantly like an intimate union of two persons, is much less intuitive. This was, however, Rousseau's view, and his "solution" to "the fundamental problem of political life" depends on its cogency.

In any case, the existence of such an interest is one thing; the wisdom of making it one's own, of "placing oneself under the supreme direction of the general will," is another. It is fair to say that, in general, the appropriateness of general will deliberation is much more problematic than the claim that general interests exist. Hardly anyone today believes that marriages are important for their own sake, rather than for the sake of the marriage partners, conceived separately. Apart from unyielding proponents of family values or committed believers in the sacrament of marriage, it would be hard even to imagine anyone thinking that it would ever make sense for Mary or John to privilege their John–Mary interest over there respective John and Mary interests. Rousseau's claim, however, is that, finding themselves in a situation in which "forces" and "obstacles" stand in mortal contradiction, self-interested individuals must act on their interests as indivisible parts of a single entity encompassing "the whole community." Should they not do so, they face the certain prospect of losing the one thing they have that is priceless, essential humanity.

Thus, Rousseau made two distinct but related claims: first, that there is a general interest for political communities, that "the whole community" is relevantly like the couple John–Mary; and second that, in the circumstances described at the beginning of Book I, Chapter 6, persons ought to deliberate with a view to discovering what their general interest is, and that they ought to act on it. In contrast to what was the case for John and Mary, the first of these claims is more difficult to defend than the second. It is far from obvious that general interests extending across entire communities, across strangers and even generations, exist. According to the argument of *The Second Discourse,* private interests are no more natural than general interests are. But a single, momentous social innovation, the introduction of private property in land, sufficed to unleash a process that brought private interests into being. A more deliberate program, of uncertain outcome, is required to do the same for general interests, as we will see. Private interests, then, are easier to form and follow than general interests are, at least for beings such as ourselves, living in the thrall of private property. This is why the citizens of just states must remain forever vigilant, if they are to succeed in placing themselves "under the supreme direction of the general will."

Without ever mentioning Hobbes by name, Rousseau argued, in effect, that Hobbesian individuals ought to forbear from acting on Hobbesian principles for Hobbesian reasons or, what comes to the same thing, that atomic individuals moved by private wills ought to undertake general will deliberations in political contexts because it is in the private interest of each of them to do so. By this reasoning, Rousseau made good on what he had promised at the outset – ". . . to bring together what right permits with what interest prescribes, so that justice and utility do not find themselves at odds" (*SC*, I, 1).

Authority and autonomy therefore can be reconciled. When individuals' wills are determined by their interests as integral parts of "the whole community," they obey only themselves at the same time that they are commanded by a legitimate authority. When this authority is obliged to coordinate individuals' behaviors coercively, thereby limiting freedom in the Hobbesian sense, it is only "forcing . . . [these individuals] to be free," as Rousseau famously explained (*SC*, I,7). This paradoxical expression would make no sense to Hobbes; it would be a plain contradiction. That it captures Rousseau's meaning precisely indicates, again, how, despite all the affinities that join Rousseau's case for sovereignty with Hobbes's, Rousseau's and Hobbes's underlying moral philosophical commitments stand unalterably opposed.

The final paragraph of Book I, Chapter 6 is ostensibly definitional, but in fact it summarizes what has been established to this point. Each individual, the text stipulates, is simultaneously a *citizen* and a *subject*. Citizens collectively comprise the *sovereign*; subjects collectively comprise the *state*. But the sovereign is not just the sum of the citizens. It is a "moral and collective" being comprised of each citizen as an integral part. It is because individuals in a *de jure* state are simultaneously citizens and subjects, law makers and law obeyers, that they can be autonomous and still live under political institutions. As citizens, they are subject to laws, but these laws are *of their own legislation.* They are therefore the sovereign's subjects, as much as the members of a Hobbesian commonwealth are, but, unlike those "slaves," the citizens of a just state are free; they are subject to no will other than the general will, which is their own. Rousseau's social contract therefore does what Rousseau had insisted any legitimate social contract must do – it reconciles authority and autonomy. Indeed, it is only when *de jure* authority exists that autonomy, which is otherwise in mortal jeopardy, finally comes into its own.

Sovereignty

It is well to distinguish *ontological* claims about the existence and nature of the general will from *epistemological* claims, about how, if the general will exists, individuals can discover what it is. The first three chapters of Book II of *The Social Contract* and also Book II, Chapter 6 are concerned with the ontological question. Book IV, Chapters 1 and 2 address the epistemological question. Since "sovereignty is nothing but the exercise of the general will" (*SC* II, 1) ontological and epistemological investigations of the general will are tantamount to analyses of the nature and limits of sovereignty.

Rousseau claimed that the sovereignty is "inalienable" (*SC*, II, 1). This, he wrote, is a consequence of the social contract itself. He was right; sovereignty is inalienable in just the way and for just the reason that autonomy is. For sovereignty just is autonomy under "the form of association" established by the social contract. Since autonomy is inalienable (*SC* I, 4), since the subordination of private wills to the general will in the circumstances Rousseau depicted is the condition for the possibility of realizing autonomy (*SC* I, 6), and since sovereignty is "the exercise of the general will" (*SC*, II, 1), sovereignty too must be inalienable. Rousseau's claim that sovereignty is indivisible (*SC* II, 2) can be defended in the same way. Sovereignty is indivisible for just the reason that autonomy is, for sovereignty just is autonomy in the "form of association" the social contract establishes.

This position is at odds with eighteenth-century theories of "divided" sovereignty of the kind that came to influence the framers of the US Constitution. For Rousseau, sovereignty is located exclusively in what American jurisprudence calls the legislative branch. The one and only thing the sovereign does is make laws. What American constitutional writers called the executive branch, the institution that executes laws, is what Rousseau called "government." According to American constitutional doctrine, the executive branch is, along with the legislature and the judiciary, an independent part of the state and therefore, in Rousseau's terms, of the sovereign, inasmuch as the state is the sovereign viewed "passively" (*SC* I, 6). For Rousseau, however, the executive is not part of the sovereign at all. Neither, of course, is the judiciary. There is, in fact, no mention of an independent judiciary in *The Social Contract*.

Government is therefore not at issue in Rousseau discussion of sovereignty. In fact, government is not even directly discussed until Book III of *The Social Contract*, after Rousseau's account of the nature of sovereignty is complete. There, the main problem is how to contrive forms of government that will execute the sovereign's will without usurping the sovereign's authority. To this end, Rousseau recommended sensitivity to local traditions and circumstances, and he discussed a variety of other factors pertinent to the design of executive institutions. Read today, his reflections seem, on the whole, anachronistic. But at least one very pertinent lesson does emerge from the protracted discussion of governmental forms in Book III: that governments ought to be as varied as the peoples they govern, that what is right for one state is almost certainly not right for another. There is, in short, no set of governmental institutions appropriate in all times and places, in marked contrast to the social contract itself which is "everywhere and always the same" (*SC*, I, 6).

Rousseau's claim that the general will cannot err (*SC* II,3) is, again, an ontological claim, not an epistemological one. It is tantamount to the contention that there is a general will for "the whole community." Rousseau might have said as well that the private will cannot err; and, in the sense in question, Hobbes would have had to agree. To say that the private will cannot err is to say that individuals have private interests; in other words, that there always is something that is best for them viewed atomistically, Similarly, to say that the general will cannot err is only to say that there is a general interest. It is not to say that the state is somehow always infallible. The idea that the general will cannot err is contentious because the equivalent claim, that a general interest exists for "the whole community," is. It is not contentious because it ascribes extraordinary epistemological powers to "the whole community." To hold that the general will cannot err is to assert nothing at all about general will detection. Allowing that general interests exist, the question of how they can reliably be discovered is yet to be addressed.

Before turning to what Rousseau did say about this epistemological question, we must first look at his account of the nature of laws, the subject of Book II, Chapter 6. We know that the sovereign's task is to make laws, that the sovereign "speaks" in laws. Indeed, the sovereign just is "the whole community" assembled together as a law-making body. Anticipating Kant, Rousseau claimed that laws are distinguished by their form, not their content; that they are "general in their object and general in their source" (*SC* II, 6). The claim that laws are general in their object amounts, in the first instance, to the idea that laws cannot name particular individuals, that they must pertain to "the whole community." The claim that laws are general in their source is Rousseau's way of saying that the whole people must legislate or, what comes to the same thing, that sovereignty cannot be "represented." The rationale for this conclusion is plain. Individuals are free if and only if they obey laws they have legislated themselves. It therefore follows that anyone who fails to participate in the making of a law fails to fall under its scope. Individuals in this situation may find it prudent to obey laws they did not participate in making, but they are under no normatively compelling obligation to do so. Thus there is at least the suggestion in Book II, Chapter 6 that the social contract is incompatible with representative government, a suggestion taken up and expanded in Book III, Chapter 15, where Rousseau famously berated the English for forfeiting their liberty by electing representatives to Parliament. In fact, Rousseau's position on representative government is more complicated than these texts suggest.[4] Were Rousseau taken at his word, the state of *The Social Contract* would have to be small enough for the entire citizenry to assemble and deliberate about the general will. It would therefore be hard to establish a just state even in a small city. In a territory the size of real world political communities, it would be impossible.

To claim that form, not content, distinguishes genuine laws from

---

[4] For an indication of some of these complexities, see Richard Fralin, *Rousseau and Representation: A Study of the Development of His Concept of Political Institutions* (New York: Columbia University Press, 1978).

enactments that appear to be laws but really are not seems preposterous on its face. How could the fact that everyone participated in a law's enactment, in conjunction with the fact that the law speaks in general categories only, suffice to make it binding *de jure*? It took a reader of Kant's genius to realize that the attention Rousseau paid to the form of the law rather than to its content, however problematic it may seem in political contexts, signaled a great advance in moral philosophy. What Kant understood was that Rousseau's focus on form captured precisely the idea behind the moral point of view as it has been understood at least since the Golden Rule was first declared in Biblical times (see chapter 1). The Golden Rule would have agents *do unto others as they would have others do unto themselves*; it would have agents abstract away everything that distinguishes them from one another and then reflect on what to do from the standpoint of all concerned. In short, the Golden Rule mandates impartial or agent-neutral deliberations; deliberations that all affected parties can acknowledge as their own. This is just the idea that Kant later expanded upon and clarified by formulating a series of categorical imperatives – a priori principles that purport to establish a grounding for normativity itself. Kant's idea is of Rousseauean origin; it is implicit in the notion of general will deliberation and therefore, as Kant himself acknowledged, in the idea of law. General will deliberators assess alternatives from the standpoint of generality. More precisely, because Rousseau's concerns were political rather than moral philosophical, they deliberate about alternatives that arise in the assemblies of the people, not as particular individuals with private wills, but as citizens with general wills, as indivisible parts of freely constituted *sovereign* communities that assemble from time to time to legislate. It is the fact that individuals deliberate as citizens that gives the decisions they reach normative force. This is why their decisions *obligate* persons *de jure;* why they compel compliance for reasons that transcend mere prudence. Again, Rousseau nowhere explained the moral philosophical bases for this position, and nowhere drew out its implications. These tasks fell to Kant and his successors. But Hegel was right to insist that Rousseau "discovered" the idea that Kant would later explore; that his accounts of political authority and political obligation exhibit the very first intimations of "the moral vision of the world."

Rousseau and Liberalism

Strictly speaking, Rousseau's theory of sovereignty is no more liberal than Hobbes's was; it acknowledges no principled limitations on the use of public coercive force. There is nothing, Rousseau insisted, that a sovereign may not rightfully do (*SC* II, 4). This conclusion too follows directly from the social contract; the sovereign's right to control the "body politic" is as absolute as was the right of individuals to control themselves in a state of nature, for it is that very same right in "the form of association" that the social contract establishes. In light of the discussion of law that Rousseau would mount in Book II, Chapter 6, two chapters after declaring the sovereign's power absolute in principle, we might say as well that the sovereign people may legislate as it pleases, without any restrictions whatsoever. Nevertheless, Rousseau's theory of sovereignty, unlike Hobbes's, has liberal implications. It implies support for some restrictions on the use of state power. It does so, however, for democratic, not liberal reasons. In a word, Rousseau's account of sovereignty is friendlier to liberalism than Hobbes's was because Rousseau was a democrat, while Hobbes was not.

The difference is most evident in those aspects of public life that pertain directly to the legislative process. Consider, for example, the traditional liberal concern to protect free speech and other expressions of "private conscience" from state interference. Rousseau's theory of sovereignty implies a strong presumption for limiting the sovereign's power to interfere with individuals' lives and behaviors in this domain, just as liberals would like. To be sure, there is no principled reason why the sovereign may not regulate or proscribe speech. But there is an instrumental reason why no sovereign would do so in the normal course of events.[5] Free speech is indispensable for sound deliberation in the popular assemblies where laws are made. There is therefore at least a presumption that it be protected from interference, including state interference. Of course, this argument pertains, in the first instance, to political speech, not to speech in general. But in this respect Rousseau's position is not that different from standard liberal views. It is a tenet of mainstream legal theory that even such a paradigmatically liberal document as the US Constitution's *Bill of Rights* accords priority to political speech over, say, commercial speech, which is subject to certain forms of regulation, and also over other categories of speech that enjoy more constitutional protections than commercial speech does. Moreover, because it is always difficult and sometime impossible to mark off political speech from other forms of expression in a principled way, it is wise, even for proponents of

---

[5] Rousseau would permit any number of exceptions to what the theory of sovereignty implies, but only in dire emergencies, when the very existence of "the whole community" is threatened. See, for example, *SC*, IV, 6.

free speech in the political arena only, to support institutional arrangements that protect speech more generally. With regard, then, to at least this one core liberal conviction, Rousseau was close to the liberals – in practice, if not in theory. Similar considerations apply to other, related liberal concerns that affect the political process – freedom of the press, for example and perhaps even the freedom to assemble together to discuss issues likely to arise in the popular assemblies. In the end, though, Rousseau did not always support these and other freedoms with the consistency and fervor that liberals do. But, contrary to what one might think, the fact that Rousseau would have individuals place themselves "under the supreme direction of the general will" was not the reason why. Quite the contrary. What Rousseau said about the nature of sovereignty points in the opposite direction.

Still, Rousseau was not quite a liberal despite himself. To account for this fact, however, one would have to look beyond the very abstract account of sovereignty provided in Book II of *The Social Contract*. Rousseau's illiberalism emerged, in the main, in the course of his reflections on institutional arrangements in particular kinds of societies, a topic he addressed throughout his political writings, and especially in his speculations on the best institutional arrangements for societies governed by just states – a topic broached, but not much developed, in Book IV of *The Social Contract*. It is fair to say, at least for just states, that Rousseau's illiberalism was motivated by the need to make it the case that individuals accord priority to their general over their private interests. This is why, to cite just one very conspicuous example, Rousseau would proscribe partial associations and, more generally, suppress group identifications that mediate between the individual and "the whole community." His thought was that it is necessary to eliminate everything that stands between the individual and the state in order to enhance the likelihood that, when individuals deliberate, they do so with the interests of "the whole community" in mind – not their own interests conceived atomistically, and not the interests of the groups with which they are identified or with which they voluntarily affiliate. Rousseau would eliminate the latter danger by suppressing these groups themselves. I will return presently to some of the implications of the fact that Rousseau identified the interests of groups of citizen-subjects in civil society with the interests of atomic individuals in a state of nature, viewing them both equally as obstacles in the way of general will deliberation. His doing so is key to understanding the politics of *The Social Contract*.

Political Obligation

Hobbes's account of sovereignty was *private* interest-driven, and so was his theory of political obligation. This is why the one is not quite the inverse of the other. In Hobbes's view, when the sovereign seeks to take a subject's life, the subject no longer has any (private) interest in obeying the sovereign. The sovereign can, of course, rightfully do anything and can therefore rightfully take his subject's life, but then the subject whose life is in jeopardy is under no obligation to comply with the sovereign's commands. Where there is no private interest, there is no obligation. For Rousseau, on the other hand, political obligation is absolute in principle in just the way and for just the reason that political authority is (*SC*, II, 5). This is what one would naively expect. But Rousseau's rationale for this position is subtle, not naive – much more than was Hobbes's case for his ostensibly more nuanced account of political obligation.

To gain a purchase on Rousseau's theory of political obligation, it will be instructive to think of the body politic, as Rousseau did, by analogy with the human body. Each is composed of members or parts, but each is also an integral whole. Arguably, it makes sense to talk, say, of the interests of a finger as opposed to the interests of the body of which the finger is a part, just as it makes sense to talk of the interests of individuals conceived atomistically, even after they have placed themselves "under the supreme direction of the general will." Thus we can say that fingers, like the citizens of a just state, have private interests. But, even if fingers had volitional capacities, it is inconceivable that it would ever be rational for a finger to make its private interest the object of its will, for there are no imaginable circumstances in which fingers ought to place themselves under the "supreme direction" of their private wills. This conclusion seems right because it is part of our intuitive understanding of the world that fingers are so thoroughly integrated into entire bodies that the their private interests have no standing against the interest of the whole body. Thus it seems unexceptionable to say that if the whole body wills, as it were, that one of its fingers should perish – say, to save the body from an infection or a cancer – then, because the finger is an integral part of that body, its will too is that it should perish. Rousseau thought that political communities governed by a just state would be equally integrated wholes and therefore that, in political contexts, constituent members of "the whole community" would also put the interest of "the whole community" over their own private interests. This is why he claimed that it followed from the social contract that if the sovereign wills that an individual should die – in other words, if an individual's death is in the general interest – then it is the interest of the condemned individual to die (*SC*, II, 5). Death is plainly not in that individual's private interest. But the general interest is each individual's interest as a citizen; and it is that interest, not any private interest, that ought to govern this and all other cases of political consequence. To be sure, in this instance, the conclusion is counter-intuitive. But in Rousseau's defense one might say that this is because human social relations outside *de jure* states, so far from forging genuine communities of the kind the social contract envisions, fragment social life, for just the reasons *The Second Discourse* made plain. The idea that political communities could be as thoroughly integrated as individuals' bodies are is therefore at odds with the lived experience of persons outside just states; in other words, with *everyone's* lived experience. As we will see, in Rousseau's larger scheme, it falls to actual politics, not to political philosophy, to counter this tendency, and to build the communities that the social contract foresees.

When the sovereign seeks to take an individual's life, the individual's private and general interests are diametrically opposed. But, again, it is the general interest that ought to prevail. Here, then, is yet another point at which Rousseau and Hobbes part ways. For Hobbes, there are only private interests. But it follows from Rousseau's account of the social contract that private interests have no rightful place in a just state, where the general interest, a notion unknown to Hobbes, alone determines individuals' wills. This is why when "the prince," executing the sovereign's will, says to any citizen-subject that "it is expedient for the state that you should die," [that individual] . . . should die." Where *de jure* authority relations exist, even life itself is "a conditional gift of the state" (*SC*, II, 5).

Rousseau was therefore right to hold that his account of the nature and limits of political obligation follows directly from the social contract itself. But his way of making this point is, to say the least, provocative. To hold that condemned individuals really want to die, that their true desires and their private interests can diverge to this extent, is to conjure up the specter of regimes enslaving entire populations in order, ostensibly, to make them free. Even so, we ought to hesitate before concluding, on this account, that Rousseau's theory of political obligation – and therefore his political philosophy generally – has totalitarian implications.[6]

[6] For a contrary view, see, among others, J. L. Talmon, *The Rise of Totalitarian Democracy* (Boston: The Beacon Press, 1952). For reasons to hesitate before using the term "totalitarian" in the way that Talmon does, see chapter 1, note 8.

For just as it would only be in exceptional circumstances that it is in the interest of the whole body that one or more of its fingers should be cut off, it would only be in exceptional circumstances that the general interest would oppose the private interests of any of its constituent members to such an extent that it would require their being put to death. In a well-functioning state, the private interests of citizen-subjects and the general interest would co-incide or at least overlap to a degree that the individual's obligation to obey the sovereign would be beyond dispute, even from Hobbes's strictly (private) interest-driven perspective.

It is, then, only in the limiting case that Rousseau focuses on in Book II, Chapter 5, where the (popular) sovereign seeks to take an individual's life, that Rousseau and Hobbes disagree about what a citizen is obligated to do. Their disagreement on this question is of only minor practical importance, inasmuch as the situation will seldom arise. But their disagreement is of enormous theoretical importance. Hobbes and Rousseau disagree about *why* it is rational for individuals to obey political authorities. Rousseau would ground normative political philosophy on the coherence and possible applicability of the idea of general will coordination, "taking men as they are and laws as they might be" (*SC*, I, intro.). Hobbes's political philosophy cannot even countenance this distinctively Rousseauean notion, let alone endorse it.

Discovering the General Will

The first two chapters of Book IV of *The Social Contract* deal, finally, with the problem of discovering what the general will is. Rousseau's claim is that majority rule voting is key; that the method of majority rule, implemented in the right way and under the right conditions, is a reliable general will discovery procedure.

It will be convenient to think of majority rule voting as a "device" for combining individuals' choices to produce social choices, where each individual counts equally in the determination of the social choice. Pictorially, if $I_1, I_2, \ldots I_n$ represent the votes of individuals 1, 2 ... n, and S represents the social choice, then

$$I_1 \longrightarrow$$
$$I_2 \longrightarrow \boxed{\text{Method of Majority Rule}} \longrightarrow S$$
$$I_n \longrightarrow$$

The method of majority rule combines or aggregates individuals' choices to produce a social choice. For anyone in the sway of this picture, simple majority rule voting will always be the preferred decision procedure, other things being equal, because the outcomes it generates are uniquely sensitive to individuals' choices among the alternatives in contention; the social choice S is strictly a function of the individuals' choices $I_1, I_2, ..., I_n.$. A decision procedure that required super-majorities or, in the limiting case, unanimity for a law to pass, would be biased in favor of the status quo. A decision procedure that required less than a simple numerical majority would accord undue power to minorities of voters; at the limit, it would license dictatorship, the rule of one. Needless to say, minority rule voting and, especially, outright dictatorship offend democratic sensibilities. However, super-majority rule voting can seem attractive for some kinds of decision-making, even to majoritarian democrats. When it does, though, it will be for extra-democratic reasons. Thus (conservative) wisdom dictates that we not allow "constitutions," the rules of the game under which political communities operate, to be highly susceptible to changes in public opinion. Constitution writers might therefore want to build in biases against changes in constitutional arrangements – by requiring, for example, that super-majorities ratify proposed changes before they can take effect. Few, if any, majoritarian democrats would hesitate to trade off some measure of popular control for enhanced stability of this sort.

In the mainstream political culture today, individuals' choices represent preferences for alternative outcomes in contention. Then if everyone's preference genuinely counts equally, it is natural to conclude that majority rule voting generates *fair* outcomes, outcomes that represent the actual distribution of preferences within the voting community. But this was emphatically not Rousseau's view. To combine preferences is to aggregate private wills; it is to do precisely what a just state may not do. For Rousseau, then, individuals' choices do not represent preferences, but rather judgments – about the general interest. Fairness is therefore not at issue in majority rule voting; correctness or, better, truth is. Rousseau employed the method of majority rule to discover what the general will requires. Majority rule voting, in his view, is a decision procedure that gets the right answer to the question "What ought we, the whole community, to do?"

Intuitively, it seems odd to say that elections produce true or false outcomes. Assuming that votes represent preferences, when Jones beats Smith in an election, the result only reflects the fact that more voters preferred Jones to Smith than Smith to Jones. We do not think that Jones's victory reveals a true, preference independent, answer to the question – "who ht to win this election?" In the mainstream view, then, voting is like *~aining*. It is a process in which different forces contend for competi-~advantages within a framework that everyone has a common (private) ~est in maintaining. Assuming that all the parties in a bargaining situ-~ are competent bargainers, where a bargain is finally struck reflects ~lance of forces among the contending parties. Similarly, in the politi-~ai case, when a vote is concluded, the outcome reflects the distribution of private interests in the society. The difference is just that, in bargaining, the contending parties seldom confront one another on an equal footing; typically, power advantages are brought to bear and are reflected in the outcome.[7] However, in voting, if there is equality of citizenship, no one has more electoral power than anyone else; each voter has one and only one vote. Then the outcome will represent the actual distribution of preferences within the voting population, everyone's preference counting the same. Needless to say, in real world conditions, preferences count equally only in a formal sense. In the all-important background circumstances leading up to elections, equal citizenship is undermined by inequalities of political influence. But it is nevertheless a theoretical *desideratum* for those who see majority rule voting in the way that the mainstream political culture does. It is an ideal to which official proponents of democracy pay homage, even as they acquiesce in its transgression.

To understand how Rousseau viewed voting, it will be useful to reflect on voting exercises that in no way resemble bargaining situations. Jury voting is an example. When jurors vote, they express their opinion about a matter of fact – for example, whether or not a defendant being tried for a crime is guilty as charged. This is not at all the same thing as expressing preferences for one or another outcome. A juror might wish that the defendant go free, but nevertheless believe in the defendant's guilt, and vote accordingly. Thus, even the mainstream political culture provides a model of "disinterested" voting, of voting not dictated by private interests. But if this model is to be applied, it must be the case that there really is a matter of fact that voters seek collectively to discover. In the jury case, there plainly is a fact to be determined. Rousseau's claim is that what the general interest is is similarly a matter of fact, one that the people assembled together to legislate can discover.

Rousseau's use of majority rule voting is therefore at odds with standard, majoritarian understandings of majority rule voting. On the stand-

---

[7] An exception, as noted in chapter 1, is the bargaining that leads individuals to concoct a Hobbesian sovereign. That negotiation presupposes the relative equality of persons, and therefore begins from an initial condition of (near) equality.

ard view, the whole community ought to do what the majority decides because it is committed to the method of majority rule as a decision procedure – perhaps for the sake of fairness, perhaps for some other reason. The majority, however, is neither right nor wrong in the decisions it reaches. Indeed, since political decision-making is relevantly like bargaining, not jury voting, there is nothing it could be right or wrong about. The majoritarian's reasons for doing what the majority says are therefore independent of the "rectitude," as Rousseau would say, of its choices. For Rousseau, on the other hand, there is a right answer to the question "What ought we, the citizenry, to do?" – there is a general interest – and what it is is logically independent of what anybody, including a majority of the voters, thinks it is. Rousseau's contention, then, is that, as a matter of fact, the majority will discover what the general interest is, provided it deliberates properly in the conditions that obtain in a just state. This is why, paradoxically, those who were in the minority on some issue remain free (autonomous) when they obey the majority; why, in fact, they would be unfree if they failed to do so. The majority, Rousseau insisted, discovers what voters on the losing side, along with citizens on the winning side, truly want; it discovers what they want *as* citizens. Thus, despite what would seem to be a plain contradiction, the method of majority rule, according to which the majority determines the minority, is compatible with and even indispensable for the autonomy of each and every citizen.

It therefore follows that even those who opposed a law in the assembly of the people, are bound by it because, in the end, despite their vote, it was their will that the measure they voted against should have won. The minority wants what the majority wants, the general interest. There is a consensus on ends. What the majority and minority disagree about is only what it is that they both want. If Rousseau was right, minorities are always comprised of those who are wrong about this matter of fact. Its members have false beliefs about what the general interest is. Here is Rousseau's remarkably concise defense of this contention:

> How can the opponents [i.e. the minority on some vote] be both free and be placed in subjection to laws to which they have not consented? . . . I answer that the question is no put properly. The citizen consents to all the laws, even to those that pass in spite of his opposition, and even to those that punish him when he dares to violate any of them. The constant will of all the members of the state is the general will; through it they are citizens and free. When a law is proposed in the people's assembly, what is asked of them is not precisely whether they approve or reject, whether or not it conforms to the general will that is theirs. Each man, in giving his vote,

states his opinion on this matter, and the declaration of the general will is drawn from the counting of votes. When, therefore, the opinion contrary to mine prevails, this proves merely that I was in error, and that what I took to be the general will was not so. If my private opinion had prevailed, I would have done something other than what I had wanted. In that case I would not have been free. (*SC*, IV, 2)

What is most problematic in this passage is, again, the claim that there is a general interest – in other words, that there is a right answer to the question "what ought we, the whole community, to do?" Rousseau's position depends on there being a right answer to this question. This view is not only at odds with the prevailing consensus in the mainstream political culture; it is also highly implausible. It is worth noting too that neither in *The Social Contract* nor anywhere else does Rousseau defend it directly. But, as we will see, he does deal with this issue in a way. What he would do, in short, is make it true – by promoting a politics that forges the kind of community in which there actually is a strong consensus on ends, a community in which citizens genuinely do seek to discover general interests.

Rousseau's other claim – that, *if* there is a general interest, the majority will discover it – is less doubtful, despite what may at first appear. Rousseau did not expressly defend this claim. But an argument is available nevertheless. It was supplied by the Marquis de Condorcet, and there is some (inconclusive) reason to think that Rousseau may have been aware of it. Condorcet proved a theorem pertaining, not surprisingly, to the jury system; in other words, to the model of voting that Rousseau endorsed. He demonstrated that if a juror has a better than 50 percent of being right, the probability that the vote of the entire jury will be right rises exponentially as the majority increases. More precisely, if each members of the group is right in proportion v *(verité)* of the cases and wrong in proportion e *(erreur)* so that $v + e = 1$, then if in a given instance h members of the group give one answer and k members another, where $h > k$, the probability that the h members are right is given by the expression:

$$\frac{v^{h-k}}{v^{h-k} + e^{h-k}}$$

For example, if $v = 60\%$ and $e = 40\%$ – not an unreasonable assumption for experts in ascertaining the general will – and if $h = 51$ and $k = 49$, the probability that the majority h is right is

$$\frac{60^2}{60^2 + 40^2}$$

or approximately 69 percent. A majority of only 2, in other words, has a 9 percent greater chance of being right than a single individual in a group whose members have a 60 percent chance of being right. And, as the majority increases, the probability that it will be right increases exponentially – rapidly approaching (though never strictly reaching) unity. Condorcet's theorem does not establish the *infallibility* of majority rule voting, even when all voters set out in a genuinely disinterested way to determine what the whole community ought to do; no probabilistic argument could do that. In this respect, Condorcet's theorem on jury voting is not exactly on point, inasmuch as the passage of Rousseau's just cited does seem to ascribe infallibility to the majority of voters. But Rousseau did not need to make such a bold and unlikely claim. To establish his position, he needed only to show that majority rule voting is, in fact, a highly reliable general will detector. Condorcet's theorem does support that conclusion. It shows that *if* there is a general will, the majority, properly interrogated, will very likely discover it.

However, we are only entitled to think of majority rule voting as a truth discovery procedure if individuals do, in good faith, combine their independent "opinions" about what the general will is. The point of many of the practical political recommendations Rousseau advanced in *The Social Contract* and elsewhere is to make this otherwise improbable condition true.

Into Politics

The social contract presupposes a degree of social unity that does not exist in a state of nature, but that is nevertheless a possibility for its inhabitants, "taking men as they are and laws as they might be." If there is to be a just state, this possibility must be actualized. Thus Rousseau's account of political authority implies a political project, an effort to construct a community in which individuals do in fact place themselves "under the supreme direction of the general will."

Politics, for Rousseau, is a struggle waged for what eighteenth-century political writers called the "opinion" of citizens or, in terms more suitable to Rousseau, for control over individuals' dispositions to will either according to their private or their general interests. Rousseau attacked this problem in a generally ahistorical way. In recommending institutional arrangements for the just state, he was less concerned to propose measures appropriate in one or another historical conjuncture than to suggest policies allegedly suitable for all times and places. It is as if Rousseau thought that the struggle for opinion is largely unaffected by particular circumstances. This characteristic of his reflections on politics renders many of his views on institutional forms anachronistic. I will therefore not dwell on the actual recommendations he made, but only reflect briefly on their underlying rationale. Two aspects of Rousseau's thinking about social, political and economic institutions warrant particular attention: the first bears on his illiberalism, on those aspects of Rousseau's thinking that drew him away from positions suggested by his theory of sovereignty; the second has to do with his utopianism or, what comes to the same thing in this case, with his views about the nature of the economic institutions of a just state.

Rousseau's overriding aim, again, was to enhance the likelihood that, in the assembly of the people, citizens will make the general will, not their private wills, their own. To this end, he would have those societal institutions that shape opinion be organized in such a way as to encourage the development of the requisite dispositions. Thus, despite all his philosophical idiosyncrasies and his extreme originality, Rousseau stood firmly in the ongoing (small r) republican tradition in political philosophy. This school of seventeenth- and eighteenth-century political thinkers took the Roman republic as their model. It was their view that the ancient Romans were a public-spirited and patriotic or, in republican terminology, a "virtuous" people. They therefore encouraged the development of civic virtue, attaching preeminence to public concerns over private ones, and to the well-being of the whole community over the well-being of the individuals who comprise it. Civic virtue, so conceived, was then held to be a condition for the realization of the values republicans endorsed; freedom, above all. As we have seen, Rousseau's account of general will coordination was motivated by more immediately philosophical considerations. But it is nevertheless plain that, in their own idiosyncratic way, Rousseau's conclusions mirror characteristic republican positions. Rousseau too would have individuals suppress their private wills for the sake of the whole community of which they are a part. Rousseau too saw virtue as an indispensable precondition for freedom (autonomy).

Many of Rousseau's positive proposals follow from his conviction that a virtuous citizenry is a prerequisite for a just state. Thus he would encourage public spectacles and other events involving mass participation in order to foster social solidarity and a corresponding common, civic identity. He would institute forms of education that emphasize love of country and its history and that instill local traditions and cultural practices in the minds of the young. He advocated a civil religion that would encourage group solidarity through its simple and uncontentious doctrinal commitments and public rituals, while at the same time undermining extra-national loyalties encouraged by universalist religions like the Roman Catholic Church (see *SC*, IV, 8). Through these and a host of other positive measures, Rousseau sought to promote patriotism; love of the community envisioned in the social contract through which alone individuals are finally and fully free. In enlisting state institutions in this endeavor, Rousseau blatantly transgressed liberal norms. As will emerge in later chapters, a genuinely liberal state neither favors nor disfavors particular conceptions of the good. In the liberal view, then, state institutions ought never to be used to indoctrinate the citizenry. Rousseau, however, would have the state do precisely what liberalism forbids: he would have it inculcate a particular vision of the good society.

But even more than in his plans to shape "opinion," Rousseau's illiberalism is evident in what might be called his negative political proposals. As remarked, Rousseau would not allow the formation of social groups that mediate between the individual and the whole community. His fear was that group affiliations would foster loyalties that would, in turn, weaken individuals' dispositions to identify their own interests with the interests of the whole community. But to suppress partial associations, it is necessary to infringe a host of freedoms liberals hold dear: above all, obviously, the freedom to enter into voluntary associations, but also all that follows from this freedom – including perhaps even the freedom to assemble outside the assembly of the people itself. Thus it is not only through state sponsored indoctrination but also through a panoply of proscriptions and suppressions that Rousseau would turn individuals into patriots; persons of such overweening virtue that their overriding concern, in legislating but also more generally, is the well-being of the whole community. To get what he thought autonomy requires, the individual whose simplicity of "manners and morals" (*moeurs*) and whose civic high-mindedness makes general will coordination at the level of the whole community possible, Rousseau would violate liberal norms assiduously. Despite his commitment to open discussion in the assembly of the people, Rousseau never recoiled from this position. He advocated using state power as need be to shape citizens into the required mold. He was committed to forging the conditions for rightful political authority by any means necessary.

In the end, however, Rousseau's illiberalism is most evident in his vision of the good society itself. Paradoxically, for autonomy's sake, the good society of Rousseau's imagination would be one whose citizenry is bereft of individuality or, more precisely, of significant individual differences. The reason why is plain: virtue, as Rousseau and other republicans conceived it, is inconsistent with a robust individualism. This is why, like other republican thinkers, Rousseau preferred Sparta, the city of patriots none of whose names are remembered, to Athens, the city of conspicuous individuals, some of whom will be remembered for all time. I will return to this thought in chapter 4, to draw a contrast with John Stuart Mill's very different vision of the good society. Mill, whose intuitions in this matter define the liberal idea, wanted individual differences to flourish. He endorsed "rugged individualism." Nothing could be further from Rousseau's political agenda. For Rousseau, conformity, even uniformity, is the order of the day. Liberal individualism divides; the just state requires unity above all.

In the just state, as in the ideal polities of other eighteenth-century republican thinkers, small, independent and generally self-sufficient producers, agricultural and artisinal, populate society. With their own needs met, these yeoman farmers and artisans devote themselves, in the main, to common concerns and to the pursuit of the public good. Modern industry is therefore absent, as is all that follows in its wake – the subordination of the countryside to the towns, luxury, self-indulgence and increasing inequality. Thus Rousseau, like other republican writers of his time, implicitly opposed the impending capitalist organization of Europe because he understood that capitalism would transform society in ways that would make general will coordination even more difficult than it already was. But the economic system Rousseau envisioned for the society the just state superintends was nevertheless a capitalist one. Despite all that Rousseau had to say about the harms private property generates, he never proposed an alternative to it. And although the economic order Rousseau favored was populated by self-sufficient producers who exchanged only their surplus products, he never thought to proscribe or even to regulate market exchanges. Thus Rousseau left a place *outside the state* for private interests to flourish and even to govern individuals' behaviors.

The economic system Rousseau imagined was roughly what Adam Smith would later call "the early and rude state of society" or what Marx would designate "simple commodity production." It was an economic structure with private property and market exchange, but without class divisions based on individuals' differential relations to their society's means of production. In economies of this sort, producers own their own means of production. Everyone, therefore, is a capitalist. But there are no class divisions and consequently no social or economic inequalities based on class. This is what mattered to Rousseau; like everything else that draws people apart, class divisions threaten the direct and unmediated relation Rousseau would establish between the individual and the state. But this is a utopian vision. For Smith and Marx, the idea of a capitalism in which all direct producers own their own means of production served only as an analytical device. It was not intended as a description of a possible real world economy. Rousseau, however, *prescribed* precisely this economic structure for the just state.

It is at least arguable that it is not utopian to hold that whole communities can freely place themselves under the supreme direction of the general will. But because the economic system Rousseau envisioned is unfeasible in real world conditions, it *is* utopian to maintain that communities comprised of individuals directed by a general will could produce and distribute goods in the way that Rousseau thought they would. The kind of capitalism Rousseau proposed is intrinsically unstable; a point that both Smith and Marx would later make plain. Market-driven exchange in a regime of private property fuels concentrations of wealth. And, wherever the relevant technologies exist, wealth, if it can be freely deployed, underwrites the rise of modern industry and, along with it, the aspects of modern life that Rousseau abhorred. Thus Rousseau endorsed private property and market exchange, at the same time that he militated against its inevitable consequences.

The state founded by the social contract is a timeless, Platonic idea. But the politics that is indispensable for forging the conditions for its possibility, "taking men as they are," can only be historically situated. To imagine relatively stable institutional arrangements for a just state, it is necessary to take account of the dynamic properties of its institutions. For all his attention to historical and local differences in Book III of *The Social Contract*, where his subject was governmental forms, and in Book IV and elsewhere, where he discussed institutional arrangements that affect opinion, Rousseau was singularly blind to this exigency when it came to economic structures.

The problem inherent in the economic vision Rousseau advanced comes to a head in his insistence that the state ought to limit inequalities of wealth – so that "no citizen should be rich enough to be able to buy another, and none so poor as to be constrained to sell himself" *(SC*, II, 11). Rousseau's choice of words is telling: it suggests that he wanted to proscribe the wage bargain, the defining characteristic of emerging, real world capitalism. In the wage bargain, propertyless proletarians sell, if not quite themselves then their capacities to labor, to property rich capitalists, in exchange for a wage. The wage bargain is the motor of capitalist development, as all the classical economists along with Marx would eventually insist. A private property, market regime without a market in labor power itself, is therefore unthinkable. However this seems to be precisely what Rousseau had in mind. But even if this is a tendentious reading of what Rousseau said, the basic problem remains. Viewed dynamically, the economic system that Rousseau thought the just state requires undermines the just state. It does so in two, interconnected ways. Because it is based on private interest, it fosters a character type inimical to republican virtue. Because it exacerbates economic inequalities, it leads to the formation of economic classes, providing individuals with a group interest, the interest of their class, to compete with the interest of the whole community. Since this interest is not a general interest, and since there are only private and general interests in Rousseau's scheme, group interests are effectively assimilated to private interests, of a piece conceptually with the interests of atomic individuals in a state of nature. This sort of group interest is therefore in principle as much a threat to sovereignty as untrammeled individual acquisitiveness is. In practice, it is an even greater danger, inasmuch as its emergence is an inevitable consequence of the very structure of the society that the just state superintends. In sum, then, the economic system of the just state puts that state in jeopardy for two, related reasons: for its direct effects on individuals' characters, and, even more insidiously and intractably, for its propensity to divide "the whole community." There is no way, in the end, to square this circle. Rousseau's effort, however ingenious, ultimately fails. But the ingenuity of the attempt is revealing. The core of Rousseau's politics lies in the interconnection of its disparate parts. The utopian economic structure he envisioned and the various non-economic measures he proposed to shape opinion complement one another. Citizens cannot be effectively inculcated with civic virtue unless there is an economic structure in place that prevents the formation of overriding class interests. But the economic structure Rousseau proposed has just the opposite effect. It therefore requires extensive operations at the level of opinion to counter its own internal tendencies – to keep it from developing into a full-fledged capitalism. Thus, at the same time that the measures designed to produce a virtuous citizenry depend upon an economic system that does not generate class divisions, the economic system Rousseau proposed requires a virtuous citizenry to block this outcome. This is an untenable configuration of countervailing conditions. If it could be made to work at all, even for a short time, it would be because somehow just the right balance is struck between, on the one hand, those institutions and policies that militate against private interest formation at the level of opinion and, on the other, those factors that depend on private interests in the underlying economy. That this balance could be struck at all is unlikely; that it could be maintained indefinitely is a utopian dream.

It is, then, to an unrealizable vision of institutional arrangements and practices that Rousseau's account of political authority leads. But because it is far from plain that there are no feasible alternatives to private property and market arrangements or that there is no way other than Rousseau's to imagine a classless society, it is not at all plain that this is the inevitable destination of Rousseau's notion of general will coordination at the level of whole communities. In chapter 6, we will encounter this idea again.

3
Locke

The reader who turns to John Locke's (1632–1704) political philosophy after Hobbes's or Rousseau's is bound to notice a diminution in philosophical rigor and depth. But readers are also likely to find Locke more "reasonable" than Hobbes or Rousseau, more inclined to adopt positions that seem workable and right. I would venture that this reaction, the sense that with Locke we finally enter the real world of politics, is, at least in part, an historically conditioned response. Locke was an influential political thinker – with the founders of the United States, of course, but also with their British counterparts and with early liberal thinkers generally. His political philosophy therefore speaks directly to the political arrangements those political actors whom he influenced helped to shape; institutional forms under which people in liberal democratic countries live. Hobbes's authoritarian statism and Rousseau's vision of moral and collective bodies moved by a general will have much less connection to our lived experience. What follows here, however, will not address many of the aspects of Locke's political philosophy that continue to resonate today. I will concentrate instead on two distinctively philosophical innovations of his: the first, having to do with the use Locke made of a notion already found in Hobbes, the idea of extra-legal *rights;* the second with Locke's way of combining liberal and democratic concerns. It was not until the mid-nineteenth century that full-fledged liberal democracies, regimes devoted both to liberal and democratic values, came into being, even in those parts of the world where Locke's political philosophy was most influential. Inasmuch as political ideas follow political forms and practices, it was not until Locke had been dead nearly a century and a half that mainstream political theory took an unequivocal liberal democratic turn. But the general strategy liberal democrats would assume was anticipated in Locke's political theory and, more importantly clarified by Locke in a way that continues to merit close attention. In this regard, I will also look briefly at Locke's defense of representative government. Twenty-first century readers will find what Locke had to say about political representation highly anachronistic. But his views about democratic governance do contrast instructively with Rousseau's and also with the views of many contemporary liberal democrats. My discussions of Locke's account of rights and of his anticipations of liberal democratic theory will focus, particularly, on the way Locke's ideas have come to be appreciated and developed in influential, contemporary strains of political philosophy. I will therefore have little to say about Locke's disputes and alliances with his own contemporaries. In Locke's case, even more than in Hobbes's, it can be instructive to disengage some of his ideas – specifically, those that are of the most contemporary philosophical interest – from the historical specificity of his own immediate concerns.

Rights

Individuals have rights relative to one another. Rights therefore cannot exist outside societies. As remarked in chapter 1, a Robinson Crusoe, alone on his island, would be utterly without rights, for there would be no one to whom he could make rights claims. Very generally, then, rights are addressed to others and imply what legal scholars call *correlative obligations* on the part of others to do or forbear from doing certain things. In this sense, rights talk is *forensic;* it has an irreducibly legal or adversarial dimension. To assert a right is to make a claim that one believes societal institutions ought to respect and also, in one way or another, to enforce. In legal contexts, rights talk is relatively unproblematic; it is a way of articulating the rules that regulate individuals' conduct, "the rules of the game." In a real game, like chess, a player has a right, say, to move a bishop only diagonally and only in specifiable circumstances – for example, when it is the player's turn. Similarly, within a legal framework, one has a right to demand certain behaviors on the part of others, including the state, in virtue of the laws under which one lives. This understanding derives from Roman jurisprudence. Until the seventeenth century, it was the only use of *rights* that the political culture acknowledged. The extension of rights talk beyond strictly legal contexts, to articulate non- or extra-legal demands, is a distinctively modern innovation. Like so many other political ideas current today, it was a creature of the English revolutions of the seventeenth century. Locke, however, was the first to make the idea the centerpiece of a distinctive political philosophy.

In Hobbes's state of nature everyone had an unlimited right to everything. No one, then, had particular rights. Thus Hobbes's state of nature was ruleless, inasmuch as rights claims specify rules that constrain individuals' behaviors. Even so, Hobbes could have used rights talk to articulate his view of life in political communities or "commonwealths." He could have maintained that, within political communities, individuals have legitimate claims against others to do or forbear from doing certain things. But, then, these rights would follow from the social contract that puts the state of nature to an end. For Locke, however, rights come first. They precede the social contract. Legitimate political institutions must therefore accommodate to these rights, not follow from them. Put metaphorically, for both Hobbes and Rousseau, particular rights are *theorems*; for Locke, they are *premises*.

To claim that rights already exist in the state of nature is not just to say that people believe that they do. It is to maintain that the rights in question are unalterable moral facts. This is why Locke and his followers spoke of "inalienable" rights. To claim that a right is inalienable is to say that, unlike the unlimited right to everything that Hobbes ascribed to individuals in a state of nature, individuals have particular rights that cannot be alienated or, as Hobbes would say, "laid down." A Lockean social contract will therefore be a contract of partial, not total, alienation. As such, it underwrites the idea that sovereignty is limited in principle, that subjects are immune from certain kinds of state interferences. Specifically, the sovereign's power is limited by the rights that individuals retain. In this respect, Locke differed significantly from both Hobbes and Rousseau, for whom the sovereign's power is unlimited in principle because the contract that establishes sovereignty is a contract of total alienation. When they institute sovereignty, individuals in a Hobbesian or Rousseauean state of nature hold nothing back. But in a Lockean state of nature, they must hold *inalienable* rights back. They therefore cannot alienate everything, and where they have not alienated rights that were antecedently theirs, they remain sovereign over themselves, just as they were in the state of nature. Lockean rights therefore establish a *space* into which the state cannot rightfully intrude. As we will see (in chapters 4 and 5), there are other, perhaps better ways to defend limited sovereignty. Liberalism can do without Lockean rights. But Lockean rights claims do limit the sovereign's power, and therefore do succeed in making a theory of sovereignty liberal.

To gain a better understanding of what Lockean rights are, it will be instructive, again, to turn to the international arena, as we did in chapter 1. The comparison is apt because, in that domain, no world sovereign rules over sovereign states, just as in a state of nature, no national sovereign rules over individuals. On what might be called a Hobbesian view of international affairs, because moral constraints can only follow from antecedent agreements, states are always in principle at war with one other, even if they are not in overt conflict. In the international arena, therefore, anything goes. However, on a Lockean view, because states, like individuals in a state of nature, have morally primary rights, anything does not go; there are some things that states cannot rightfully do to one another. If, for example, there is a morally primary right not to have one's territory invaded, a state that invades another's territory acts wrongly. If this moral fact is known, it might to some degree constrain the behavior of potential aggressors, diminishing the likelihood of overt conflicts. If so, hostilities would likely erupt only infrequently at the international level, not just for the Hobbesian reason, because otherwise warring parties are able to establish relatively stable balances of power, but also in consequence of this moral fact. Even so, the temptations of national interest always threaten to overwhelm the dedication to act rightfully. Then, in the absence of a suitable rights-enforcement mechanism, battle would erupt anyway, and there would be no effective redress. There is, therefore, a Lockean way to argue for a world sovereign that is nearly as compelling as the Hobbesian way. A world sovereign is needed to enforce rights that already exist. With respect to international affairs, this argument may or may not be decisive. But it is instructive. As we will see, individuals are motivated to leave a Lockean state of nature for just the reason that underlies this (putative) Lockean case for world sovereignty. They will want to leave the state of nature because they recognize a permanent need to have their morally primary rights enforced.

But even if the existence of rights in a Lockean state of nature does not preclude the need for sovereignty, it does change the sovereign's role. A Lockean sovereign makes laws, just as a Hobbesian or Rousseauean sovereign does. In this sense, a Lockean sovereign too assigns rights. But the extra-legal, particular rights that matter most, the rights that the social contract aims to protect, already exist before a sovereign comes onto the scene. A Lockean sovereign is therefore not, in the main, a rights maker in the way that a Hobbesian or Rousseauean sovereign is. A Lockean sovereign is mainly a rights enforcer. Because individuals' interests often lead them to violate even those rights claims that they acknowledge, they need a rights enforcer to maintain order, even if they do not need one to establish rules that constitute order. Just as in Hobbes's state of nature, therefore, rational, self-interested individuals will, if possible, contrive a mechanism that represses their natural disposition to act in ways that, left unchecked, would lead to a war of all against all. The only such mechanism conceivable is, again, one that uses or threatens force to assure compliance to its rules. On this point, then, it hardly matters that Locke, unlike Hobbes, thought that the most important rules that the state should enforce are specified by rights that individuals in the state of nature already enjoy. What matters more is that there be a coercive apparatus in place to assure that compliance is widespread and, therefore, that order is maintained.

But if Locke and Hobbes were of one mind on the need for states, their views of the nature of the authority the state wields differed considerably. For Hobbes, the rules under which individuals ought to live are just those that the sovereign commands, whatever they happen to be. Rules have normative force because they are enforceable, because the sovereign, the peoples' authorized representative, is powerful enough to issue enforceable commands. For Locke, on the other hand, enforcement is necessary mainly to secure rights that pre-exist the establishment of sovereignty. It is their presence in the state of nature, not the fact that the sovereign's police stand ready to enforce them, that gives these rules normative force. Therefore, political authority *de jure* and political authority *de facto* do not necessarily coincide. Might and right were distinct notions for Locke, just as they were for Rousseau. But might is indispensable if right is to prevail, just as Rousseau thought it was.

The first liberals were concerned to protect individuals from state interference with religion, a cause that animates liberal politics to this day. But the morally primary rights that Locke and other early liberals cared about most were property rights. Locke sought to protect against state interferences with commerce, and to defend private property and the right of individuals to accumulate wealth virtually without limitation. However, what makes a position liberal is not *what* it seeks to protect from state interference, so much as the fact that it seeks to protect *something*. From Locke's time to our own, the focus of liberal concerns has evolved. Today, it is only "libertarians" who view property rights in the way that Locke did. Mainstream liberals nowadays are more concerned, say, with privacy than with property. But even if contemporary liberals would reject Locke's unabashed defense of private property rights and commerce, their positions too are susceptible to a Lockean rationale. Locke's idea was that rights claims, whatever they may be, morally *precede* political arrangements. Thus the social contract does not ground the most important of the rights that it protects. Quite the contrary. The rights that individuals retain when they enter into the social contract lie beyond the scope of the sovereign's rightful authority. The sovereign is a protector of these rights, and nothing more.

The State

Could rights be enforced *privately* – that is, without the state? One might, at first, think so. There could be, for example, a division of labor in which those who are good at, say, commerce, engage in commercial pursuits, while those who are good at fighting become rights defenders – and maybe also, when the occasion arises, rights aggressors. A good merchant and a good fighter, working together, might be able to accumulate more wealth than either could independently, doing everything for themselves. Those who hit upon this scheme might do very well indeed, at first. But then, as in the story Rousseau told in the *Second Discourse*, others would follow their example. In time, therefore, the problem everyone faced in the state of nature, how to have their property rights protected, would reemerge – but at a higher and more dangerous level of violence. Individuals would find themselves mired in a civil war with rival gangs, private armies, fighting to mutual ruin. In these circumstances, there is a compelling reason for private armies to confederate or even to merge, again solving the rights enforcement problem temporarily, but only by reanimating a process of imitation that will again inevitably make the original problem worse. Ultimately, therefore, the logic of the situation requires that there be a single rights enforcer. This, of course, can only be the state, the form of political authority that *monopolizes* the means of legitimate violence.

Locke would have individuals in a state of nature arrive at this solution to the enforcement problem they all confront by means of a social contract. But as the thought experiment just sketched suggests, he could also have had them "back into" a state – by allowing the logic of private rights enforcement to unfold.[1] By looking at the contractarian idea this way, and then by focusing, as Locke did, on rights enforcement rather than on rights creation, we can gain a better understanding of what is essential to the contractarian program, and what is superfluous to it. We can see, for example, that a social contract is less central to contractarianism – or, at least, to Locke's version of it – than one would suppose.

---

[1]   This alternative route to a statist conclusion was first proposed by Robert Nozick in *Anarchy, State, and Utopia* (New York: Basic Books, 1974), chapter two.

And we can see more clearly than in traditional contractarian accounts why only *one* supreme authority can rule over a particular territory or population. The rights enforcement business is a natural monopoly. The state, therefore, must be One. If it is to serve its purpose, political authority cannot be diffused; it must be concentrated into a single institutional nexus.

A Lockean state is not limited to the enforcement of pre-existent rights claims. As remarked, in addition to this core task, states can rightfully make rules, and therefore ascribe rights that individuals did not already possess in the state of nature. No doubt, states must do so to some extent, if they are to operate effectively. And because Locke, like nearly everyone else, was a Hobbesian statist, he also thought that states may rightfully do whatever is required to supply those public goods that everyone, or nearly everyone, wants (see chapter 1). However, in the execution of these tasks, there is one overriding constraint: states may never exceed their rightful authority by impinging upon morally primary rights. Inasmuch as states are contrived to protect morally primary property rights more than any other, these rights limit what states may do. To better understand the Lockean state, therefore, it is necessary to fathom Locke's position on private property.

In general, it is easy to fault Locke's political philosophy for its arbitrary rights ascriptions. Locke, it can seem, assumed what he wanted to establish, and then hid this circularity, even to himself, by building his conclusions into the rights claims he asserted. The strategy of ascribing morally primary rights to individuals in a state of nature invites this charge. I would submit that it is largely justified. But, with respect to property rights, it must be said that Locke did try to defend the rights he invoked. It is even fair to say that, in the course of doing so, he developed a *theory* of private property. To this day, this effort of Locke's to justify private ownership and market exchange represents perhaps the most sustained attempt ever contrived to defend capitalist property relations.

Property

Locke set forth his theory of property rights in chapter 5 of *The Second Treatise of Government*. His aim in that text was to defend the right of individuals to own resources, external things, privately and (almost) without limitation. Locke's account, however, confounds two distinct issues relevant to this larger ambition. The first has to do with how unowned things can rightfully be privately appropriated. The second has to do with what individuals can rightfully do with the things they own. Inasmuch as there are very few unowned things in the world today (or in Locke's day, despite the convictions of European colonizers), the first of these issues would seem moot, especially inasmuch as Locke's immediate objective was to justify the holdings generated by capitalist markets. One would therefore expect that the second issue, concerning rightful transfers of things that are already owned, would be Locke's prime concern. Curiously, however, Locke had very little to say about ways of transferring already owned things. Most of chapter 5 is about the rightful appropriation of previously unowned things.

However, this focus was not entirely off-mark. Locke plainly did have a view about rightful transfers of already owned things. He endorsed uncoerced market exchange and gift-giving, voluntary transfers unblemished by force or fraud. Locke never quite supplied an explicit defense of this position, but the broad outlines of one are clear enough, given Locke's dedication to taking morally primary rights seriously. Exchanges and gifts, because they are voluntary, are justified insofar as they violate no one's rights. Or, to put the matter positively, individuals may rightfully do whatever they want with the resources they own, provided only that what they do does not adversely affect the rights of anyone else or of themselves. Thus individuals may rightfully exchange what they own in market transactions, so long as the rights of those who are not parties to the exchanges they make are respected; or, if they choose, they may give what they own away. However, this rationale only applies to what individuals already legitimately own. Locke therefore needed to establish how individuals can legitimately own anything, how the just acquisition of previously unowned things is possible.

Implicitly, Locke's account of property rights provides a basis for a theory of distributive justice, a point Robert Nozick made very clear several decades ago.[2] Locke's core idea, again, was that individuals' holdings are rightfully theirs if and only if these holdings have the right history or, more precisely, if and only if they were acquired cleanly, without the violation of any morally primary rights claims. Thus a theory of justice of the sort that can be teased out of Chapter 5 of *The Second Treatise* unwittingly mimics the structure of a deductive argument in formal logic. A deductive argument is a string of sentences $S_1, S_2,....,S_n$, where every sentence that is not a premise of the argument, a sentence assumed to be true for the argument in question (whether or not it is itself the conclusion of some other argument), follows from preceding sentences by rules

[2] See Nozick, *Anarchy, State, and Utopia*.

of inference that preserve truth values. The conclusion of the argument, S_n, is just the last sentence in the string. A deductive argument is *valid* if each sentence that is not a premise does indeed follow from preceding sentences according to logical rules. It is *sound* if it is valid and if its premises are true. A conclusion of a sound argument will therefore be true. We can think of Locke's efforts to establish a theory of just initial acquisition as analogous to efforts to establish the truth of the premises of a deductive argument; and we can think of market exchange and gifting as analogues to truth-preserving rules of inference. Then just as the conclusion of an argument that is valid and that follows from true premises is true, a distribution that follows from justice-preserving rules of transfer will be just, provided only that what is transferred was, at the outset, rightfully acquired.

If we focus, as Locke did, on just initial acquisition, it is fair to say that Locke's starting point was not one that would command widespread assent today, even if it were reformulated in a secular guise. It is the allegedly revealed claim that "God gave the world and all that dwells therein to Man"; in other words, that human beings collectively stand in a proprietary relation to the rest of nature. Locke then claimed what others before him, including Hobbes, maintained – that human beings have a fundamental and infrangible right to self-preservation. On this basis, he went on to infer that individuals can rightfully appropriate whatever they need for self-preservation from the common stock, from what they own jointly with everyone else, provided that, in so doing, they do not diminish anyone else's capacity to do the same. In this way, Locke justified *limited* private ownership, against a background of collective world ownership. Nature itself belongs to human beings collectively, but parts of it can be appropriated privately when and insofar as private ownership is necessary for self-preservation. It is plainly a long way from this defense of very limited private appropriations to the unlimited private property rights Locke wanted ultimately to defend. To arrive at the desired destination, then, Locke needed to enlarge his arsenal of premises. Thus he was obliged to advance even more contentious claims than those that got him this far.

Of these additional premises perhaps the least problematic was what some philosophers today call *the thesis of self-ownership*. Locke claimed that human beings stand in a proprietary relation to themselves, that they own themselves. Despite its name, this thesis advances no contentious metaphysical claim. Locke's idea was not that there exists some entity, the self, that somehow owns the body and powers with which it is associated. The claim is only that with respect to individuals' bodies and powers, the owners and ownees are one and the same. So understood, Locke's contention was that individuals own themselves in the same way that, in a regime of private property, individuals own external things or that, in economic systems in which the ownership of *other* persons is permitted, masters own slaves. His idea, in short, was that individuals have virtually unlimited rights to *control* and *benefit* from the exercise on their own bodies and powers. Inasmuch as property rights are decomposable into rights to control assets and rights to benefit from them, and inasmuch as Locke evidently regarded individuals' bodies and powers as assets, his claim literally was that individuals have property rights in themselves, in their own bodies and powers.

These rights, as Locke conceived them, are virtually unlimited. But they are not quite absolute. Locke seems to have modeled self-ownership on chattel slavery. Slave owners could do almost anything they wanted to their slaves, and they had unlimited rights to benefit from their slaves' labor. Similarly, Locke thought that individuals could rightfully do almost anything to themselves and that they have a virtually unlimited right to benefit from their own bodies and powers. Thus, self-ownership, as Locke understood it, encompasses more rights than prevailing understandings of private property normally include. To be sure, many of the external things that people own are theirs to do with as they please or to benefit from without qualification. But in many other cases, property rights over external things are limited, especially when the assets owned have some non-trivial effect on others. This is true even for some personal possessions. In most contemporary societies, for example, individuals may own their own dwellings, but they cannot do literally anything they want in them or to them. They may not use their houses, say, for commercial purposes, unless zoning laws permit this use; they may not be able legally to demolish their houses or to make additions to them or even to alter their appearance fundamentally. But however extreme a self-ownership theorist Locke may have been, it was not his view that self-ownership rights are literally without limit. Property rights can never be absolute in this sense, at least not in any political community organized on principles of mutual respect. Thus when we do have unlimited property rights in external things, as we do, say, with our furniture, if not with the houses in which our furniture is kept, we still cannot rightfully use what we own to harm others by violating their rights or otherwise affecting their fundamental interests adversely. Neither can we rightfully harm others with our bodies and powers. Self-ownership, as Locke understood it, conveys virtually unlimited revenue and control rights, but it is not equivalent to the unlimited right to everything that everyone in a Hobbesian state of nature enjoyed. Indeed, it is partly because individuals do own themselves that it is not the case that a Lockean state of nature is a universal war of all against all. Self-ownership limits the behaviors of others in ways conducive to peace; it renders individuals unfree to violate other individuals' bodies and powers.

The thesis of self-ownership reflects a view of the world according to which everything, even oneself, is owned. The thesis is therefore susceptible to criticism by those who find this world view and the self-understanding it implies historically limited or otherwise defective. Even so, the self-ownership thesis is intuitively appealing. Among other things, it explains the widespread and deeply entrenched intuition that individuals' bodies and powers cannot be "invaded" without their consent. This is a compelling conviction; one that even seems to swamp other moral imperatives. Thus it would almost certainly be better, according to any likely moral theory, that in a two-person world in which one person has, say, two functioning kidneys and the other is about to die of kidney failure, that the healthy person give up a kidney to the person about to die – especially if, contrary to fact, the removal and transplantation of kidneys was an easy, painless, and costless undertaking. Then the imagined kidney transfer would be the right, even the morally obligatory, thing to do. Nevertheless, there is the intuition that, even if morality does require this transfer, it is wrong, in this case and in cases like it, to *force* individuals to do what they ought to do, wrong to take their kidneys by force. One way of making sense of this conviction would be to maintain that "takings" of this sort violate morally primary rights that individuals have in virtue of their ownership of themselves.

Self-ownership also explains some prevailing intuitions about revenue rights. Most people nowadays would probably hold that if Jones and Smith are in all relevant ways similar, and if they labor under similar conditions, but if Jones works for 10 hours on some (remunerative) task while Smith works at the same task for 5 hours, that Jones ought to receive a greater monetary reward than Smith, perhaps even twice as much. More generally, the idea is that differential expenditures of effort generate entitlements to differential rewards, in proportion to the effort expended. This intuition too is explained by the thesis of self-ownership, by the idea that one has a (virtually) unlimited right to benefit from one's own body and powers. No doubt, these intuitions can be faulted. I would hazard too that they can also be explained in other, perhaps better, ways. Even so, the idea that individuals own themselves is not as easily dismissed as, for example, Locke's claim that human beings collectively own nature because God made it so. I would suggest that if the self-ownership thesis ought to be rejected., the reason for doing so is neither that it is implausible on its face nor that it is without explanatory power. It is because the larger moral vision that motivates it, the idea that there genuinely are morally primary rights, is found wanting.

In any case, what Locke must do is go from limited private ownership of external things and self-ownership to unlimited private ownership of external things. This task elides together questions pertaining to legitimate initial acquisition and legitimate transfer, with the emphasis, wittingly or not, on the former problem. But, for now, the better to reconstruct the argument of chapter 5 of the *Second Treatise*, it will be well to go along with Locke's own confounding of these distinct issues.

In Locke's case for according individuals unlimited private property rights to parts of the external world, self-ownership plays a crucial role. His idea was that when individuals mix their labor with external things, they effectively transfer their ownership of their own labor to that part of the external world that they "improve" with their labor. To its evident discredit, this position seems to appeal to what anthropologists call "sympathetic magic," to the idea, common among so-called primitive peoples, that properties are transferred through contact, as when something becomes ritually unclean or "polluted" when it touches something that is already in some ritually meaningful sense unclean. However, the idea is not entirely unintuitive to moderns. Thus I suspect that most people, in Locke's day and in our own, would be inclined to think that some unowned and unimproved things – a piece of wood found in the forest, for example, or even a parcel of land – becomes the property of whoever improves it substantially by working on it. But whether or not this speculation is correct, it is plain that, for Locke, labor or, more precisely, its productive expenditure, is crucial to legitimate initial acquisition. This is why standardly, though misleadingly, the entire Lockean theory of property is called a labor theory.

Locke was fatally vague about how much labor is required to generate claims on external things and also about how to identify or individuate external things themselves. Here, as elsewhere, he relied on intuitions that he left carelessly unexamined. Extreme cases are readily identifiable, however. Spitting into the Pacific Ocean would hardly make the spitter its owner. On the other hand, an individual who lands on a small, unoccupied Pacific island and then, through toil, transforms nearly every inch of it from a barren landscape into productive agricultural land might well be thought the rightful owner of the island. In most cases, however, it is not clear how to identify the boundaries of the items with which the admixture of labor is supposed to confer ownership rights. Nor is it clear

how much labor individuals need to perform to become owners of unowned things, or even what kinds of labor they must expend. Presumably, rubbing one's finger up and down a found piece of wood or running
to exhaustion on an unowned piece of land would not do. Mere expenditures of effort are therefore not enough. But, apart from vague indica-
tions that labor must somehow be productive, that it must improve the
item in question, Locke had nothing helpful to say about what suffices to
confer ownership. Again, we are left to rely on unexamined intuitions.

Locke insisted that in appropriating parts of the external world privately, we leave "enough and as good" for others. Taken literally, this is
an impossible condition to meet. Unless the world of privately unowned
things is so large as to be inexhaustible, anything that is privately appropriated diminishes the common stock. No doubt, what Locke meant was
that private appropriators may not *significantly* diminish other peoples'
opportunities to appropriate parts of the external world. But this celebrated *Lockean proviso* would still be difficult to satisfy in the vast
majority of cases in a finite world like our own. This is why Nozick, in a
desperate effort to make Locke's position defensible, altered the terms of
the proviso. For Nozick, it is enough that, in appropriating parts of the
external world, individuals leave others at least as *well-off* as they were
before; in other words, that the private appropriation of unowned things
not diminish anyone else's well-being. However, this revision goes against
the grain of Locke's moral philosophy. For Locke, institutional arrangements are justified if and only if they respect morally primary rights;
improving well-being therefore matters, if at all, only after this condition
is met. Were someone, then, to make a convincing case that, say, the
abolition of private property would make people better off, Locke would
be unmoved because his defense of private property is based on the claim
that private ownership is an inalienable right; and, for him, rights claims
take precedence over other considerations, no matter how compelling.
However, Nozick's revision does make the intuition that underlies the
Lockean proviso, that the harmless appropriation of unowned things is
morally defensible, more plausible than Locke's own formulation does.
It does so, though, at the cost of introducing a consideration foreign to
Locke's way of thinking into the very heart of his theory.

Locke also maintained that individuals can rightfully appropriate only
what they can productively use. This contention is already implicit in the
idea that laboring on something unowned makes it one's own, so long
as the proviso is satisfied. If, to appropriate X, an individual must first
have transformed X through labor, and if, as Locke vaguely but unmistakably implied, the requisite sort of labor is productive labor, labor that

improves the material on which it is employed, then, since *does* implies *can*, X must be capable of being used productively, of being improved, by whoever appropriates it. It also follows that anything that an individual cannot productively use cannot be rightfully appropriated by that individual. Therefore, if Locke's theory specified how much and what kind of labor is needed for a person to become an owner of an unowned thing, and if it made clear just how to individuate prospective candidates for ownership, it would provide a theoretically well-motivated upper limit on private appropriations. So long as these notions remain vague, however, the claim that individuals can only rightfully own what they can productively use remains vague as well. But if we set this difficulty aside and grant that we can tell, well enough, when Locke's productive use condition is satisfied, we are still some way from justifying an unlimited right to own external things privately. At most, Locke would have shown that, in the face of collective world-ownership, individuals can privately appropriate some external things – what they need for self-preservation *and* what they can put to productive use. This last consideration takes Locke closer to his destination. But it still leaves him with a long way to go. Given human limitations, the restriction on private ownership remains severe. Individuals could not, for example, rightfully own more land than they are able to work themselves. In Locke's time, this was not very much land at all, and even today, with the mechanization of agriculture and a host of new technologies, an individual can only do so much. Allowing, then, for all the indeterminacies and shortcoming of Locke's argument to this point, he is still far from defending a right to accumulate limitless wealth.

It is a social convention that comes to Locke's rescue. Once human beings agree to introduce a universal medium of exchange, money, they are able to expand the range of external things that they can utilize productively to a point where effective limits on private appropriation and accumulation cease to obtain. Individuals can only work so much land through their own efforts, but once they can use money, they can put limitless amounts of land to productive use by hiring others to work it for them. In short, with money in the picture, they can satisfy Locke's productive use condition without having to be able to put what they own to productive use themselves. It is only thanks to money, then, that unlimited private accumulation becomes morally possible. Though property rights themselves exist in a state of nature, it takes a social convention, the institution of a universal medium of exchange, to put these rights to use in behalf of the form of society Locke sought to defend.

With money in the story, the focus inevitably turns from the initial appropriation of unowned things to property transfers. For even if it is morally permissible for individuals to appropriate privately more than they can physically work themselves, it is only in consequence of just transfers that individuals can become able, in fact, to make this right operative. Unlimited private accumulation is not a feasible consequence of just initial appropriation, nor is it likely to result from the voluntary transfer of unwanted surplus products, whether through gift giving or barter. For Locke's profoundly commercial vision to be realized, there must be markets of the kind that depend on money as a universal medium of exchange – labor markets and markets in credit and all the other essentials of a capitalist economic system. Here, then, is yet another reason why Locke was a statist. A state of nature could never be a full-fledged capitalist society. The problem is not just that, in the absence of a sovereign power, property rights, though widely acknowledged, would often be ignored. It is also that, in a state of nature, there would be no reliable way to maintain exchange relations of the required kind. For that, money must be in circulation, and money, because it is a human artifice, based on convention, cannot be sustained without a state. In Locke's view, then, the state is necessary for security, just as it was for Hobbes. But it is also an indispensable condition for capitalism, for the good society of Locke's imagination.

This latter consideration, however, is only implicit in Locke's thought. Although he was an ardent defender of private property and market exchange, Locke's understanding of capitalism was primitive, at best. It is especially telling that, despite his focus on productive labor, he had nothing of consequence to say about the sources of wealth. Insofar as a view can be ascribed to him, it would have to be a vague and largely undeveloped version of the mercantilist consensus of his time, according to which "the wealth of nations" is mainly a consequence of trade, of buying cheap and selling dear. But, of course, this is a mistake, as political economists after Locke made clear. National wealth does not result from trade *per se*, but from investments in resources capable of expanding productive capacities – a condition that money, an artifact unknown in the state of nature, finally makes possible.

Because Locke confounded the issues of just initial acquisition and just transfer, it is not clear to what extent he would have his proviso, that owners leave "enough and as good" for others, apply after the introduction of money and the unlimited private ownership it makes possible. It is clear, however, that, even if we do not take Locke at his word and interpret the proviso to mean only that accumulators do not significantly undermine the capacity of others to accumulate too, the proviso would undo Locke's case for unlimited private ownership if it is applied after money has been introduced. For if it was implausible to think that individuals could leave anything like "enough and as good" for others when they mix their labor with unowned things, it is inconceivable that they could do so with the wealth generating mechanisms of modern capitalism in place. Perhaps this consideration was the principal motivation for Nozick's revision of the Lockean proviso. Nozick's aim, even more than Locke's, was to justify capitalist economic arrangements. But he could hardly do so with a theory encumbered by a proviso that effectively proscribes the unlimited private ownership that the theory intentionally defends.[3]

However, Locke's theory has a certain internal integrity that later day Lockeans, like Nozick, breach at their own risk. In ascribing normative force to individuals' well-being and then in integrating this ascription into the conceptual architecture of morally primary rights, Nozick created an opening for a kind of justifying theory that has nothing to do with justice, as Locke conceived it. According to this way of thinking, economic structures are justified on efficiency grounds; that is, for their effects, direct or indirect, on individuals' well-being. To take this approach to heart is, however, to move the discussion of economic systems onto a very different philosophical terrain from the one Nozick set out to revive. Nozick remained too tied to Locke's moral philosophical vision to move onto this other terrain himself. Whether or not this fidelity to Locke puts the soundness of his own defense of capitalism in jeopardy, it clearly does set him apart from many other contemporary libertarians. For this reason, and also to better grasp the logic of Locke's own position, it is worth reflecting briefly on where the non-Lockean element Nozick introduced into Locke's theory of property leads.

Those who would defend capitalism or any other economic structure on efficiency grounds would first have to specify the content of the feas-

---

[3]   Contrary to what many of Nozick's libertarian followers suppose and what even Nozick himself may believe, Nozick's case for capitalism only supports a purely "clean" capitalism – in which property is rightfully acquired and then rightfully transferred. If only because real world initial accumulation was based more on conquest, plunder, murder, and mayhem than on suitable admixtures of labor with unowned things, existing capitalism could hardly count as clean – even if, contrary to fact, the market exchanges that have structured production and trade in the intervening centuries took place unblemished by force or fraud or subsequent theft. Actually existing capitalism falls so far short of the ideal that it is hardly bolstered by Nozick's arguments, a point that even those who find his justification of clean capitalism compelling should readily concede.

ible set of alternative economic systems in contention. They would then have to propose and justify some non-equity metric against which these systems could be compared. Finally, they would have to show that, as a matter of fact or plausible empirical speculation, one or another member of the set of feasible economic structures fares better than its rivals with respect to this metric. Thus one might argue that capitalism and socialism are distinct and feasible ways of organizing economic life; that they ought to be compared with respect to their ability to enhance, say, overall productivity, where productivity is defined in some theoretically well-motivated way; and then, finally, that capitalism fares better than socialism or vice versa with respect to this standard. I will say no more here about arguments of this kind, except to observe that this way of thinking about capitalism and its rivals is at odds with the core Lockean idea that capitalism is justified because it, and it alone, is what justice requires. In efficiency arguments, consequences matter. In Locke's argument, all that matters is that morally prior rights are respected, regardless of the consequences.

The State and Society

Locke's account of limited sovereignty and also his defense of private property and market exchange imply a distinction that is characteristic of liberal political philosophy – a sharp separation between the state and *civil society*. This division would have been unthinkable for Rousseau. For him, as for political philosophers in the classical tradition generally, politics is a component of the human good; one that permeates all aspects of human life. But Locke, like Hobbes, falls on the side of those for whom politics is a necessary evil. To be sure, just as Locke's account of the state of nature was more benign than Hobbes's, so too was his understanding of the evils of political life. But it is nevertheless plain that, for Locke just as for Hobbes, the state is in no way an indispensable part of the good for human beings. Its role is to superintend civil society, especially the commercial sphere; not to make people realize their special excellence or to become more of what they potentially are. Thus the state is necessary, in Locke's view, for Hobbesian reasons: because civil society cannot reliably take care of itself, given human nature and the human condition.

But in their respective ways of adhering to the non-classical, Christian view of political life, Locke and Hobbes parted ways. As remarked, Hobbes's understanding of human nature was essentially a secular version of the Christian doctrine of Original Sin. For him, therefore, human self-realization was an ill-conceived goal. Human beings in a state of nature, in their "natural condition," already are self-realized; this is why the state of nature is a state of war. The very last thing one would want, therefore, is for the institutions the sovereign establishes to encourage the free expression of what is essentially human. The best that human beings can hope for, instead, is to accumulate riches and honor in relative security – in other words, to satisfy the desires their natures occasion. For Locke, however, *outside* the state, in civil society and especially in the commercial arena, self-realization is a feasible and estimable goal. Even more than Hobbes, Locke wanted institutions arranged to facilitate the accumulation of wealth. But, unlike Hobbes, Locke did not defend this goal on the grounds that what matters normatively is only desire satisfaction and that, given human nature, riches are inevitable objects of human desire. He did not expressly defend it at all.

However, given Locke's enthusiasm for the commercial life and his penchant for cobbling doctrines together into a "reasonable," if not altogether consistent, synthesis, it would not be unfair to ascribe to him the view that the accumulation of wealth is a way of realizing an intrinsic human excellence. Locke, it appears, thought of commercial activity in more or less the way that "classical" political philosophers thought of other self-realizing but non-mercantile human endeavors. Locke's political philosophy therefore straddles, or rather confounds, Christian and classical elements. But however inconsistent the various strains of Locke's thinking may be, what emerged, in the end, was a more hopeful, less puritanical, vision of ideal institutional arrangements than Hobbes imagined. Locke was a Hobbesian or Christian in the sense that, for him, no good comes directly from political engagement; only less bad. But because the political sphere is sharply delineated and separated from the rest of human life, especially from the world of commerce and wealth accumulation, Locke effectively maintained that human beings can and should self-realize *outside* the state. Hobbes's political philosophy was based on taking Sin seriously, on the dark side of Christian theology. Locke's thinking reflected the cheerful but confused optimism of popular Christianity. He was the philosopher of Sin Light.

The Minimal State

In contrast to more standard views of rightful state activity, for Locke, there are, in effect, only two legitimate state functions. The first, of course, is to enforce morally primary rights. The second is to provide for public goods, a notion that Locke, like Hobbes, implicitly invoked. A state that restricts its activities strictly to the former function is, let us say, a *super-minimal* state. Locke's ideal state would then be a *minimal state*, one that performs both. This designation is apt because it underscores how little of what states, even liberal states, usually do that Locke would allow. For Locke, everything that does not involve either rights enforcement or public goods provision must either be done by individuals themselves or be relegated to the non-state institutions of civil society.

As discussed (in chapter 1), public goods are goods that require the efforts of many to produce and that are of such a nature that, if they exist at all, their benefits spill over to individuals independently of the contributions they make towards their production. Textbook examples include defense of the national territory and fire protection in congested areas. Because it would be impossible or, at the very least, difficult and therefore inordinately expensive to defend some citizens but not others, to defend those who pay for defense but not those who don't, or to put out a fire in the apartment of subscribers to a volunteer fire service, but not in their neighbors' apartments too, these goods, if they are supplied at all, must be supplied to everyone in the relevant community. Assuming, as Locke did, that people are basically Hobbesian – in other words, that they are generally self-interested and instrumentally rational – public goods provision has a Prisoners' Dilemma structure. Because the goods in question are of such a nature that it is possible to benefit from them without incurring the costs of producing them, no one has an incentive to contribute to their production voluntarily. Rather, everyone prefers free riding on the contributions of others to contributing themselves. But, as we have seen, if everyone free rides, the good will not be produced, and everyone will be worse off than they might otherwise be. The only way, then, to provide public goods is to coerce individuals to contribute towards their production. This is why the state, the institution with a monopoly of the means of legitimate violence, is indispensable for public goods provision. Locke endorsed the converse position too – that public goods provision is a legitimate state function. In holding this view, Locke evinced his characteristic reasonableness. To this day, public goods provision is the least controversial of state functions.

To say that something is a public good is only to say that it has a public goods structure. It is not to say that it is actually something that citizens want. The public will want some public goods and not others, and it is for the political process to make the relevant determination. However, in Locke's view, public goods provision is an appropriate state function only when the non-state coordinating mechanism he favored, the market, is inadequate to the task at hand. If, like Locke, we view markets as quasi-natural institutions, it follows immediately, insofar as what is natural is better than what is artificial, that it is better to rely on markets than on the state to coordinate individuals' affairs. The state, after all, is an artifice contrived to neutralize the otherwise devastating consequences of untrammeled human nature. Markets, on the other hand, accord with the natural human disposition to trade. But markets are unable to produce public goods because they cannot provide incentives sufficient to elicit the contributions required for their production. Therefore, if public goods are to be provided at all, the state must provide them. For Locke, this is a doubly distressing necessity. Markets are preferable to states not only because, unlike states, they arise naturally rather than by convention, but also because, unlike states, they are freedom preserving. Inasmuch as Locke valued freedom in the Hobbesian sense, "the absence of External Impediments," he was obliged to conclude that a good society would assign coordinating roles to markets rather than states whenever possible. States operate by restricting freedom, by making persons unfree. In markets, on the other hand, no one does anything that they do not want to do. Market transactions represent individuals' free choices – in the Hobbesian, non-Rousseauean sense of the term to which Locke subscribed.

There is, however, a countervailing consideration, at least for anyone who believes, as Locke did, that states rightfully supply public goods. It could be argued that the distinction between the Lockean minimal state and the *activist* state of mainstream liberalism collapses, because all that mainstream liberal states do, beyond discharging their responsibilities as rights enforcers, is provide public goods. Consider, for example, welfare state measures that libertarians oppose: poor relief, say, or social insurance programs that provide old-age pensions or health care or compensation for unemployment. The goals of these programs require the efforts of many to produce; arguably too, their benefits spill over into the general population independently of individuals' contributions towards their production. They therefore have a public goods structure. If, then, they are generally desired by the citizenry, as their enactment through democratic collective decision procedures would imply, they would have to be seen, even by Locke and his followers, as institutional arrangements concocted to provide public goods. But these and similar state policies would nevertheless be anathema in a minimal state. One reason why is that, in valorizing markets and denigrating states, Locke introduced a bias against state activism. A more theoretically grounded reason is that public goods provision is limited by the imperative that underlies Locke's political theory, the need to respect and defend morally primary rights. This is why contemporary followers of Locke, like Nozick, insist that states cannot rightfully *redistribute* market generated distributions. If individuals own external things in the same way that they own themselves, state takings of owned external things would be as illegitimate as state takings of peoples' kidneys or other body parts. The minimal state is therefore precluded from redistributing market-generated holdings. But social insurance programs and poor relief, even if they do provide public goods, are redistributive in their effects. Thus must therefore be proscribed. Purportedly, then, this is the difference between Locke's minimal state and the state of mainstream liberalism. Mainstream liberals generally endorse capitalist economic arrangements, just as Locke did. They would therefore have markets generate initial distributions of privately owned external things. But then they would have the state redistribute the market generated distribution, at least to some extent – in order to make people better off or for the sake of justice, conceived in a non-Lockean way, or equality or for some other reason. This is what Locke's libertarian followers today cannot abide.

But because Locke *is* for rights enforcement and for (some) public goods provision, and because these state functions require resources, Locke cannot be against taking property in general. A Lockean minimal state would have to tax its citizens. The aim, then, would be somehow to tax but not to redistribute market generated shares. It is far from clear, however, that this is a coherent position. The problem is that public goods provision almost always has redistributive effects. Except in virtually unimaginable limiting cases, benefits, even as they spill over irrespective of contribution, will not and cannot spill over *equally* to everyone. The army that defends the national territory may not be able to protect some individuals but not others. But it affects individuals differently, and these difference can and typically do have redistributive consequences. Similarly, it is neither necessary nor, in many cases, possible for everyone to contribute equally towards the production of public goods. We may all be taxed for the support of national defense, but we are not and probably cannot all be taxed equally – either in the sense that we all contribute the same amount absolutely or that we all contribute the same proportion of our incomes. Public goods are redistributive in this way too. Locke and his followers oppose state organized redistributions of market generated outcomes. But implicitly, though perhaps unwittingly, they permit redistributions that are inevitable consequences of public goods provision. It is incumbent on them to show why the kinds of redistributions they permit are morally acceptable, while the more straight-forward redistributions they oppose are not. I would propose that they cannot meet this challenge.

In a desperate effort to do so, they could resort to a version of the doctrine of double effect. Developed by Catholic casuists in the Middle Ages and by Thomist philosophers in recent years, the doctrine of double effect holds that it is permissible to perform acts likely to have evil conse-quences – the killing of civilians in war, for example – provided the act is performed for good or at least legitimate purposes. Similarly, a neo-Lockean libertarian could argue that it is permissible to violate otherwise unbreakable property rights, provided that the reason for doing so is warranted, and provided that the resulting redistributions are unintended, even if they are foreseen. But this way of arguing strains credulity. Locke's followers today implicitly take a different tack. Their inclination is to reduce public goods provision to the barest minimum, thereby minimiz-ing – and so, to a degree, obscuring – what would otherwise be an intrac-table problem for their position. This is why the state Locke envisioned and the state his followers continue to endorse, though a minimal state is, in practice, almost, but not quite, a super-minimal state, one that *only* enforces morally primary rights. Between that state and the state of main-stream liberalism, there is a clear difference. Neo-Lockeans, like Nozick, exploit this difference in order to block their slide into mainstream liber-alism. But it is far from clear, given their (unavoidable) commitment to the idea that public goods provision is a legitimate state function, that they are entitled to do so.

Political Legitimacy

No state can count as legitimate, in Locke's view, if it violates morally primary rights. But there is also another condition for political legiti-macy that Locke upholds. No state can rightfully command others if those who fall under its jurisdiction do not *consent* to its authority. In this respect, Locke endorsed the fundamental contractarian idea – that the source of political authority is ultimately the citizenry itself. Locke's political philosophy therefore stands in the contractarian tradition, as much as does Hobbes's or Rousseau's. But, as was characteristic of his thinking generally, Locke's contractarianism is *softer* than theirs. His understanding of consent has nevertheless come to be the dominant un-derstanding today. As one might expect, it is not an unproblematic understanding. But like so many other elements of Locke's political philosophy, it does strike a reasonable chord, at least to those accustomed to living under institutions shaped by Locke's ideas.

Not surprisingly, Hobbes and Rousseau occupy extreme positions with respect to consent and therefore political legitimacy. For Hobbes, self-interested, rational individuals have no option but to acquiesce to the sovereign's power wherever it exists, or to concoct it wherever it does not. Beyond that point, questions about legitimacy cannot arise. Rousseau's conditions for political legitimacy, on the other hand, are so stringent as to turn consent into active, though possibly unacknowledged, agreement with the sovereign's will. For Rousseau, because sovereignty resides in the people assembled together to legislate, citizens are obligated to obey laws only if they have actively participated in their legislation. As discussed (in chapter 2), citizens do not have to have actually voted in favor of particular laws to be obligated by them. But they must have voted and, in so doing, expressed their opinions about what the general will is on the matter in question. Then since the majority discovers the general will, in obeying the majority, citizens do what they really want. Needless to say, neither of these positions correspond to ordinary understandings of consent in the way that Locke's view does.

For both Hobbes and Rousseau, the social contract is a *pact of association*, an "act by which a people becomes a people" (see Chapter Two). For Locke, however, it seems that a people already exists before the social contract; presumably because the rights individuals possess in the state of nature bring them into a form of association. Locke thought of the social contract as a *pact of government*, an "act by which a people selects a king," not a pact of association. This is why Locke's politics is not inherently anti-revolutionary, as Hobbes's was. Unlike Hobbes's pact of association, Locke's pact of government can be broken – as it was said to be, for example, by the British monarchy in its relations with its North American colonies, according to the US *Declaration of Independence*. But we must not exaggerate Locke's differences from Hobbes. Locke was a liberal of a generally conservative bent. His social contract, though breakable, is not easily broken. It remains in force so long as the people collectively consent to the rule of those who govern them or, at least, to the institutional forms through which these rulers came to power. Except in cases of dire tyranny or oppression, the plain expectation is that consent is conferred.

Characteristically, Locke failed to provide an account of what is required to indicate consent. It is clear, though, that he did not think that consent must be *explicit*. *Tacit* consent will do. But the idea of tacit consent is desperately in need of clarification. Does simply remaining within a political community suffice? That might be a plausible view if there were somewhere else for a non-consenting citizen to go; somewhere, that is, without the kinds of institutional arrangements to which non-consenters might object. It would be especially compelling if a citizen could somehow go back to a state of nature. But since these exit options are generally unavailable, the fact that an individual has not left a political community would hardly seem a sufficient ground for inferring that consent is given. A more demanding view, reminiscent of the position Socrates put forward in Plato's dialogue *The Crito*, is that consent is conferred when individuals accept benefits from the state that governs them. Something like Socrates' view is probably what Locke had in mind. But a host of questions need to be answered in order to make this thought viable. One would have to specify, among other things, just what kinds of benefits, when accepted, indicate consent. Is simply living under a regime of law benefit enough, as Socrates believed? Or must there be other benefits in addition? And what exactly counts as accepting a benefit? If Jones gives Smith a gift that in some sense benefits him, a gift Smith neither asked for nor wanted but that Smith does not or cannot return, did Smith consent to the transfer? Philosophers who address these questions nowadays, especially if they are liberals, typically do so in the spirit of Locke's political philosophy. But Locke himself had hardly anything to contribute directly to their elucidation.

Locke was not unabashedly committed to the view that consent, even when it is explicitly offered and therefore plainly conferred, establishes right. He even maintained that there are agreements that individuals cannot rightfully make for reasons distinct from the overriding requirement that morally primary rights be respected. Here, too, Locke's position is more plausible than his argument in its behalf. Consider, for example, Locke's discussion of slavery in chapter 4 of *The Second Treatise*. Locke opposed pacts of voluntary slavery. He reasoned that because slavery is based on a right of conquest, which is "a continuation of war," and because individuals cannot "wage war" on themselves, individuals cannot freely become the slaves of others; they cannot sell themselves into slavery. This is an obscure argument, but it does clearly register the view that there are limits to the rights consent can establish, limits that exceed the boundaries fixed by the inalienability of certain rights.

It should be noted that Locke's position on slavery is, in any case, rather odd. On the one hand, one would expect a partisan of the view that consent confers legitimacy to permit pacts of voluntary slavery. On the other hand, one would expect a self-ownership theorist to forbid them. Locke, however, did neither. What he opposed was *selling oneself* into slavery, not slavery as an institution. Indeed, Locke thought that involuntary slavery, based on a right of conquest, was morally permissible. Thus he joined that longstanding tradition in political and legal theory that Rousseau rejected in Book I, chapter 4 of *The Social Contract*, according to which conquerors can rightfully take slaves among conquered peoples. Locke thought that individuals who acquire slaves by this means or, subsequently, through rights-preserving market transactions, are entitled to own them, just as people generally are entitled to own external things, provided they come by them in the right way. This was how Locke, along with many of the founders of the American republic, his intellectual descendants, were able to rationalize chattel slavery. They held that the African slaves were won in war; that they were a conquered people.

But, again, according to Locke, individuals cannot sell themselves into slavery – not for Rousseau's reason, because liberty (autonomy) can never be advantageously exchanged, but because the idea of a pact of voluntary slavery is somehow conceptually flawed. Whatever we make, finally, of Locke's uncertain rationale for this position, it is worth observing that it is compatible with Locke's commitment to the legitimacy-conferring status of consent that consent is not always sufficient for establishing legitimacy. If we generalize this thought, the way is open to proscribing many more transactions than Locke himself did or than his libertarian followers today are wont to do. In Locke's view, doing what slaves do, serving another for an indefinite period of time for no wage, is not wrong in itself. What is wrong is *capitalizing* on one's ability to be a slave. The example is chilling, but it illustrates an important general point. There are a number of activities that in themselves are almost certainly not wrong, but that, following Locke's lead, we might nevertheless want to exclude from the marketplace. Sexual "services" are an obvious example. One does not have to think that sex or, more precisely, sex outside of marriage is morally impermissible to oppose prostitution, the buying and selling of sex. Commercial gestational surrogacy is another example. No one objects on moral grounds to a woman carrying a fetus to term, but some people do think that it is wrong for a woman to do so for a fee. The idea, in short, is that taking advantage of the capacity to X can sometimes be impermissible, even when X itself is not. Locke only broached this subject, and did hardly anything to clarify it. In practice, he was no more disposed to impose limits on market arrangements than his libertarian followers are. Even so, his work provides a focus or, at least, a starting point for thinking about what the limits of consent might be.

Because Locke's sense of what is reasonable accords so well with contemporary sensibilities, his work is a suitable starting point for many questions central to political philosophy as it is practiced today. This is why, in contrast to Hobbes or Rousseau, his general purchase on political legitimacy seems beyond reproach. It anticipates the liberal and democratic commitments of contemporary political philosophers. Unlike Hobbes's or Rousseau's, Locke's theory has both a liberal and a democratic component. It is liberal because it requires that the political sphere be circumscribed, that there be an area of individuals' lives and behaviors that is immune from state interference. In the view of mainstream liberals today, Locke marked the boundaries of this area incorrectly, and he justified his claim for non-interference in an unsatisfactory way. But the idea that political legitimacy depends, in part, on respecting the inviolability of a non- or extra-political sphere of human life is an idea that Locke bequeathed to modern political thought. Locke's theory is democratic too, at least according to contemporary understandings of the term. The point is not just that Locke vested legitimacy in the consent of the governed. Hobbes did too, and Hobbes was no democrat. Locke's innovation was to locate consent in ongoing institutional arrangements, not just in the social contract itself. In this respect, Locke's position resembles Rousseau's. But, for Rousseau, the idea that consent is conferred in each and every act of legislation was a strict consequence of a coherent, well integrated, rigorously developed philosophical theory. For Locke, it is a position taken up almost arbitrarily, because it seems right.

Locke's notion of consent is fraught with difficulties, many of which Locke seems barely even to have recognized, let alone resolved. But in this instance good sense again came to Locke's rescue. Like nearly everyone today, Locke was partial to the method of majority rule. Because he was, many of the difficulties that attend his notion of consent are neutralized or obscured. For it seemed to Locke, as it does to many people nowadays, that a state in which the majority rules is unquestionably legitimate because its laws reflect the will of its people. The situation is in fact more complicated, as we will see, but the idea that democratic procedures confer legitimacy has become part of the common sense of our political culture. This too is Locke's legacy. Locke passed this notion on as part of a larger vision of proper governance, a theory of representative government, that effectively joins all the elements of his political philosophy together into a workable, if not entirely coherent, institutional framework.

Representative Government

For Rousseau, when citizens vote they express their opinion as to what the general will is and then, if all the necessary background conditions obtain, the majority discovers the right answer. For Locke, however, votes represent preferences for alternative outcomes in contention, not opinions about a putative matter of fact. Thus Locke's view, though bland and unmotivated, is, by contemporary standards, mainstream and sensible, while Rousseau's position is exotic, if it is intelligible at all. For Locke, as for Hobbes, politics is driven by private, not general, interests. Like Hobbes, Locke had no notion of a general will. For him, therefore, preferences for alternative outcomes straightforwardly represent the only kind of interest there is, and the method of majority rule combines these interests fairly. Majority rule voting is therefore an ideal decision procedure, one that should be modified or overridden only if there are compelling reasons for insulating some kinds of decision-making from the vagaries of public opinion and collective choice.

Locke did not quite argue the case, but something like the following rationale seems to have been what he had in mind. Individuals establish sovereignty because it is in their interests that it exist, that there be a political community governed by a supreme authority. More specifically, individuals' interests in rights enforcement lead them to establish a universal rights enforcing agency, the state. But if interests prescribe that there be states, should not interests also dictate the form of the state or, more precisely, its method for making social choices? Unlike Hobbes, Locke thought that the answer to this question is Yes. The state's reason for being implies a commitment to collective choice rules that maximize preference satisfaction, and therefore to the method of majority rule.

It would therefore seem to follow that Locke should favor direct democratic rule, just as Rousseau did, for it is only by combining individuals' votes on matters of concern to them that overall preference satisfaction is maximized. However, Locke did not think that citizens ought to enact the laws that govern them. Rather, he would have them vote periodically for representatives who would then, in turn, do the requisite law making. Majority rule voting is, of course, the preferred decision procedure at both levels of this process. But it is only in representative assemblies or legislatures that votes on particular issues are directly combined. In the election of representatives, citizens only decide who will combine interests on their behalf.

In the governing structure Locke envisioned, representatives represent their constituencies poorly if they vote as mere delegates, beholden to the views of the constituents who elected them. The best representatives are those who do what they think right, without undue concern for their constituents' preferences. Of course, representatives are accountable to their constituencies, and beholden to them for their electoral success. They therefore cannot ignore their constituents' views altogether. But it was not Locke's intent that constituencies first decide what they want, and then transmit this information to their representatives, who then legislate accordingly. His preference instead was for representatives to act independently. Indeed, a bias for independence is built into the very structure of representative government. When citizens select representatives, usually at intervals of several years, they can only make overall choices between a handful of candidates, often no more than two. How a representative voted on a particular issue, or how a proposed candidate is likely to vote, is therefore unlikely to have a significant effect on individuals' decisions about how to cast their ballots, except of course, for those comparatively few citizens for whom a particular issue or set of issues is of overriding importance.

Despite his own involvement in the emerging party politics of his day, Locke's account of representative government ignores the role of political parties. There is no doubt, however, that political parties affect relations between representatives and their constituents profoundly. The overall impact of this institutional form on popular control of the legislative process is, however, unclear. To the degree that representatives are accountable to their parties and not just to their constituencies, the party system probably distances political representatives from the citizens they represent even more than they would otherwise be. On the other hand, insofar as citizens are able to participate in the political process indirectly by participating directly in the activities of political parties, they do gain a measure of control over the legislative process that they might not otherwise enjoy. But whether, on balance, one or another sort of party structure makes citizens more or less involved in law-making, the basic fact remains – representative government, as it exists today, is anything but a straightforward preference aggregating mechanism.

A natural way to think about representative government is to view it as a second-best approximation of direct democracy, where direct democracy is an impracticable ideal. Because it is not possible, except in very small communities, to assemble the whole people together, much less to have them deliberate, representative government, one might suppose, is the best a democrat can hope to institute. However, this is not what Locke thought, nor is it what many contemporary liberal democrats believe. If it were, it would follow that the more representatives eschew independence and vote as delegates instead, the better the system of representative government would be, the closer to the ideal. But Locke's view was just the opposite. He supported independence on the part of elected representatives, just as his philosophical descendants do today. Ironically, in this respect, Locke's position resembles Rousseau's. For Rousseau, representative government was less a feasible implementation of an impracticable ideal than a betrayal of it. Thus Rousseau would have societies resort to this expedient warily, if at all. Implicitly, Locke held a similar assessment of the relation between representative and direct democracy. He too denied that representative government is a second-best approximation of an unrealizable ideal. But he then drew the opposite conclusion. For him, representative government, because it differs from direct democracy in the ways that it does, is an ideal in its own right. It, not direct democracy, is the ideal one ought to hold.

The two poles of Locke's political philosophy converge on this conclusion. Because there are morally primary rights that states may not, under any circumstances, infringe, it is crucial, above all, that political institutions make support for morally primary rights, especially property rights, as secure as can be. And because human beings are able to do well for themselves only in civil society, outside the political sphere, it is best that political institutions support civil society; in other words, that they be designed so as to guard against the temptation to expand state power beyond its proper, very limited, confines. Thus it is necessary, above all, to guard against what Rousseau wanted to promote, the democratization of the social order, and to limit, as much as possible, its prerequisite, a highly politicized citizenry. What better way to accomplish these objectives than to put the principal beneficiaries of the institutions of civil society, men of property and those who identify with their interests, in power; to assign the tasks of legislation, execution and also judicature mainly, perhaps even exclusively, to them. Governance is a necessary evil. But if it is to be done well, it is best that only the right people govern, and it is best too that public servants undertake their tasks under conditions favorable to themselves. So far as possible, therefore, members of the political class should face incentive structures similar to those that motivate actors in the larger civil society. Politics should become a career among others, not an affair of the citizenry at large. Contrary to what Rousseau and other political philosophers in the classical tradition believed, political actors ought to be professional politicians. So far from permeating every aspect of human life, it is best that politics be cordoned off and relegated to a political class.

This is, in fact, what has happened in the liberal democracies that began to appear by the middle of the nineteenth century. Liberal democratic states accord with Locke's general vision of proper governance, even if they are not the minimal states of Locke's imagination. Thanks to the revolutionary upheavals in England and then, especially, in France, the *demos*, the popular masses, have entered the political arena irreversibly. Some measure of democracy – of government of, by, and for the people – has therefore become indispensable for the *de facto* legitimacy of any regime that would rule effectively or even survive for all but the briefest period. But Locke's intuitions have proven prescient – a very minimal recourse to democratic decision-making procedures is enough to assure legitimacy. Thus, in liberal democracies today, because the people select their representatives in free, competitive elections, the *de facto* legitimacy of existing institutional arrangements is secure. No matter, then, if all the people really do is ratify choices already made within the political class. The idea, after all, is not to empower the people but to use the idea of popular empowerment to legitimate liberal protections; and, for this end, periodic free elections evidently suffice. This is why the liberal component is robust in contemporary liberal democracies, and the democratic component barely in evidence. This was Locke's idea too; it was how he foresaw proper governance. The contrast with Rousseau is striking, not least in the political implications of their respective positions. Rousseau's just state required a highly politicized citizenry. Locke's requires that the popular masses be as little involved in governance as is feasible, given how deeply entrenched democratic values have become. For Locke, civil society, not a politicized citizenry, ought to dominate the state.

In Locke's view, representative assemblies are better able than the people themselves to protect morally primary rights, especially property rights, and to support civil society because legislators are wiser than ordinary citizens. Political wisdom is a skill to be cultivated. One must know how and when to govern; and, above all, how to govern lightly, lest civil society suffer unnecessary state interferences. These skills, Locke thought, lie beyond the competence of the *demos,* the popular masses. Thus Locke stands closer to Hobbes than to Rousseau; his sensibilities were antidemocratic. Rousseau had faith in the peoples' ability to discover the general will; Locke had little faith in the ability of ordinary people even to attend to their own interests well. Above all, he feared for the enforcement of property rights and the defense of market arrangements. Before the emergence of liberal democratic institutions with their anesthetizing effects on democratic aspirations, this was, no doubt, a reasonable fear.

In any case, it is why Locke favored restricting the franchise to adult male property-holders. Locke offered no arguments against extending the franchise to women. Perhaps it seemed obvious to him, as it did to nearly everyone else in his time, that women's place was in the private sphere of the family, not in public life. But Locke did have a reason for restricting the franchise to property holders. His idea was that only people who have the leisure to cultivate the capacities required to vote competently should be legally entitled to vote. Then, since the requisite degree and type of leisure is available only to those with income from property, especially landed property, only property holders should vote. Plainly, this position reflects both class bias and a view of the condition of agricultural and urban workers that is long out of date, if it ever was even remotely accurate. But, again, Locke's was a reasonable view in his day. Allowing that mental capacities themselves are distributed by nature more or less equally among human beings, as Hobbes thought they were, Locke and his co-thinkers thought that the servile condition of the propertyless masses rendered them unfit either to vote competently or, more evidently still, to govern. Because democratic impulses were still underdeveloped in Locke's day, this observation did not underwrite a call to change society, as we might expect. It did not suggest to Locke that the conditions of labor had to be improved in order better to enlighten and then empower the citizenry. Rather, it seems to have been Locke's view that it is inevitable that the vast majority of human beings be assigned to lives of burdensome toil, that political competence will therefore always be the possession of the fortunate few, and that political institutions must accommodate to this stubborn and inexorable fact.

One cannot help but suspect that Locke's claim that differential political capacities correlate with class position in the way that he maintained was only a cover for his real concern – the worry that the propertyless masses, if politically empowered, would fail to respect the interests of property holders, the class with whose interests Locke identified. As remarked, this fear was part of the political common sense of Locke's time. It was not until long after Locke's death that the perceived tension between liberalism and democracy became muted in the minds of political philosophers and ordinary citizens. No doubt, a very large part of the responsibility for this sea-change had to do with the development of institutions consistent with Locke's vision of proper governance, with representative government itself. In any case, the transformation has been profound. At the present time, "liberalism" and "democracy" are commonly, if carelessly, used interchangeably. In Locke's day, the idea that respect for rights, especially property rights, and government of, by and for the people come to the same thing, that liberalism and democracy articulate the same fundamental idea, was unthinkable.

Locke's insistence that the franchise be severely restricted was undemocratic. But, in another respect, his views were potentially more democratic than those current in the mainstream political culture of many contemporary liberal democracies, including the United States. For Locke would permit legislative assemblies, parliaments, to do more or less as they please, unencumbered by judicial or executive "checks and balances." Within the political sphere, a Lockean legislature, like a Hobbesian or Rousseauean sovereign, exercises supreme authority over the territory or population it governs. A Lockean legislature is therefore potentially a more powerful instrument of popular rule than legislatures with more circumscribed powers. Among other things, the right of judicature ultimately resides within it. Thus its decisions, unlike those of the legislative branch of the US government, are immune from review by extra-legislative, judicial institutions. There are obvious risks, especially for liberals, in diminishing the political independence of the judiciary. But a countervailing consideration, of great importance to democrats, is that the range of what is susceptible to political contestation is enhanced when legislatures alone exercise sovereign power. The American model sharply restricts what legislatures may do, turning many issues that might otherwise be addressed in representative assemblies, into legal questions to be settled by courts. In a Lockean, parliamentary system, the executive apparatus too is a creature of the legislature and therefore ultimately subject to its will. In the American model, on the other hand, the executive branch, like the judiciary, is a distinct and independent division of the government. In short, for Locke, as for Rousseau, sovereignty resides exclusively with those who make laws. This is what one would expect a democrat to think. Of course, unlike Rousseau, Locke channeled authority away from the people into representative assemblies, just as liberal democrats later would. But Locke's theory of representative government, because it gives legislatures free reign over the political sphere, invests more power in the people, at least potentially, than do the representative institutions established by the Constitution of the United States. It should be noted, finally, that the democratic implications of Locke's theory are substantially enhanced by a fairly recent development in the real world of politics; one that, in his own time and place, Locke opposed: the extension of the franchise to all adult citizens.

If supreme authority resides in representative assemblies, as Locke maintained, how can people be sure that their rights will be protected and that the institutions of civil society will receive the support they are due? The answer is that there is no alternative but to trust representative assemblies to behave as they should. In the end, democracy, even the pale democracy Locke endorsed, rests on faith in the people. Locke's faith was weaker than Rousseau's. He had no confidence in the capacity of the popular masses to rule themselves. But Locke was confident that a properly cultivated class of professional politicians could rule wisely on their behalf. Thus Locke was, at most, a reluctant democrat. Even so, he realized that the true foundation of a legitimate state in a democratic era can only lie in the democratic dispositions of its citizens, a point Rousseau would later make emphatically clear. This lesson holds even for the liberal democracies we know today; regimes that, despite the extension of the franchise, are, if anything, even paler in their democratic commitments than the state Locke envisioned. Institutional safeguards are important. But they can never substitute for a democratic citizenry.

However, faith in the *demos* is reasonable only if there is reason to think that the people are capable of fulfilling their allotted role. Locke realized that the requisite capability is not automatically present in each and every citizen; competence must be cultivated. In setting forth his views on representative government, he brought this theme to the fore, perhaps without quite realizing its importance. Ironically, this contribution of his to modern political philosophy has come to play a larger role in subsequent liberal and democratic theory than has his core conviction, his belief in the existence of morally primary rights. As we will see, competency thresholds were a central concern for John Stuart Mill. They matter in John Rawls's political philosophy too, and in modern, mainstream liberal theory generally. Both Mill and Rawls, however, rejected the idea of morally primary rights, and so do the mainstream liberal traditions their work has shaped.

4

Mill

All distinctively modern political philosophies take individuals' interests as their points of departure. But they deal with these interests in different ways. Contractarians would uphold individuals' interests by imagining how idealized, rational agents would look out for themselves in hypothetical states of nature. Hobbes was a contractarian; his social contract was a pact individuals enter into because it is straightforwardly in their interests to do so. Rousseau was a contractarian too, though in a more obscure way, inasmuch as his social contract was not so much a pact of mutual advantage as a way of articulating what the moral point of view, the point of view of impartiality or *generality*, requires. Rights theorists uphold individuals' interests by according priority to morally primary rights, interests that take precedence over other considerations. Locke was a rights theorist, though he made use of the device of a social contract too. John Stuart Mill (1806–73) was neither a contractarian nor a rights theorist. He represented the third major, modern moral philosophical position, utilitarianism. Utilitarians would accommodate individuals' interests in a very direct and commonsensical way – by seeking to have them be as well satisfied as possible.

At the beginning of *On Liberty*, Mill declared that the principle of utility would be his supreme moral principle, and went on to deride the very idea of "abstract rights independent of utility" (*On Liberty*, hereafter *OL*, 1). Mill was determined, in other words, that his liberalism be undergirded by a moral philosophy very different from Locke's. Their liberalisms differ in content too – among other things, Mill was less interested in property and commerce than Locke was, and more concerned with what would nowadays be called "civil rights," especially freedom of thought and expression, and tolerance of diverse life-styles and experiments in living. But, for both Locke and Mill, liberalism, the doctrine that there are areas of individuals' lives and behaviors that are rightfully immune from public, especially state, interference, rests on a prior moral philosophical foundation. Each, therefore, saw political philosophy as a sub-field of moral philosophy generally, as that aspect of moral philosophy that deals with political concerns.

Mill's Reformism

Just as it is instructive to acknowledge Hobbes's anti-revolutionary politics as a key to understanding his political philosophy, it is instructive to think of Mill and his utilitarian predecessors – Jeremy Bentham and John Stuart's father, James Mill, among others – as radical reformers in the context of early nineteenth-century English politics. Just as it is instructive to acknowledge Hobbes's desire to think about politics and society in a way that is joined systematically to what Hobbes took to be the discoveries of Gallilean physics, it is instructive to think of the utilitarians' project as an effort to put moral and political theory on a scientific basis by showing how in principle all moral and political questions can be decided in a rationally compelling way.

These goals of the classical utilitarians were interconnected. The political antagonists of the radical reformers were British Conservatives, Tories, who believed that questions of institutional design and also of personal conduct were generally not amenable to rational adjudication, but were best left, instead, to traditional elites, who, in consequence of their superior virtue, were equipped with the right intuitions. The utilitarians' principal philosophical opponents were the moral sense theorists preeminent in the Scottish Enlightenment, defenders, in their own way, of an intuitionist methodology in ethics. Not all the moral sense theorists were Tories, but the affinities between their philosophical orientation and Tory political ideas resonated with the classical utilitarians.

There is a sense too in which the classical utilitarians were also, like Hobbes, anti-revolutionaries, though in a much less categorical way. Like the conservatives they opposed and also like the socialists who were, by Mill's time, emerging into a significant intellectual and political current to the Left of reformism, early nineteenth-century British reformers were, in large part, shaped politically and intellectually by the French Revolution and its aftermath. The reformers were friendly to many of the causes the French revolutionaries advanced, but hostile to revolutionary politics. They wanted the old regimes of the world transformed – not by their insurgent victims, but by political elites bent on maintaining continuity with received governing structures. In the reformers' hands, therefore, utilitarianism and eventually liberalism became doctrines of permanent reform, of change – sometimes substantial, more usually incremental – imposed from above. The liberalism that emerged out of this political and philosophical tendency was, like Locke's, dedicated, above all, to the principle of limited government. But, unlike Lockean liberalism, post-Revolutionary liberalism, the political theory of the English reformers, developed into a full-fledged, *progressive* ideology, a system of ideas organized around the notion of progress implicit in contemporaneous understandings of the French Revolution. But these progressives were steadfastly opposed to the revolutionary impulse that motivated the more radical of the French revolutionaries; they opposed the idea of the victims of the regime in place taking their own affairs in hand.

Like other centrists, the reformers drew criticism from both the right and the left. The conservative right opposed their desire for change. The revolutionary left saw in the reformers opposition to revolution nothing more than an expression of the principle that everything must change in order to remain the same. However, the reformers themselves sought to steer a principled course. In their view, changes, including radical changes, are often warranted. Even revolution is not out of the question, when non-revolutionary means for changing the system of governance are unavailable and when it is possible, as it was in the American case but not in the French, to keep the popular masses within bounds. But change is best when it is imposed by elites within the existing legal and institutional framework.

In part because the revolutionary specter had almost vanished in England by the early and mid-nineteenth century, and in part because the reformers themselves were more hostile to their Tory compatriots than to the utopian socialists and the fledgling working-class movement that was taking shape before their eyes, the utilitarians' principal antagonists were to their right, not their left. Their views are therefore better understood as anti-conservative than anti-socialist. But the conservatism that Mill and the others opposed was not exactly Hobbesian conservatism. Hobbes opposed radical change on the grounds that human nature and the human condition make it inordinately risky. Because sovereignty is such a fragile achievement, so contrary to the free expression of human beings' natural inclinations, no one should do anything to jeopardize it, lest everyone fall back into a devastating war of all against all. Opposition to established authority is therefore always to be suppressed in Hobbes's view. To this day, most conservative thinkers, especially on the

European continent, ground their conservatism on a similar view of human nature. Like Hobbes, they take Sin or rather its secular equivalent, a human nature that threatens perpetually to undermine civil order, seriously.

The conservatives the English reformers opposed were different. They were indifferent to the nature of Fallen Man. As remarked (in chapter 1), their conservatism was grounded instead on a view of the nature of governance as an activity. Their guiding idea was that good government and radicalism stand unalterably opposed. In their view, governing more nearly resembles cooking or carpentry than geometry. It is an activity in which a reservoir of accumulated wisdom and good sense, built up over generations and materialized in techniques, implements and traditions matters more than rational insight or deductive acuity. The French revolutionaries were moved by what Pascal, in another context, called *l'esprit de géometrie*. They overthrew the old regime in order to build a new world on rational foundations, much as geometers overthrew existing beliefs about spatial relations in order to start over from firm, rationally irresistible foundations, and much as the philosophical rationalist, René Descartes, taking geometry as his model, resolved to doubt whatever could not be established with certainty, thereby overthrowing all of his own beliefs, until he discovered his own existence as a thinking thing, a belief Descartes thought logically impossible to doubt. On that foundation, Descartes then proceeded to reconstruct philosophy and science from the beginning. But, for the English conservatives, because governing is an activity that depends on accumulated wisdom, not first principles, rethinking its foundations or otherwise tampering extensively with received understandings raises the prospect of going disastrously wrong. In their view, therefore, revolutionaries and others who favor fundamental and abrupt changes in political life mistakenly import a "rationalist" attitude into politics, a way of thinking that is appropriate in geometry and perhaps also in "first philosophy," but not in political affairs. In the post-Revolutionary conservative view, the French revolutionaries erred not so much in their objectives, as in their dedication to building a new world on the ashes of the old. They ought instead to have been guided by what Pascal called *l'esprit de finesse*, a more spontaneous, less deliberative, mental attitude – finely attuned to extant traditions and received ways of conducting social and political life.

This distinctively English conservatism reflected ways of thinking that were already deeply entrenched in English political culture and in the political culture of the English-speaking world. Consider, for example, the Common Law principle of *stare decisis*, let the precedent decide. The idea is that, as far as possible, the way legal cases were decided in the past ought to govern how new cases are decided in the present. Continental jurisprudence is, on the whole, more "rationalistic" in style and perhaps also in substance. The jurisprudence of the English-speaking countries, in contrast, is officially dedicated to maintaining continuity with the past, even as lawyers and judges apply the *state decisis* principle creatively, innovating perhaps as much as any continental magistrate would. Basic to this way of thinking is the idea that received ways of doing things are good enough, even when they are almost certainly not as good as could be. Change is therefore never out of the question, but it is best that it be evolutionary change, undertaken gradually and with proper attention to ongoing traditions and practices. Needless to say, this attitude will be more attractive to those who do reasonably well under existing arrangements than to those who suffer under them. It will be attractive too to those who, in their psychological constitution, are disinclined to take risks. The reformers, however, were undaunted by the pervasiveness of the mentality they opposed, and unmoved by its attractions. Their desire to place deliberations about individual conduct and about the nature of social institutions on a sound, scientific basis was therefore, in context, nearly as revolutionary as the more overtly revolutionary doctrines they opposed.

On Liberty exemplifies this political orientation perfectly. At the same time, however, it registers some differences from classical utilitarianism, differences Mill was generally disinclined to acknowledge. Mill's departures from classical utilitarianism are evident in his principal treatise on moral philosophy, *Utilitarianism*, a work that first appeared in 1861, just two years after the publication of *On Liberty*. It will therefore be useful to remark on some aspects of the utilitarian philosophy Mill set forth in that text, in order better to understand what Mill took the supreme moral principle invoked in *On Liberty* to be.

What Utilitarianism Is

At the beginning of *Utilitarianism*, Mill declared his aim to be to establish "a criterion of right and wrong." He set out, in other words, to identify universal principles that would ground judgments of rightness and wrongness. Mill argued that the need for such principles was conceded even by his intuitionist opponents. They too wanted to be able to say what sorts of actions are right or wrong. However, the intuitionists could do no more than assemble their intuitive judgments and compile them into categories. Mill, however, wanted a general account of right and wrong-making properties. Part of what motivated him was the conviction that morality is a coherent system, and therefore that genuine moral dilemmas cannot exist. Inasmuch as there is nothing to prevent intuitions from conflicting, intuitionism encourages the opposite view, the idea that morality is internally conflicted. If it were possible, however, to identify right- and wrong-making properties, the way would be clear for thinking of the moral order as a harmonious whole in which no conflicts exist. This conclusion would be irresistible, if it should turn out, as the utilitarians maintained, that, in the final analysis, there is only one such property.

Unlike many moral philosophers, Mill did not set out to discover general principles of right- and wrong-making by reasoning up from particular cases, relying on his own intuitions or what he took to be peoples' intuitions generally. He sought, instead, to discover principles directly – and then to decide particular cases from the top down, relying on whatever general considerations his principles would endorse. Mill was led to this strategy by what he took to be the nature of moral properties. Moral properties, he thought, contrast with ordinary perceived properties of objects. Grass is green; we might even say that greenness is a basic property of grass. No doubt, this fact can be explained. But the explanation is not part of grass's greenness, any more than the fact that left-handedness can be explained is part of the property of being left-handed. Right and wrong, however, are apparently not basic properties of actions because actions are neither right nor wrong in themselves. They are only right or wrong in particular contexts. Mill, then, reasoned that this could only be the case if there is a fundamental right or wrong-making property that applies not to actions *per se*, but to acting in situations. He therefore concluded that a universal principle or "general theory" of rightness and wrongness, an account of what it is that makes actions right or wrong, is built into the very idea of a moral property.

A large part of the appeal of utilitarianism is its claim that this general theory is a simple one; that there is, in fact only one right and wrong making property. If this view could be sustained, it would constitute a major philosophical and practical breakthrough. There would then be a single, rationally compelling principle governing all normative deliberations! In place of the chaos intuitionism threatened, order would reign. The utilitarians would then have done for the "moral sciences," what Newton had done for natural science. After millennia of confusion and false conviction, they would have put morality and public policy on a firm, rationally compelling foundation.

Mill sometimes harmlessly elided the two issues, but we should take care nevertheless to distinguish utilitarianism as an account of right action, a theory of individual conduct, from utilitarianism as an account of how institutional arrangements should be, a public philosophy. In the former case, utilitarianism addresses the following question: "What is it that makes an action right or wrong"? In the latter case, it addresses the question: "How should societies organize social practices and institutions?" The former question, about right action, falls squarely within the domain of ethics. Utilitarianism is therefore an ethical theory. The latter question, about social practices and institutions, falls within the domain of social and political philosophy. Utilitarianism is therefore also a political philosophy or, more precisely, a justifying theory that underlies positions within social and political philosophy. Thus, in *On Liberty*, Mill asked what should society's practices be with respect to public, coercive interferences with individuals' lives and behaviors? His resolve was to assess this question by appeal to "the principle of utility"; in other words, to develop an account of the limits of sovereignty or, more precisely, since he was also concerned with non-state societal interferences, of individual liberty, that is justified on utilitarian grounds. It is possible, of course, to think that utilitarianism is a sound public philosophy but a false ethical theory, or vice versa. To be committed to it in one of these domains does not imply support for it in the other. Mill, however, was a utilitarian in both, at least according to his own self-representations.

The basic idea behind utilitarianism is simple and direct: it is *to maximize (moral) goodness*. Because utilitarianism is a *moral* theory, it maintains that what is morally good is good in an impartial or agent-neutral way, good from the moral point of view. Utilitarians then identify the moral point of view with the perspective of the moral community as a whole. This position gives expression to a distinctive view about what morality involves, about how the moral point of view ought to register in an ethical theory. It is because utilitarians subscribe to this understanding that they want to maximize the good *for the whole community*. A common reproach leveled against utilitarianism is directed precisely at its view of impartiality. The charge is that because utilitarians adopt the perspective of the whole community and seek to maximize the good *for it*, they fail to accord proper respect to moral personality as such. Utilitarianism, the argument goes, is prepared to sacrifice individuals' interests or otherwise to treat individuals *unfairly* for the sake of maximizing moral goodness overall.

Utilitarians also have a distinctive conception of *the whole community*. It is an understanding that is both individualistic and egalitarian.

Their idea is that the whole community is comprised of the individuals who constitute it, and that all individuals count equally as members of it. In calculating the good for the whole community, therefore, utilitarians literally add together the goods for every individual, each individual counting the same. Utilitarians identify the good with *well-being* or *welfare*. These are place-holder terms, typically used interchangeably. In principle, then, utilitarians may disagree about the nature of the good. We will find, in fact, that, on this issue, Mill broke ranks with his utilitarian predecessors. But, like them and like most utilitarians after him, Mill did identify the good with well-being, at least officially, and this is not an innocuous claim. Well-being is both an individualistic and a passive notion. To hold that the good for the whole community is the logical sum of individual welfares is to claim (or assume) that the good is always a good *for individuals*, and it is to say that the good is something they *consume* rather than something they *do*. It is also to claim that there are no goods that need to be taken into account in ethical or (normative) political deliberations that are goods of any other sort. This is a strong claim, but it is not quite as strong as may at first appear. Utilitarians need not insist that all goods are welfarist. They are only committed to the view that non-welfarist goods ought to play no role in normative deliberations.

Utilitarianism holds that individual welfares are in principle quantifiable, that they are susceptible to being compared along a single dimension. That dimension is *utility*. Utility is a measure of welfare. Utilitarians therefore want to maximize utility for the whole com-munity or, more precisely, to maximize the value U_s, where U_s is the logical sum of the utilities of each of the *n* individuals in the whole community, $U_1 + U_2, + \ldots + U_n$. For a utilitarian, then, normative deliberations are about *aggregating* goodness or, what comes to the same thing, maximizing utility. The aim of a utilitarian deliberator is to amass the greatest possible amount of overall goodness, subject only to the constraint that, as bearers of utility, all individuals count the same. The issue at stake is *how much* overall goodness there is. All other considerations are secondary. Therefore, utilitarians are interested in *distributional* questions, including questions pertaining to the distribution of welfare itself, only indirectly – insofar as distributions causally affect how much goodness there is.

As remarked, it is one thing for a moral theory to have a utilitarian structure, and something else for it to be committed to one or another view of what the good is. Historically, though, utilitarians, especially the generation of utilitarians before Mill, the generation of Bentham and James Mill, famously identified the good with pleasure or happiness.

Their view, *hedonism,* persists to this day. But even utilitarians who object to hedonism in its original, Benthamite form, as Mill expressly did,
and utilitarians who stray even farther from the hedonistic fold, as I will
suggest that Mill, perhaps unwittingly, also did, usually agree that the
good is one or another kind of *natural* property. The dominant view, in
other words, is that whatever is intrinsically good is part of nature. It is
therefore fair to say that, with very few exceptions, utilitarians are *ethical naturalists.* One can be a utilitarian, though, and not an ethical naturalist. For example, G. E. Moore, one of the founders of modern analytic
philosophy, was a utilitarian. He was as committed as Bentham or Mill
to enhancing overall goodness by maximizing social utility, taking social
utility to be the logical sum of individuals' utilities. However, Moore
famously opposed ethical naturalism, insisting that the very idea rests on
what he disparagingly called the "naturalistic fallacy."[1] In direct opposition to Mill, Moore maintained that the good can only be a non-natural
property; one, however, that, like the bare properties of physical objects,
individuals are able directly to apprehend.

Problems for Utilitarians

As an ethical theory, a theory of *right action*, the basic utilitarian claim is
that an action is *right* if and only if, of all the actions the agent could
perform, it has the consequence of generating the most utility overall. As
a political philosophy, the corresponding idea is that institutional arrangements and social practices are justified if and only if, of all the alternatives in contention, they too generate the most overall utility. Thus, in
both ethics and political philosophy, utilitarianism is a *consequentialist*
theory. For utilitarians, only the consequences of actions or of institutional arrangements matter. Indeed, for utilitarians, only some consequences matter – utility consequences, consequences for individuals'
welfares.

Again, if U_s represents social utility, the utility of all individuals in the
community, and U_1 represents the utility function for individual 1, U_2,
the utility function for individual 2, and so on up to the nth individual,

---

[1]   Moore thought ethical naturalism fallacious because it is always meaningful, he
insisted, to ask of any naturalistic property with which an ethical naturalist might
identify the good, whether or not it is, in fact, good. See G. E. Moore, *Principia
Ethica* (Cambridge: Cambridge University Press, 1903) and *Ethics* (Oxford: Oxford
University Press, 1912).

then what utilitarians want is to maximize the value of U_s, where $U_s = U_1 + U_2 + \ldots + U_n$. This formulation supposes that there is a theoretically meaningful way of assigning cardinal numbers (1, 2, 3 ...) to welfare, however welfare is understood, so that individuals' welfares can be added together, as the theory requires. There are therefore two measurement problems that must be addressed: (a) how to measure utility *intra-personally*, within the person; and (b) how to measure utility *inter-personally*, between persons. To measure utility intra-personally, there must be a theoretically well-motivated way to assign cardinal numbers to individuals' welfares, so as to measure not only how alternative states of the world can be ranked with respect to their welfare consequences, but also the degree of welfare differences in alternative states of the world. To measure utility inter-personally, it must be possible to express these intra-personal measurements in a common unit. Otherwise, it would be impossible meaningfully to add the numbers together, as utilitarianism requires. These measurement problems have been addressed with considerable ingenuity over the past two centuries, especially by economists, and some progress has been made, on both fronts, in measuring utility in highly restricted and stylized conditions. Still, the general problem remains.

It is often said that inter-personal utility comparisons are the main obstacle in the way of developing a satisfactory utilitarian theory. Inasmuch as it has become a tenet of modern philosophy, after Descartes, that individuals cannot even in principle have direct cognitive access to minds other than their own, it would seem impossible even in principle to compare utility measurements across individuals. Thus utilitarianism seems to run aground on the problem of other minds. Whoever takes this problem seriously would almost certainly cavil at the thought that the utilities of different individuals could be expressed in a common unit, even if the problem of measuring utility intra-personally were somehow solved. This is not the place to dwell on methodological issues pertaining to the measurement of utility. I would only say that however perplexing these problems may be, they are almost certainly not fatal to the utilitarian idea. There is little doubt that we can and do compare utilities interpersonally all the time, even if only very crudely. We can often tell, for example, that John would get more satisfaction from a piece of pie than Mary would, and this fact can register in our deliberations. Therefore, even if a satisfactory way of measuring utility precisely remains permanently elusive, the fact that we do make coarse-grained inter-personal utility comparisons may suffice to establish the theory's cogency, Cartesian hesitations notwithstanding. The utilitarians' guiding idea, that deliberators ought to seek to maximize the logical sum of individuals' utilities, is probably secure enough.

Of course, a full-fledged utilitarian theory must address a host of questions: among others, how to determine the scope of the utilitarian principle. If pleasure or pain is what matters normatively, it would seem arbitrary to restrict utilitarian calculations only to human beings, inasmuch as the world abounds with sentient creatures, as capable as human beings of feeling pleasure and pain. But if the problem of inter-personal utility comparisons seems intractable, the very idea of inter-species comparisons must strike even the most resolute utilitarian as hopeless. In any case, Mill never thought to include anything non-human in utilitarian calculations, and neither did any other utilitarian before the rise of the environmental movement late in the twentieth century. Another problem utilitarians must confront is whether to aim to maximize total or average utility. How this question is resolved bears particularly on public policies pertaining to population size. Is it better to have many people at very low levels of utility or fewer people at higher levels – when, as would likely be the case, there is more total utility, but less utility on average, in the former condition? This is a twentieth or twenty-first century problem, about which Mill also had nothing to say. The moral arithmetic of Mill and the other classical utilitarians seems outdated in other respects too. For example, if it is consequences that matter, how far into the future should utilitarian deliberators look? This is an urgent problem in a world in which there are utility consequences that are only likely to emerge after considerable periods of time have elapsed. But given the level of technological development a century and a half ago, the prospect of delayed or distant consequences hardly impinged on Mill's imagination.

Finally, it should be observed that utilitarianism is a prospective, not a retrospective ethical or political theory. Its concern is normative deliberation, not the goodness or badness of states of affairs, viewed as timeless objects. Deliberation is necessarily forward looking. Therefore, in making normative assessments, utilitarians can only take *expected* consequences, not *actual* consequences, into account, because actual consequences are necessarily unknown to deliberators. Utilitarianism cannot will away this inexorable fact. It is why even the best laid plans of utilitarian deliberators sometimes go astray.

"The Permanent Interests of Man as a Progressive Being"

In the first chapter of *On Liberty*, immediately after stating that he would "forgo any advantage that could be derived . . . from the idea of abstract right as a thing independent of utility," Mill went on to add: "I regard utility as the ultimate appeal on all ethical questions; but it must be *utility in the largest sense, grounded on the permanent interests of man as a progressive being*" (*OL*, 1, *emphasis* added). This passage is key to understanding Mill's justifying strategy in political philosophy.

Officially, Mill was a hedonist, as he declared at several points in *Utilitarianism*, as when he wrote: "Questions about ends are . . . questions [about] what things are desirable. The utilitarian doctrine is that happiness is desirable, and the only thing desirable, as an end; all other things being only desirable as means to that end" (*Utilitarianism*, hereafter *U*, chap. 4). Mill even seemed to endorse Benthamite hedonism as, for example, when he declared: ". . . actions are right in proportion as they tend to promote happiness; wrong as they tend to produce the reverse of happiness. By happiness is intended pleasure and the absence of pain; by unappiness, pain and the privation of pleasure . . ." (*U*, chap. 2). In other words, only pleasure and the absence of pain are *intrinsically* desirable. Everything else that is desirable is desirable only insofar as it enhances pleasure or, what comes to the same thing in Mill's usage, insofar as it diminishes pain.

But Mill cannot be taken at his word. In Chapter 2 of *Utilitarianism*, immediately after endorsing Bentham's view, Mill deliberately distanced himself from it, by introducing a distinction between what he called *higher* and *lower* pleasures. Bentham's was a quantitative hedonism, according to which the only differences between pleasures or pains that matter for utilitarian calculations are differences in degree or intensity. For Bentham, then, the only relevant normative fact was how much of this one intrinsic good there is. But this position leads to conclusions that are at odds with intuitions that even Bentham would have been loathe to abandon. To use one of Mill's examples, in Mill's day, pushpin, a game similar to bowling, generated more, indeed much more, pleasure overall than poetry did. Yet Mill was adamant that poetry was better, more valuable, than pushpin, a judgment Bentham would likely have endorsed too, were he not forced to deny it by his commitment to "the greatest happiness" principle. To retain both utilitarianism and the intuition that poetry is better than pushpin, something must give. One solution would be to insist that whenever utilitarianism underwrites the "wrong" conclusions,

conclusions opposed to the intuitions of cultivated reformers, it is society, not utilitarianism, that is at fault. If the reformers could then somehow justify their confidence in their own intuitive judgements without abandoning their utilitarian principles, they could say that the fact that pushpin, not poetry, provides "the greatest happiness" is a reproach to a social order that encourages the development of pushpin preferences over poetry preferences in the vast majority of its people. This reproach would then underwrite a call for reform. Mill did not frame his discussion of higher and lower pleasures in these terms. But inasmuch as he was prepared to indict societies for the preferences and attitudes they encouraged, as he famously did in *The Subjection of Women*, he might not have been averse to drawing this conclusion.

In any case, Mill's more immediate reason for distinguishing higher from lower pleasures was philosophical, not political. For reasons having to do with the justification of moral theories, he was determined to reconcile his utilitarianism with his own intuitive judgments, judgments in which he had the utmost confidence. Like other utilitarians, Mill rejected intuitionism in moral philosophy. He set out to do what his moral intuitionist opponents thought impossible – directly to discover a "general theory" of right and wrong from which conclusions about what to do would follow. Mill therefore implicitly rejected the method, dear to philosophers today, of teasing general conclusions out of considered intuitive reactions to particular cases. Nevertheless, Mill understood that conformity to considered intuitions is indispensable for justifying claims in moral philosophy, including claims about general criteria for rightness and wrongness. He underscored this point explicitly in Chapter 4 of *Utilitarianism*. How else but by testing their claims against their own judgments, can moral philosophers defend their assertions? In the sciences, empirical evidence supports or infirms hypotheses. In moral philosophy, there is no pertinent empirical evidence; there are only considered judgments. Thus it is a problem for utilitarianism that it implies that pushpin is more valuable than poetry or, to take another of Mill's examples, that it entails that it is better to be a "contented pig" than "Socrates dissatisfied" (*U*, II). This problem must somehow be addressed.

Mill addressed it by transforming Bentham's quantitative hedonism into a *qualitative* hedonism that acknowledges differences among pleasures that are irreducible to differences in degree, and that is therefore able to assign more value to poetry than to pushpin and to a life dedicated to Socratic pursuits than to the shallow endeavors of contented pigs. To this end, Mill argued that because desires are based on different degrees of knowledgeable acquaintance with their objects, desires vary with respect to how informative they are as indicators of value. The more acquaintance there is, the better. Thus Mill proposed a test for drawing distinctions among pleasures: "Of two pleasures, if there be one to which all or almost all who have experience of both give a decided preference, irrespective of any feeling of moral obligation to prefer it, that is the more desirable pleasure" (*U*, chap. 2). The desires of *experienced* judges, then, are the basis for distinguishing higher from lower pleasures. Their views, not the views of the uninformed, provide evidence for judgments of value. This is an epistemological thesis, a claim about how knowledge of value is best ascertained. In conjunction with the empirical claim that knowledgeable judges, like Mill himself, do in fact accord more value to poetry than to pushpin, it warrants the conclusion that there really are qualitative differences among pleasures; and therefore that the utilitarian calculus should accord more weight, perhaps even decisively more weight, to higher pleasures, like poetry, than to lower pleasures, like pushpin.

The distinction between higher and lower pleasures pertains, strictly speaking, to values, not choices. Mill's discussion is sometimes insufficiently attentive to this difference. It can therefore seem disconcertingly high minded. Mill might even be thought to have implied that experienced judges would generally (or always) opt for higher over lower pleasures in their own choices. This is almost certainly a false prediction, and it is unnecessary for his argument. All Mill needed to hold was that experienced judges would in fact categorize values in the way he thought they should, and that they would be right to do so. It is compatible with this conclusion that even the most knowledgeable judge might, from time to time, prefer playing pushpin to reading poetry. Similarly, one can admire the life of Socrates without giving oneself over entirely to the anguish of Socratic inquiry, abandoning all the shallow pleasures experienced by contented pigs.

Qualitative hedonism is, of course, still hedonism, even if it is not Benthamite hedonism. However, Mill's discussion of higher and lower pleasures introduces considerations that point in a direction beyond the conceptual horizons of even the revisionist, qualitative hedonism Mill expressly endorsed. These implications become clear, finally, in Mill's political philosophy. For it is there that a distinctively Aristotelian element in Mill's thinking stands revealed. In describing the higher pleasures as he did, as *doings* or *functionings* rather than as states of mind or even states of affairs of the world, Mill implied that what matters normatively is incompatible with the notion, implicit in any imaginable hedonism, that individuals are mere *bearers* of utility, *passive* recipients of the good. For Mill, instead, individuals are beings whose *activities* are essential components of the good or, at least, of those higher goods that knowledgeable observers are able to detect.

Pushed to the limit, this thought puts not only hedonism but utilitarianism itself in question. It does so in two ways. First, it strains the idea, implicit in the very structure of utilitarian theories, that individuals' utilities can be logically summed. As we have seen, that understanding accords well with welfarist understandings of the good, even when, as in G. E. Moore's case, the good is conceived in a non-naturalistic and therefore non-hedonistic way. But if the good is identified with doing certain sorts of things, rather than with being in certain conditions – in other words, if, following Aristotle's lead, it is conceived in a non-welfarist way – then it is not clear that utilities can be added together at all. What could the common metric be? Because Mill remained officially in the utilitarian camp, he never faced this question. But the moral theory he seems, at least sometimes, to have had in mind does pose it.

In addition, the Aristotelian aspect of Mill's discussion of higher and lower pleasures suggests that there are potentialities in human beings, such as those that make it possible to detect how poetry is better than pushpin, that ought to be cultivated for their own sake rather than for any other end, and that are therefore good in themselves. If so, then Mill, again like Aristotle, was what philosophers today would call a *perfectionist*. Perfectionism – the view that there exist activities and/or ways of being that are good in themselves, and not just for the sake of some other end (like pleasure) – is a rival to utilitarianism. It implies that there are many intrinsic goods, not just one, as utilitarians believe, and it even suggests that these goods may be incommensurable.

To be sure, both as an ethicist and as a public philosopher, Mill was a consequentialist. He thought that, from a normative point of view, only consequences matter. And, as his utilitarian commitments require, his underlying justifying strategy was individualistic and egalitarian. In his view, the good for the whole community is decomposable without remainder into the goods of the individuals who comprise it; and, in calculating consequences, each individual counts the same. In these respects, he was unequivocally of one mind with more traditional utilitarians. But in other respects Mill seems to have strayed so far from the fold that his professions of utilitarianism ring hollow.

In any case, what matters is what Mill did, not how he represented his views, and this question will probably remain controversial for as long as his work is studied. I would submit that Mill's underlying moral philosophy is, in the end, an amalgam of utilitarian and Aristotelian positions that never quite cohere satisfactorily. It would be misleading to say that, despite his self-representations, Mill was not really a utilitarian at all; he plainly was, even if there are aspects of his thinking that utilitarianism cannot accommodate. But he was an Aristotelian too. The positions are incompatible. Nevertheless, their amalgamation, in Mill's hands, was often more fruitful than debilitating.

Mill's (implicit) Aristotelianism consisted, in the main, in his commitment to self-realization, to the actualization of distinctively human capacities. In much the way that a flower realizes its own special excellence when it grows and is sustained under ideal conditions, people realize their own distinctive excellences when they actualize their capacities, including especially those functionings that make them reliable detectors of value. For Aristotle, what is good in itself is the actualization of capacities. So too for Mill. But Mill went beyond Aristotle. He not only upheld the intrinsic value of realizing particular capacities but also historicized the idea, in its applications to human beings. The conditions that cause a flower to become all that it can be are timeless. At any point in natural history, the flower need only have the right degree of sunlight, the right soil, and the right level of moisture to actualize all of its potentialities. But the conditions that lead human beings to self-realize are historically contingent. They rise as the level of technological, intellectual and moral development rises. In Mill's view, "man . . . [is] a progressive being" (*OL*, 1). In other words, there is irreversible technological, intellectual, and moral progress. Self-realization, as Mill understood it, tracks the level of development of human civilization. Therefore, since history is progressive, the excellences peculiar to human beings expand as history unfolds.

The Principle of Liberty

The central contention of *On Liberty*, according to Mill's own account, is that the only justification for interfering coercively with the life, behavior or expressions of private conscience of individuals is to prevent harm to others (*OL*, 1). This is his principle of liberty. He stated it forthrightly in the first chapter of *On Liberty*.

> The object of this essay is to assert one very simple principle, as entitled to govern absolutely the dealings of society with the individual in the way of compulsion and control, whether the means used be physical force in the form of legal penalties or the moral coercion of public opinion. The principle is that the sole end for which mankind are warranted, individually or

collectively, in interfering with the liberty of action of any of their number is self-protection. That the only purpose for which power can be rightfully exercised over any member of a civilized community, against his will, is to prevent harm to others. His own good, either physical or moral, is not a sufficient warrant. He cannot rightfully be compelled to do or forbear because it will be better for him to do so, because it will make him happier, because, in the opinions of others, to do so would be wise or even right. These are good reasons for remonstrating with him, or reasoning with him, or persuading him, or entreating him, but not for compelling him or visiting him with any evil in case he do otherwise. To justify that, the conduct from which it is desired to deter him must be calculated to produce evil to someone else. The only part of the conduct of anyone for which he is amenable to society is that which concerns others. In the part which merely concerns himself, his independence is, of right, absolute. Over himself, over his own body and mind, the individual is sovereign.

This principle is justified, in turn, by the principle of utility. Thus the claim is that, by adhering to the principle of liberty rather than to any alternative principle, by establishing institutional arrangements that are maximally tolerant, "the permanent interests of man as a progressive being" are most likely to be advanced.

As the cited passage makes plain, Mill's concern was with *coercive* interferences, not with attempts at remonstrance, reasoning or persuasion. In the main, the institution that interferes coercively with individuals' lives and behaviors is the state. Thus Mill, like Locke, was largely interested in rendering individuals immune from particular kinds of state interferences or, equivalently, in specifying the rightful limits of sovereignty. But Mill's thesis also applies to "the moral coercion of public opinion." Thus the principle of liberty straddles the state/civil society divide characteristic of liberal political philosophy. For Mill, the state is only one institution among others, and the principle of liberty applies to them all.

Mill's thesis is directed at those who already acknowledge a *presumption* against coercive interference, who think that coercive interferences need to be justified, while non-interference, liberty in the Hobbesian sense, does not. The burden of proof, in other words, is on whoever would defend interfering in one or another domain. This assignment of a presumption was already implicit in Hobbes's underlying imagery – in the idea that it is natural for atomic individuals to pursue their own "inertial motions." By Mill's time, the intuition that this imagery suggests had become so deeply entrenched that Mill's way of assigning the burden of proof was uncontroversial. But it should be acknowledged, even so, that it is not unthinkable to assign the burden of proof differently. In any case, for Mill, liberty is the baseline condition, the natural state; it does not need to be defended. Restrictions on liberty do.

Mill's position is susceptible to at least two different interpretations, which I shall call the *weak* and the *strong* interpretations, respectively. Of these, the weak interpretation is more in line with Mill's own formulation of his thesis. However, it will emerge that the stronger interpretation is very likely what Mill ultimately wanted to defend.

According to the weak interpretation, there is a presumption against coercive interference, and the only kind of *reason* that can be invoked to overcome this presumption is one that appeals to the prevention of harm to others. This is not to say that, in Mill's view, interference is mandatory whenever harm to others is possible or even likely. The claim is just that then and only then can the invocation of legal penalties or "the moral coercion of public opinion" be justified. Whether actually to interfere is a question for further utilitarian calculation, for weighing the advantages of interference against the costs. For example, promise breaking plainly falls under the scope of Mill's principle. A broken promise harms whoever expected the promise to be kept. According to Mill's principle, then, the state can rightfully punish promise breakers. But it would almost certainly be unwise, from a utilitarian point of view, for it to do so. If it did, the practice of promise making would be damaged, probably beyond repair, and the considerable advantages that accrue from the existence of this practice would then be lost to the political community. On the other hand, where murder or assault or robbery are concerned, state interferences are not only permissible but, on any likely utilitarian calculation, mandatory.

In maintaining that the prevention of harm can swamp the presumption against coercive interference, Mill presumably had only *significant* harms in mind. Minor harms won't do. But there is hardly anything in *On Liberty* or anywhere else in Mill's writings that can serve as a sufficiently rigorous analysis of harm to provide guidance for dealing with difficult cases. In applying Mill's principle, therefore, we have only our intuitions upon which to rely, and we are unlikely, in any case, to get much help in deciding many of the questions that vex our generally liberal political culture today. Should, for example, behaviors that offend racial minorities be susceptible to state or societal interference? *On Liberty* provides little guidance. It only advances a view about how this question, and others like it, ought to be addressed. It implies, in this instance, that preventing the giving of offense to (some) individuals is not a ground for regulating other individuals' behaviors; that, before regulation can be considered, the offended party must be recognizably *harmed*.

This is not a trivial claim. But even its most ardent defenders would have to concede that, pending a fuller analysis of harm, it is insufficiently elaborated to settle this question or any of a host of similarly contentious issues that perplex contemporary liberals.

In Mill's view, it is only harm to *identifiable* others that justifies coercive interference – not harm to society at large, harm that is irreducible to harms to particular individuals. The idea that identifiable others must be harmed before coercion is justified is admirably austere, especially when joined with the requirement that harms must be significant. But, like some of the traditional utilitarian exercises in moral arithmetic noted earlier, the resulting position seems dated. Nowadays, more than in Mill's time, there is reason to be concerned not just with significant harms to particular people, but also with minor harms done by many individuals, sometimes to no one in particular, that are cumulatively as devastating in their effects as any of the harms Mill had in mind. Many of the human activities that degrade the natural environment fall under this description. An individual who throws a piece of litter onto a highway harms no one in particular and does nothing very consequential in any case. But when many individuals litter, the cumulative effect can only be described as a significant harm – to many unspecified individuals, perhaps even to society at large, and to the natural environment as well. Mill's principle provides no way to deal with or even to identify harms of this kind.

As a professed utilitarian, one would expect Mill to permit interferences for the sake of making individuals better off, so-called *paternalistic* interferences. The utilitarian idea, after all, is that institutions should maximize overall goodness, where goodness is construed in a welfarist sense and where overall goodness is the logical sum of individual welfares. But, as the passage cited above makes clear, Mill did not think that paternalistic reasons overcome the presumption against non-interference. So adamant was Mill in this conviction that he would even proscribe interventions that prevent individuals from harming themselves. For adult and competent members of "civilized communities," Mill's position is unequivocal: paternalistic interferences are never justified. Therefore, unless a case could be made that some ostensibly paternalistic interventions – laws against smoking, for example – actually prevent harm to identifiable others, Mill would oppose them. The fact that smoking harms smokers would be reason enough for a utilitarian to "remonstrate," "reason," "persuade" or "entreat" them not to smoke, but not to "compel" them or "visit [them] with any evil." For Mill to have held this view, he must have believed that the utility consequences of paternalism are generally worse than the utility consequences of non-interference for paternalistic reasons. This was, in fact, a central claim of the concluding chapters of *On Liberty*, where Mill argued both that paternalistic interferences are usually counterproductive, and also that considerable benefit can come from letting individuals find their own way.

There are a number of other reasons that people today, living in generally liberal societies, might invoke to overcome the universally acknowledged presumption against coercive interference. Among them is the one just cited, an interest in not offending others. This is a concern dear to contemporary proponents of identity politics and multi-culturalism, as well as to defenders of traditional values. Another reason is an interest in enforcing morals, where "morals" designates what proponents of this position think morality requires. Mill's principle of liberty rules out these reasons too.

The *weak* interpretation of the principle of liberty focuses on *reasons* only. It is therefore consistent with the weak interpretation that *anything* can be interfered with rightfully, so long as a compelling case can be made for doing so that appeals to reasons of the right kind. Liberals might therefore worry that, with sufficient ingenuity on the part of defenders of one or another sort of intervention, interferences that are plainly at odds with Mill's intentions might nevertheless be made to fall under the scope of the principle. It would only have to be shown that the activities one wants to regulate somehow constitute harms to identifiable others. This worry could, of course, be mitigated by a tradition of reasonable, casuistical interpretation, in much the way that similar worries about well-established legal principles are mitigated by a tradition of judicial interpretation, guided by standards of reasonableness and a determined effort to ascertain the intent of the framers of the laws in question. In any case, the prospect that the weak interpretation might be abused or that it might be used to underwrite conclusions that Mill never intended are not decisive reasons for rejecting it. These possibilities do point to a difficulty with it, however.

The *strong* interpretation, on the other hand, requires little or no interpretation to make Mill's intentions clear. It holds that (significant) harm to (identifiable) others marks off an *area* or *sphere*, a *private sphere*, within which coercive interferences are always and everywhere illegitimate. Everything else falls in the *public sphere,* where interferences are allowable but, again, not required. Thus the strong interpretation retrieves the spirit behind one of the core convictions of Lockean liberalism. For Locke, because individuals have inalienable rights in a state of nature, there is a clearly delineated private sphere into which the state may never rightfully intrude. The strong interpretation of Mill's principle aims at a similarly precise specification of a private sphere, but without the dubious theoretical apparatus of Lockean rights and without recourse to a social contract.

The expressions "private sphere" and "public sphere" are useful for capturing Mill's idea, but it should be noted that the words "private" and "public," in these expressions, do not mean what they do in ordinary speech. The private sphere is that *space* that is rightfully immune from state and societal interference. This space is populated by activities that are eminently public in the ordinary sense of the term Without quite putting his point in these terms, Mill assumed, in Chapter Two of *On Liberty*, that speech and other forms of expression fall within the private sphere. But the kinds of expressive activity he wanted to protect are clearly public in the ordinary sense. What Mill had in mind was speech directed at others, speech in the public forum. Only what one says to oneself, when no one else is in earshot, would count as "private" in the colloquial sense. But the regulation of private speech, so defined, is of little interest to anyone. What is of great interest, however, is speech that is public in the colloquial sense. It is this kind of speech that Mill wanted to ensconce in the private sphere.

In short, the problem with the strong interpretation is that it is unclear how the notion of harm can be invoked to mark off a private from a public sphere in the intended way. Mill grappled with this issue indirectly throughout *On Liberty*, especially in its later chapters. It is significant that he never confronted the problem directly. He certainly never solved it. I will go on to show, however, that Mill needed the strong interpretation to do the work he intended the principle of liberty to do. I will suggest too that he never quite succeeded in making a case for the principle of liberty, understood in this way, because, in the end, there is no case to be made. First, though, it will be well to follow Mill's lead by turning to the problem of free speech, just as Mill did in Chapter Two of *On Liberty*, after setting forth the principle of liberty in its full generality in Chapter One. A defense of free speech, even if successful, would amount to much less than a defense of the principle of liberty itself. But to defend free speech is to defend one of the most important limitations on state and societal interferences of interest to Mill and to liberals before and after him.

Freedom of Speech

At the very beginning of Chapter 2 of *On Liberty*, Mill proclaimed: "If all mankind minus one were of one opinion, mankind would be no more justified in silencing that one person than he, if he had the power, would be justified in silencing mankind." These stirring words set the tone for the arguments that follow.

Mill formulated his defense of free speech in a way that was officially true to his announced justifying strategy. His position was that maximal tolerance of speech and other forms of expression is justified on utilitarian grounds; that the relevant utility consequences of tolerance are better than those of any rival policy. Mill's, then, was not a rights based defense. As he made clear when he inveighed against the idea of "abstract rights independent of utility" (*OL*, 1), he would have nothing to do with Lockean rights claims. Neither was Mill's support for free speech a "rules of the game" defense of the kind that is officially assumed when free speech issues devolve into constitutional questions to be settled judicially. In the political culture of the United States, free speech issues are typically cast as legal arguments about the implications of the First Amendment to the US Constitution. They are resolved, ultimately, when judges "interpret" the Constitution – in effect, an insufficiently detailed rule book – that specifies the basic legal framework that governs political life in the United States. Mill's defense of free speech was different; it was unabashedly utilitarian.

His argument, however, was less than entirely transparent. For one thing, it rests on an unstated premise; one that Mill either did not notice or else regarded as too obvious to formulate explicitly. Mill assumed that the discovery of new truths or, what comes to the same thing, the growth of knowledge, is itself justifiable on utilitarian grounds. This may be true. But as was the case with the idea that only *significant* harms to *identifiable* others justify coercive interferences, a distinctly old-fashioned sensibility is implicit in this assumption. When Mill wrote *On Liberty*, it was easier than it is today to be optimistic about the connection between the growth of knowledge and "the permanent interests of man as a progressive being." As the years between Mill's time and our own have unfolded, the idea has emerged, even in "enlightened" circles, that the growth of knowledge is not an unmixed blessing. If nothing else, improvements in weaponry and environmental degradation suggest otherwise. The discovery of new truths may yet lead to the destruction of the human race, the worst possible utilitarian outcome. Today, therefore, one would have to say that Mill's unstated premise, even if true, is at least not obviously true. It is hardly so self-evident that it does not even need to be stated.

This suppressed premise therefore stands in need of defense. Mill could, of course, have introduced Aristotelian considerations at this point. He could have said that questing for knowledge is a distinctively human excellence that ought to be cultivated for its own sake. But Mill's Aristotelian perfectionism was never quite so blatant. Had he undertaken to defend his suppressed premise, his defense would no doubt have been utilitarian in nature. But Mill neither acknowledged the conviction implicit in his suppressed premise nor attempted to defend it, even implicitly. What he did instead was argue that a policy of maximal tolerance is more instrumental for promoting the growth of knowledge than any more intolerant policy would be. But it is only if this claim is joined to the assumption that the growth of knowledge is itself something utilitarians ought to further that the policy Mill favored, maximal tolerance of speech and other forms of expressions, would be justified on utilitarian grounds.

Like any consequentialist argument, this one depends on empirical speculations about the likely effects of following one or another policy. Much of Chapter Two is therefore devoted to corroborating the speculation that maximally tolerant policies consistently best their rivals. To this end, Mill advanced arguments of both an historical and epistemological nature. On the historical side, he provided what amounts to a sketch of the history of intolerance – specifically, of religious intolerance and of intolerance in scientific communities and in politics – arguing that it has generally had effects detrimental to "the permanent interests of man as a progressive being." He then contrasted the consequences of intolerance with the likely consequences of tolerance. Tolerant policies consistently win out in this competition. The epistemological dimension of Mill's argument consisted in an appeal to the fallibility of human beings' cognitive capacities. Mill drew out the consequences of this fact for social policy. His idea was that, because certainty is an unattainable goal for such beings as we are, it is always wisest, for anyone who would further the growth of knowledge, to leave all questions open. A silenced opinion might, after all, be true or partly true, whatever is believed about it at a particular moment. Then silencing it would diminish human knowledge. But Mill insisted too that even if, contrary to fact, an opinion could be known with certainty to be false, it should still not be silenced. Everyone benefits, Mill claimed, from "the lively collision" of truth with error. In other words, in Mill's view, it is generally salutary to engage with false or, more precisely, probably false beliefs. To employ metaphors that would emerge decades after *On Liberty*, in the context of twentieth-century American jurisprudence, Mill thought that contending with error improves "consumer competence" in "the marketplace of ideas."

Thus, in Mill's view, tolerance is utility enhancing both directly and indirectly. It enhances utility directly, by furthering the growth of knowledge, thereby making individuals better off. It enhances utility indirectly by improving individuals' abilities to benefit from tolerance, thereby improving the efficacy of the marketplace of ideas. This last consideration calls attention to the crucial role that *competence* plays in Mill's argument. Tolerance is beneficial if and only if human beings exceed a certain competency threshold. The further beyond that threshold they advance, the more beneficial tolerance becomes. But if individuals fall below the threshold, there is no reason to think that tolerance will be an improver, and therefore no reason for a utilitarian to defend it. Thus, in Mill's view, paternalism is justified for children and perhaps also for adults who, for any of a variety of reasons, including "lunacy" and "idiocy," fall below the competency threshold. It is only full-fledged "adult members of civilized communities" who stand to benefit from tolerance. Mill's argument pertains, strictly speaking, only to them.

Mill did not think that, in genuinely free conditions, a strong consensus on all or even very many issues was bound to emerge. Quite the contrary. Human diversity and cognitive shortcomings militate against any such expectation. But Mill did think there would be continual *improvement*. The phenomenon of connoisseurship illustrates part of what Mill had in mind. One can imagine a Millean theory of connoisseurship following from his account of the distinction between higher and lower pleasures. As in the more general case, this is an area in which informed judgment is crucial. Most peoples' judgments of, say, wines, will be poor, at least in non- wine drinking countries, because, thanks to a lack of knowledgeable acquaintance with wines, most peoples' wine judging capacities are poorly developed. They will therefore not be reliable judges of the aesthetic or gustatory qualities of wines. In all likelihood, though, with a better and more egalitarian distribution of resources for cultivating innate wine appreciation capacities, most people will be able to rise to a threshold level of competence. Let us call people who have crossed this competency threshold wine connoisseurs, and let us suppose that, in the case of wine appreciation, there is little area for improvement beyond the threshold level. Then wine connoisseurs will likely agree in their rankings of wines when the items in contention differ significantly in quality; and, on the view of connoisseurship that Mill implicitly endorsed, their judgments will be better than the judgments of people whose wine appreciation capabilities fall below the threshold level. In this sense, the cultivation of individuals' innate wine appreciation capacities improves outcomes. But there is no reason to expect that connoisseurs' judgments will ever converge to the point that everyone's fine-grained discriminations of the qualities of different wines of roughly equal merit will be in accord. Ultimately, there are limits on convergence that follow from differences among human beings. Similarly, Mill was confident that free expression would improve outcomes in all areas of contention in which competent people can reasonably disagree. But, again, as in the special case of wine connoisseurship, even ideal – that is, maximally free – conditions cannot be expected to lead to a thoroughgoing consensus on all issues in dispute. Human diversity blocks that outcome. It explains why, even in the best of circumstances, not everyone will see all issues in the same way. The difference from the special case of wine connoisseurship is just that in the general case, there *is* reason to expect major improvements in individuals' judgments after they have crossed the relevant competency threshold levels. Therefore, some views will be better than others, even if they are not incontrovertibly better. Mill could therefore hold that, for example, utilitarianism is sounder than Lockean rights theory; that the choice between these moral philosophical doctrines is not, as in the case of wine appreciation, only a matter of taste. But, at the same time, he would have to concede that, even with the best of arguments, he could not persuade literally everybody to think as he did; and therefore that some reasonable people might be drawn to Lockean rights theory in preference to his own views.

For a somewhat different reason, a similar conclusion about the unlikelihood of convergence holds even in areas in which opportunities for rational disagreement are more limited. Thus Mill seems to have thought that it is unlikely, even in the sciences, where disputes are in principle susceptible to decisive rational adjudication, that there will ever be a complete convergence of views. Because human beings' cognitive capacities are as limited as they are, it is unlikely, no matter how much science progresses, that any of our theories will be so good as to be insusceptible to further revision. But as long as this is the case, reasonable disagreements remain possible and even likely. In scientific disputes, though, the expectation is that some positions will be ruled incontestably out, even if none can be ruled incontestably in, and therefore that disagreements will be framed against an ever-improving background of secure, though not incontrovertible, truths.

Mill's general brief for tolerance of speech and expression, his claim that it fosters the growth of knowledge and thereby furthers "the permanent interests of man as a progressive being," coheres poorly with the particular arguments he offered for tolerance in the three domains he discussed expressly: religion, science, and politics. It is instructive to reflect on each of these cases, for each one reveals something different and important about the nature and limits of Mill's rationale.

Viewed historically, religious toleration takes pride of place in the history of liberalism. It was, if anything, even more important to the development of liberal theory than the defense of private property and untrammeled private accumulation was. In the aftermath of the wars of religion that followed the Protestant Reformation and the Catholic Counter-Reformation, as faith waned and as the various sides fought to exhaustion, the contending parties came increasingly to accept each other – grudgingly perhaps, but with enough enthusiasm eventually to give tolerance a foothold. However, as this process unfolded, the contending religions themselves changed. They transformed themselves from "essentially social things," as Emile Durkheim put it, from the institutional, ritualistic, and doctrinal "cements" of the societies they constituted, into matters of private conscience – which is how liberalism, in Mill's day and in our own, regards them.[2] In consequence of this transformation, even strict adherents of the originally intolerant religious doctrines that dominated the Christian West become increasingly tolerant of practitioners of rival faiths. But they did not and could not come to believe that their own views are open to revision in light of "collisions" with opposing religious doctrines. For these religions teach that they are already correct and complete. Thus liberals who celebrate religious diversity would be hard pressed to say that the end religious toleration serves is the growth of knowledge. Believers especially, whether they are liberals or not, would be loathe to hold such a view. No believer believes that there are any religious truths left to discover, and certainly not any likely to come from paying careful

[2] Durkheim's account of religion as a social phenomenon marked a breakthrough in the development of modern social theory. It was Durkheim's position that all societies are held together by "religions," but that religions need not be theistic. In fact, in Durkheim's view, theistic religion is just one phase in a progression that began with pre-theistic forms of religious life and that will end with doctrinal commitments and "ecclesiastical" forms appropriate to the emerging scientific and secular age. It is compatible with this view that the old, theistic religions might survive for an indefinite period. But they would have a different, less social, function in the societies of the future than they did in the societies of the past. Durkheim's views on these matters must be teased out of his seminal study of "primitive" (especially aboriginal Australian) religions. See Emile Durkheim, *The Elementary Forms of Religious Life* (New York: The Free Press, 1995, originally published 1912), esp. chapter one and the conclusion. Students of modern political philosophy should note that Durkheim's account of the fundamentally social character of religious institutions and beliefs was anticipated by Rousseau's remarks on civil religion in Book IV, Chapter 8 of *The Social Contract*. Durkheim was intensely interested in Rousseau, as his short monograph, *Montesquieu and Rousseau: Forerunners of Sociology* (Ann Arbor: University of Michigan Press, 1960), attests.

attention to the teachings of other faiths or from defending one's own convictions against challenges posed by rival views. Religions are closed systems; they rest on the conviction that they have already gotten everything right.

There are, of course, other ways to defend religious toleration. Rights based defenses are possible, as Locke's own example illustrates. Or it might be argued that tolerance in this domain follows from a more fundamental commitment to respect for persons and their core commitments. It could also be claimed that because stability is a value in heterogeneous political communities, and because public support for one or another religious doctrine is likely to be destabilizing, that it is a requirement of political morality that public coercive institutions be neutral with respect to competing religious claims. This list is hardly exhaustive. There are many non-utilitarian ways to defend the conclusion Mill supports. But Mill's own rationale, the claim that tolerance is justified because it promotes the growth of religious knowledge, is plainly a non-starter.

Religion is a closed system, but science is open. Flourishing sciences sometimes even transform themselves entirely in short periods of time. Moreover, in science, the growth of knowledge is the main, perhaps the only, objective. But scientific communities are generally intolerant – especially of lay opinion but also, in diminishing degrees, of the views of apprentice scientists and of practicing scientists too. Even at the leading edge of ongoing research, a certain intolerance of heterodoxy reigns. One might even say, only slightly facetiously, that scientific communities, in their intolerance of dissent, more nearly resemble the intolerant religious communities of old than genuine marketplaces of ideas. But it is far from clear that the practicing intolerance of scientific communities actually is detrimental to the growth of knowledge, as a reader persuaded by Mill might think. To foster the growth of knowledge, it is necessary, above all, to have well-trained scientists, and it is reasonable to expect that the best way to increase the supply of good scientific workers is, first, to teach good science in the schools and universities, and then to keep working scientists on track with a system of institutional incentives that rewards "true believers" and punishes "heretics." A scientific community that encouraged its apprentice or practicing scientists to devote a great deal of their time, energy and resources to learning and refuting outdated or bizarre scientific theories would almost certainly be one that wasted its time, energy and resources. Such a policy would more likely impede the discovery of new truths than encourage it indirectly, by enhancing scientists' understandings of their own positions through the "lively collisions" of truths with errors. There is, therefore, a difficulty for Mill's position implicit in the apparently very reasonable practice of existing scientific communities. The scientific enterprise, dedicated as it plainly is to the discovery of new truths, works best by *not* according equal respect to the views of all adult members of civilized communities. Within limits, it works best by enforcing orthodoxy – not only in its relations with non-scientists but within its own ranks as well.

This conclusion is less of an embarrassment to Millean liberalism than first appears because the intolerance of scientific communities can be reconciled with Mill's express position. We need only stipulate that the requisite level of competence required to benefit from tolerance is much higher in science than it is in general. To be a competent consumer in the marketplace of scientific ideas, it hardly suffices to be an adult member of a civilized community. It is necessary, at the very least, to be a full-fledged practicing scientist; perhaps even a scientist working on the frontiers of ongoing research. Thus, within scientific communities, it is necessary to set the competency threshold at a far higher level than in the usual case. This effort to reconcile Mill's case for tolerance with the actual practice of scientific communities reveals perspicuously how important competency thresholds are for Mill's defense of tolerance of speech and expression. Even so, anyone sympathetic to Mill's policy positions is bound to find this conclusion troubling. To save Mill's general case for tolerance, it is necessary, at least with respect to science, to restrict its scope severely. This is a high price to pay.

Ordinary scientific norms of behavior raise other challenges to Mill's position. Contrary to what Mill's theory of tolerance requires, it is commonplace, within scientific communities, to take account not only of *what* is said but also of *who* is saying it. This deviation from the model Mill endorsed is eminently reasonable; so much so that it carries over, in varying degrees, to life outside of science too. No one has enough time to evaluate every position on its merits, especially not if they are intent on discovering new truths. To focus on who is saying what is to deploy a filtering mechanism; one that provides reliable, though fallible, information about how seriously to take particular claims, and therefore how much time, effort, and attention to devote to evaluating them. Having such a mechanism in place is efficiency-enhancing. But it is inconsistent with Mill's vision of what ought to transpire.

It might seem, finally, that in political and social matters, Mill would be on firm ground. But, in this case too, his general case for tolerance is inapt. The problem is that Mill, like other liberals, thought of the political process in a Lockean, not a Rousseauean, way. He saw it as an arena in which competing interests contend; not as a forum in which truths are discovered. To the extent that it is fairness, not truth, that is served by tolerance in political life, an appeal to the purported efficacy of tolerance for facilitating the growth of knowledge fails entirely to capture Mill's own view of the political process. For Mill, as for Locke, the goal there is not the growth of knowledge; indeed, it is far from clear that Mill thought that there are political truths at all, let alone new truths to be discovered. The point of tolerance in the political arena is to assure that competing interests are fairly represented, and therefore that the outcomes of legislation and other political processes are fair. As we have seen (in chapters 2 and 3), this is a very different aim from setting out to discover a matter of fact.

One could, however, imagine a utilitarian thinking about politics in a more Rousseauean way. This imaginary utilitarian could hold that what legislators ought to do is not to vote in ways that represent their own particular interests or the interests of their constituents, as best they can ascertain them, but rather, through their vote, to voice their opinion about what the utilitarian maximum is. This kind of utilitarian legislator would therefore do what Rousseau thought every citizen should do by voting in the assembly of the people – express an opinion about a matter of fact. The difference would only be that the general interest, the matter of fact that Rousseauean assemblies seek to discover, is not the same thing as the utilitarian maximum, the logical sum of individuals' private interests.

But, again, this was not the way that Mill thought about politics. He endorsed an "adversarial" model, according to which competing interests contend against one another, united only by a common interest in keeping existing political institutions afloat. As any reader of *Considerations on Representative Government* will see, Mill believed that it was a positively good thing for legislators to represent particular or sectorial interests because, when they do, the utilitarian maximum emerges as an unintended consequence, as if by an "invisible hand." Mill thought, in other words, that the way to arrive at the utilitarian maximum is for citizens and their representatives to act in self-interested ways, not in utilitarian ways. It is, in fact, a characteristic of utilitarianism that it can and often does recommend actions based on non-utilitarian reasons. It recommends whatever works best for maximizing utility overall. It should be noted, too, that the kind of adversarial model Mill endorsed is familiar in our political culture. For example, the Common Law tradition in legal theory holds that, in general, it is better in criminal and civil judicial processes that the contending parties face one another as adversaries than that disinterested magistrates conduct impartial investigations on their own.

Inasmuch as other defenses of free speech and expression are conceivable, the problems sketched above hardly undo Mill's conclusions. But they do suggest that his arguments for those conclusions are flawed. I would venture that at least part of the blame for this unhappy state of affairs lies with Mill's determination to fit what he had to say into a framework that is consistent with the utilitarianism he officially endorsed. In this domain especially, the price of not acknowledging his own perfectionist intuitions was high indeed.

Experiments in Living

Mill advocated maximal tolerance of individuals' lives and behaviors. A good society, in his view, is a diverse society; one that not only lives by the principle of *laissez-vivre,* but even encourages experiments in living. Thus, with respect to tolerance generally, as with respect to speech and other expressions of private conscience, Mill was no grudging acceptor of difference; he was an enthusiastic supporter. He celebrated differences in life-styles, just as adamantly as he favored differences of opinion. The more widespread the better, and the more profound the better too; the healthier for the body politic. His rationale, in both cases, was the same. It was that tolerance promotes better outcomes than rival policies. A good society is therefore comprised of *individuals*, not just in the methodological sense characteristic of modern political philosophy, but in the familiar colloquial sense too.

Mill's position contrasts with Rousseau's (see chapter 2). Rousseau would have institutions discourage the cultivation of individual differences in order to enhance civic virtue. He favored simplicity of manners and morals (*moeurs*), not "rugged individualism" or eccentricity. He abhorred luxury, in part because it sets individuals apart, and he favored the dominance of the countryside over the cities and towns, because rural life is more conducive than city life to uniformity in ways of living. Mill, on the other hand, favored the *individualism* of city life. Even today, with means of transport and communication unimaginable in Rousseau's or Mill's time, there are more opportunities in the towns and cities than in the countryside for individuals to find their own distinctive, even idiosyncratic, ways. There is more space for diversity because cities harbor a larger variety of sub-cultures through which individuals can find themselves and so, by forging their own niche, become more individualistic than their rural brethren. If the self-sufficient, yeoman farmer was Rousseau's ideal citizen, the modern, urban individual was Mill's.

The diversity Mill celebrated was diversity of life-style, not "identity." Like all liberals until very recently, Mill acknowledged no normatively significant differences among human beings. It is therefore fair to suppose that he would have looked with disfavor on the efforts of those who would accord positive value to group differences and, especially, to the notion that the permanent recognition of these differences is a component of ideal social and political arrangements. But, of course, Mill lived in a world in which the divisions that concern contemporary multiculturalists were less salient than they now are. In the mid-nineteenth century, liberal societies were more racially and ethnically homogeneous than they are today, even if they were more divided along class lines and even if gender inequalities were more pronounced as well. The social divisions prominent in nineteenth-century societies were in principle impermanent, and Mill, more than most other progressive thinkers, was committed to their demise. It was in this spirit, for example, that he pioneered the advocacy of equal rights for women. It is idle, though, to speculate about what Mill would have thought had he lived in a world comprised of heterogeneous agglomerations of peoples. He was a creature of his time and place, and his political theory reflects this fact, for better or worse. Thus the differences he endorsed enthusiastically were differences in ways of living that follow from the experimental cast of mind he favored, not from disparate cultural backgrounds or other expressions, residual or contrived, of group differences.

Mill favored experiments in living for reasons that parallel the reasons he offered in defense of free speech. His idea was that tolerance is an improver, at least for persons who have exceeded a competency threshold; that it makes outcomes better in both a static and a dynamic sense. It produces better outcomes here and now, and it makes persons more competent at pursuing their respective paths through life, and therefore better able to make outcomes better in the future. In this instance, though, it is not the growth of knowledge *per se* that is at stake. It is a particular kind of knowledge, knowledge of what is good for oneself. What ultimately justifies tolerance is its beneficial consequences for the permanent interests of man as a progressive being. Mill thought that this end is best served when individuals are left as free as can be to discover their own distinctive goods, provided that, in so doing, they do not interfere with the opportunities of others to do the same. This is why Mill would regulate only those behaviors that can harm identifiable others and, even then, only if the likely consequence of state or societal interference is better than the likely consequence of leaving individuals at liberty to do as they please.

To the extent that he genuinely was a utilitarian, Mill was committed to the view that there is, in the end, only one good, "the permanent interests of man as a progressive being," and also to the idea that, in evaluating social practices and institutional arrangements, the aim is to maximize this good overall. To talk of the good for individuals is therefore to talk about goods that matter insofar as they affect this overarching objective. Mill was convinced that in generally liberal societies where the relevant competency thresholds are exceeded, overall utility actually is maximized when each individual does what is individually best; in other words, he believed that liberal societies are relevantly unlike Hobbesian states of nature or other Prisoners' Dilemma situations. This is why he was so concerned to insure that individuals live according to their own lights. If individuals maximize their own distinctive goods, as they themselves see them, the outcome will be best for the permanent interests of man as a progressive being in general.

Mill was convinced too that there is no single right way for all individuals to live; no plan of life that is applicable to everyone. There are instead a diversity of goods for individuals, corresponding to the diversity among human beings. Political philosophy can only accommodate to this fact; it cannot legislate it away. The claim, then, is that there exist many optimal plans of life, perhaps as many as there are individuals. Uniformity is not only undesirable, then; it is impossible. The situation is similar, though more extreme, to the one that obtains with respect to free expression. As we have seen, Mill believed that knowledge grows best under maximally tolerant conditions, but also that a full-fledged rational consensus will never emerge, no matter how tolerant societies are – in consequence of human diversity and the complexity and indeterminacy of the issues in dispute. Under genuinely free conditions, inferior ideas will pass away and the remaining opinions will come to exist within an ever more *reasonable* range, but they will never literally converge. Similarly, individuals living under genuinely tolerant institutional arrangements will never all decide to live according to the same plan of life. But inferior plans will fade from the scene, as the citizens of liberal states increasingly find their own, distinctive ways. Differences will fall within an ever more *progressive,* though not necessarily narrower, range. But no matter how much plans of life improve, people will never agree about how best to live. They will not agree because there is nothing to agree about; there simply is no way to live that is best for everyone. In Mill's view, efforts, like Rousseau's, to counter this stubborn fact are bound to fail; perhaps even to fail disastrously.

At the heart of Mill's case for the beneficial consequences of tolerance, conceived statically, at a given moment in time, is the conviction that individuals are, in general, the best judges of their own interests. This is why a policy of non-paternalism for "adult members of civilized communities" is likely to have better consequences than direct paternalistic interventions. Of course, in imaginable cases, other persons, especially intimates, may know better what is best for particular individuals than they know themselves. But it is unlikely in the extreme that the state will know better or that "the moral coercion of public opinion" will. In any case, it is general policy provisions that are in contention, not particular interventions. Mill's claim is that, in contriving rules to regulate relations between individuals, on the one hand, and state and societal institutions, on the other, it is generally better to proceed on the assumption that individuals do indeed know best what their own goods are, even if they are eminently fallible. Mill concluded that societies should concoct institutional arrangements accordingly.

Viewed dynamically, Mill's case also resembles the argument he pressed for the long- term benefits of tolerance in the marketplace of ideas. Individuals left free to find their own best ways will sometimes make mistakes. The mistakes they make may be consequential, and a utilitarian cannot fail to take this prospect into account. People, left to their own devices, may harm themselves severely – perhaps even irreparably or fatally. But in designing institutional arrangements, Mill insisted that it is better that individuals be left on their own than that the state or "the moral coercion of public opinion" regulate their lives. In this way, people can learn from their mistakes, provided, of course, that they survive the consequences of their own choices, as they almost always will. And because individuals have privileged access to knowledge of their own good, they are in a better position than others, especially the state, to benefit from what experience teaches them. Therefore, in the course of a lifetime, they are likely to be better off left alone than they would have been had they been treated like children throughout the course of their lives, even if those who would treat them as children are benevolent and wise. In short, Mill's contention is that paternalism generally makes outcomes worse for "adult members of civilized communities." For those already beyond the relevant competency threshold, competence in living is enhanced by public policies that are maximally tolerant; to the long-run advantage of the community as a whole.

In Defense of Liberty

Mill supplied ample reasons for thinking that experiments in living generally do have beneficial consequences and that overall well-being is therefore greater the more tolerant societies are. But it is one thing to make a utilitarian case for tolerance and something else, a good deal more ambitious, to defend the principle enunciated in the first chapter of *On Liberty*, according to which state and societal regulation of individuals' behaviors is justifiable only in cases in which permitting persons to do as they please threatens significant harm to identifiable others. It is clear from the later chapters of *On Liberty* that Mill intended this principle in the stronger of the two senses described above; he wanted to use the notion of harm to mark off a private sphere in which coercive interferences are never permissible, regardless of societal norms, practices and expectations. But even on the weaker interpretation, according to which Mill's claim was just that only one kind of reason, the prevention of harm to identifiable others, overcomes a universally acknowledged presumption against coercive interference, the point remains. If the objective is to maximize goodness overall, why insist categorically that only interferences within a certain "space" or only interferences justified by a certain kind of reason are warranted? Why maintain that the principle of liberty or harm principle is *always* what the principle of utility recommends? I will conclude this discussion of Mill's liberalism by speculating on why, in the end, despite all the very sensible claims he registered along the way, Mill never quite succeeded in reaching his destination; why one looks in vain for a full-fledged utilitarian justification for Mill's position.

The first reason is, by itself, decisive, at least for the strong interpretation of the principle of liberty. To arrive at a critical vantage point for assessing societal norms and practices, it is necessary, first of all, to have an account of harm that is trans-historical and trans-social. It must be possible to specify what is and is not a harm, regardless of what people at given times and in particular places take harms to be. Mill, however, had nothing helpful to say about how harm could be conceived trans-historically and trans-socially. Quite the contrary. Instead of developing a concept of harm suitable for the strong interpretation, a task that is almost certainly impossible to execute, Mill explained harm in a way that reveals the indefensibility of the strong interpretation. Mill claimed, in short, that individuals are harmed if and only if their interests are infringed. But, of course, what counts as an interest that can be harmed depends on prevailing norms and practices. Religious bigots may become physically ill in consequence of their awareness of their neighbors' religious practices or beliefs. They may even suffer physically, so much so that they are unable to work or to enjoy life. Now if anything would count as a trans-historical, trans-social harm, it would be physical harm. Should we therefore conclude that the state or the moral coercion of public opinion can rightfully regulate religious beliefs and practices? Certainly not, as Mill would be the first to insist. But on what grounds? The bigots I am imagining are indeed harmed. But Mill would say that their interests are not infringed, and therefore that they have not been harmed in a way that should be of public concern. Religious beliefs and practices are matters of private conscience. They fall within the private sphere, and therefore ought not to be of concern to bigots or, for that matter, to anyone else at all. If some people suffer physically or are otherwise debilitated by the practices or beliefs of their neighbors, it is their problem to bear. They have no claim on society for redress. In other words, in Mill's view, despite their suffering, bigots are not actually harmed by the religious practices or beliefs of their neighbors. They are not harmed because no one can be harmed by the religious convictions of anyone else. No one can be harmed because no one has an interest that is infringed or, more precisely, a *legitimate* interest. In a word, it is no one else's business what religious convictions or practices others observe. But how do we know what interests are legitimate? How do we know what minding our own business involves? The answer is that we have no way of knowing, nor could we, because, in the end, there is nothing to know, no fact of the matter. Legitimacy is a context-dependent standard, an artifact of the norms, practices, and expectations that the principle of liberty is supposed to critically assess.

Thus everyone in societies like our own would agree that when one individual, say, destroys another's automobile, the first individual has harmed the second. A legitimate interest of the automobile's owner was infringed; an interest established by a property right. But, of course, for Mill, as for anyone else who is not a believer in morally primary property rights, systems of property are and can only be human concoctions. Individuals who are harmed when their automobiles are destroyed are harmed because they are the owners of these objects, and they would not be these objects' owners but for the system of property in place. Were they living in a regime in which automobiles were collectively, not privately, owned, they could not be harmed by the destruction of an automobile in the way that they are in societies in which automobiles are privately owned. Of course, were someone dependent upon a particular vehicle that is destroyed, that individual would be inconvenienced by its destruction, and therefore harmed in a way. But such persons, no matter how aggrieved, would not have been harmed in the way that they would be in a regime of private property. No property right of theirs would have been infringed, no socially protected interest. Thus it is conceivable and even likely that, no matter how inconvenienced they might be by a particular vehicle's destruction, they would have no standing in their own society to level a complaint against the automobile's destroyer; that only the vehicle's collective owner, the state or some other entity, would. But, again, systems of property are among the institutions that the harm principle is intended to assess.

The point is clear: what counts as a harm depends on what counts as a legitimate interest, and the relevant notion of legitimacy is and can only be relative to prevailing norms and practices. Mill wanted a standard, analogous to Lockean morally primary rights, by means of which societal norms and practices could be assessed. He invoked the idea of harm in his quest for this critical vantage-point. But because he did not and could not satisfactorily identify what it is to harm someone in a trans-historical and trans-social way, the standard of evaluation he sought eluded him. To suggest, as he did, that individuals are harmed if and only if their *legitimate* interests are infringed is effectively to concede defeat in this regard – unwittingly perhaps, but nevertheless unmistakably.

In sum, Mill's position is circular. He set out to distinguish the private from the public spheres by deploying an (unanalyzed) notion of harm, but he also, implicitly, used the private/public sphere distinction, understood intuitively, to characterize what counts as a harm. Mill could have broken out of this circle if he could have somehow specified what harms are by characterizing them in a trans-historical and trans-social way. But he could not do so because, in the final analysis, there is no suitable trans-historical or trans-social concept of harm available. What counts as a harm depends, ultimately, on what people take harms to be.

A similar consideration applies to the weak interpretation. Because it relies on the same intuitive understanding of harm that the strong interpretation does, it also fails to provide a norm-independent, critical vantage-point for assessing prevailing institutions and practices. The weak interpretation suffers from other disabilities as well. Even if we stipulate that we know well enough what it is for one individual to harm another, it still remains to show why this reason, and this reason alone, should count for overcoming the presumption against non-interference with individuals' lives and behaviors. To argue, as Mill did, that it is generally best to leave individuals free to do as they please does go part of the way towards establishing the desired conclusion. Allowing that societies do have interests in preventing harm to their members, and therefore that the prevention of harm to identifiable others is a grounds for coercive interference, Mill's arguments counter the prima facie utilitarian case for paternalism – the idea that, to make outcomes better overall, the state or the moral coercion of public opinion ought to interfere coercively, if need be, to make individuals better off or to prevent them from harming themselves. They therefore count against *some* additional reasons for overcoming the presumption against coercive interference that others, utilitarians especially, might propose. But nothing that Mill says establishes that *only* the prevention of harm to identifiable others should count as a reason. His arguments therefore failed to establish the conclusion he drew from them.

An example will illustrate the point. It is a direct implication of the principle of liberty, weakly interpreted, that the prevention of offense to others is not a reason that can be rightfully invoked to overcome the presumption against non-interference. But it could be argued that because civility enhances community and individual self-esteem, because these conditions are instrumental, in turn, for advancing "the permanent interests of man as a progressive being," and because, finally, in real world conditions, the requisite degree of civility is unobtainable without coercive prohibitions on giving offense, the prevention of offense to others *should* overcome the presumption against non-interference too. It could be argued, in other words, that the utility consequences of proscribing the giving of offense are, on balance, better than the utility consequences of not proscribing it. If this case could be made persuasively, then, as a utilitarian, Mill ought to permit coercive interferences to prevent the giving of offense. That he did not do so suggests that he thought that, in general, it is better to permit the giving of offense than to proscribe it. But inasmuch as this conclusion is far from obvious, it must be demonstrated or at least supported. It will not do simply to assert the harm principle and then to adhere to it dogmatically. Rather, the harm principle, the claim that *only* the prevention of harm to identifiable others warrants coercive interference with their lives and behaviors, must be defended against all likely competitors, not just against paternalism. Nowhere in *On Liberty* or in any of his other writings did Mill attempt anything of the sort. Nowhere did he venture a direct, full-scale defense of the principle of liberty.

In the end, I think the problem is that one cannot derive categorical policy prescriptions from a consequentialist theory. Insofar as Mill genuinely was a utilitarian, he was committed to doing whatever makes outcomes best. Even if we concede, following Mill's practice, that at the societal level this question is best addressed by looking to rules rather than to particular interventions, the rules in contention will always be context dependent. But it is impossible to generalize over the full array of contexts that real world conditions present. Mill wanted to be able to draw categorical policy conclusions; conclusions that hold for any imaginable society. But, for good or ill, his utilitarian convictions stood in the way. Try as he might, Mill could not succeed in overcoming the flexibility inherent in his own utilitarian outlook. Paradoxically, because his underlying justifying theory was simple and unequivocal, he could not draw sure and unequivocal conclusions about what is to be done in the complex, real world situations that citizens of modern states confront. Ironically, then, inasmuch as the utilitarians were opponents of Tory conservatism, their stance towards justifying institutional arrangements unintentionally underwrites the conclusion the arch-Tory Edmund Burke advanced in his *Reflections on the Revolution in France* – that, in the end, it is circumstances that render "every civil and political scheme beneficial or noxious to mankind."

Appendix: Repressive Tolerance

In the 1960s, Herbert Marcuse wrote an influential essay entitled "Repressive Tolerance."[3] But because political philosophy reflects political life and because, for the time being, Left radicalism has largely faded from the scene, Marcuse's essay is no longer widely read. It is unfortunate for students of Mill and of liberalism generally that this is so because "Repressive Tolerance" poses a challenge to Millean liberalism or, more precisely, to its real world applications that a defender of Millean positions today would do well to address. The challenge was largely implicit. Marcuse seldom mentioned Mill explicitly, and an uninformed or causal reader might well miss the connection. But the challenge is, nevertheless, real. In brief, Marcuse claimed that the formal or "pure" tolerance Mill advocated has "turned into its opposite," that having once played a positive role in the struggle for human emancipation, pure tolerance has become an implement of "repression," a means through which those in power dominate those whom they rule.

Marcuse's essay poses this claim in a way that genuinely engages Mill's substantive theoretical positions. Thus his was not the kind of challenge

[3] Herbert Marcuse, "Repressive Tolerance" in Robert Paul Wolff, Barrington Moore, Jr., and Herbert Marcuse, *A Critique of Pure Tolerance* (Boston: Beacon Press, 1965).

to Millean liberalism that one encounters nowadays in the work of those who would enforce civility for reasons that they believe to be in the interests of oppressed or otherwise derogated social groups. Marcuse's hesitations about tolerance had nothing to do with wanting to protect particular categories of people from speech that shows them disrespect. To this concern, Marcuse, like Mill, would likely have said that the remedy for speech that is disrespectful of subordinate groups or otherwise unresponsive to their legitimate demands for "recognition" is to work to empower these groups. In Mill's view, institutionally imposed restrictions on speech nearly always make matters worse, and there is no reason to think that Marcuse would have disagreed. Also, unlike some "postmodern" opponents of untrammeled free speech, Marcuse was no relativist, persuaded that, in the end, it is power, not truth, that determines what is taken to be the case. For reasons that are obscure or incoherent or both, postmodernists typically maintain that the very idea of determinative truths is somehow definitively superseded. They also deliberately reject the goals and standards of argument that they associate with what they disparagingly call "the Enlightenment project." Thus they oppose so-called "master narratives" of human history and related notions of progress. They are suspicious too of the very goal of making sense of things in the way that philosophers always have – by discerning conceptual structures, drawing pertinent distinctions and marshaling rationally compelling arguments, grounded, where appropriate, on relevant evidence. Postmodernists are inclined, instead, to collapse logic into rhetoric. They insist that persuasion is all that there is, and that what persuades is ultimately power, not reason. They sometimes even maintain that reason is just a form of expression of a will to power, and that it can be and often is invoked to enhance "oppression." Marcuse would have had none of this. Although he too often wrote obscurely, in an Hegelian idiom that can make even the work of postmodern relativists seem focused, he was, in the end, as anchored in the Enlightenment tradition as Mill was. As much as Mill, Marcuse believed in the possibility of human progress and in the capacity of reason to change the world for the better.

Marcuse was, in fact, an intellectual descendant of the tradition in German philosophy inaugurated by Kant that reached its apogee in the work of Hegel and Marx and that was then revived in the 1920s in the so-called Frankfurt School, a group with which Marcuse was associated. Within this intellectual and political current, the relevant standard of progress has always been the expansion of human freedom, understood in roughly Rousseau's sense – the self-emancipation of the human race. Mill's notion of progress was, of course, superficially very different. Mill was officially a hedonistic utilitarian, concerned to advance human happiness. But, as I have tried to show, his reflections on free speech and especially on experiments in living reveal that, whatever he may have believed, he was more disposed to value an historicized notion of self-realization than he was to seek to maximize happiness, on any plausible construal of that term. Thus what Mill ultimately valued and the emancipatory vision that motivated Marcuse's thinking were not as far apart as may at first appear. In any case, both Mill and Marcuse were consequentialists. They both assessed social and political arrangements according to how well they further their respective ends – "the permanent interests of man as a progressive being," in the one case; and, to the degree that it differs, human emancipation, in the other.

Both agreed too that, in ideal conditions, "pure" or formal tolerance, tolerance that takes no account of the content of speech, works to promote the consequences they would further. For both, an ideal society would therefore be tolerant of all speech and forms of expression. Implicitly, then, Marcuse would have agreed with Mill that "the marketplace of ideas" is an improver, so long as its participants are competent consumers, and he would have agreed too that, in general, the competency threshold is within the reach of most adult members of civilized communities. Marcuse was as ill-disposed as Mill to suppose that there is anything in human nature that must be systematically suppressed. Thus he did not think that human beings were in any way "hard wired" to block their own emancipation. There is therefore no need, in his view, to protect consumers from themselves in a genuine marketplace of ideas. Quite the contrary. People are disposed by their natures to adhere to attitudes and views that foster the self-emancipation of humankind.

For both Mill and Marcuse too, this contention is empirical and speculative. It rests on a prediction about the likely consequences of following one or another policy, a prediction for which epistemological facts about human beings' cognitive capacities along with lessons drawn from actual history are relevant. On epistemological issues, Mill and Marcuse were essentially of one mind; they both believed that human beings are fallible, that no one can ever be certain of being right. But they disagreed about the bearing of history. This is hardly surprising, inasmuch as Marcuse wrote "Repressive Tolerance" more than a hundred years after Mill wrote *On Liberty*. Mill had hardly any examples of tolerance to reflect upon. He was therefore obliged to dwell on the detrimental consequences of intolerance. By Marcuse's time, however, the evidence was more ample. It does not unequivocally support Mill's speculations.

It is worth noting that Marcuse spent his youth in Germany in the days of the Weimar Republic, a generally tolerant regime that did very little to suppress the rising Nazi movement. The Weimar Republic behaved towards the Nazis as it ought to have done, if Mill was right. It abstained from interfering with the promulgation of Nazi doctrine. But so far from being cast out of Weimar Germany's marketplace of ideas, Naziism won adherents. Then, with astonishing rapidity, the Nazis came to power, overthrowing the regime that nurtured their rise. For Mill and those who agree with him about pure tolerance, this is not what was supposed to have happened. The marketplace of ideas is supposed to ferret out good ideas, and eliminate bad ones. It is not supposed to be an incubator of social movements that work to the detriment of "the permanent interests of man as a progressive being."

Mill's policy provisions were based, of course, on the assumption that ideal conditions obtain: that there is a genuine marketplaces of ideas, with free entry and exit, and that there is ample consumer competence. Only then will ideas rise or fall according to how rationally compelling they are; not according to how or by whom or by what means they are promoted. The real world plainly falls short of this ideal. One can therefore always ask whether the differences between the actual world and the ideal are sufficiently pronounced as to warrant drawing different policy conclusions about the likely consequences of tolerance. Can we explain the fate of the Weimar Republic in this way? Can we say that it self-destructed because it failed to approximate the ideal situation closely enough? No doubt this would be, at most, only one factor among many that would have to be taken into account. But if it was a factor at all, then similar questions about our own society suggest themselves. How well does it approximate the ideal? And what, if anything, follows from the respects in which the actual and the ideal diverge today? Since Mill and Marcuse agree at the level of ideal theory but disagree about what is to be done here and now, it can only be because they disagree either about the extent to which real world conditions approximate the ideal, or about the practical implications of the differences that obtain, or both.

It is important to be clear, however, on the nature of their disagreement. True to the reformist origins of the utilitarian tradition, Mill's case for tolerance was addressed to well-intentioned political elites. His principal concern was state policy. Marcuse was characteristically unclear on this issue, so what he had to say can be mistakenly construed as a direct challenge to Mill's policy position. But it should be plain, despite the obscurantism that pervades his essay, that Marcuse had no wish to make institutions less tolerant of speech than they already are, and no desire to move state policies away from Mill's idea. He would have been foolish to have wanted anything of the sort, for Marcuse was a man of the Left and, by his own account, it is precisely the Left – that is, the genuine Left, the Left that is more concerned with changing real power relations than with the "inclusion" or "recognition" of excluded groups within existing power relations – that would be the first to suffer from likely changes in public policy. In any case, Marcuse's essay was not so much an exercise in political theory as a political intervention in a very specific context. In the mid-1960s in the United States, in the face of rising opposition to the Vietnam War and in the throes of the Civil Rights movement, an emerging New Left, based mainly in colleges and universities, was beginning to forsake prevailing norms of political propriety, taking up deliberately outrageous political styles in their stead. Radical students would sometimes disrupt the public speeches of corporate, government and university officials, in opposition to a longstanding tradition on the Left of categorical respect for free speech. For better or worse, Marcuse's essay defended this new political style. As such, it was not written for political elites, and its intended effect was not to reform public policy. Marcuse's audience was an insurgent group – student radicals – and his intent was to provide a theoretical justification for the political strategies they were spontaneously developing. Strictly speaking, then, one could say that, in the end, there was no actual disagreement between Mill's position and Marcuse's, because Marcuse offered no policy recommendations at all. But this conclusion would be misleading for reasons that bear importantly on how Mill's case for tolerance should be understood and assessed.

What could have prompted Marcuse to think that, in the United States of the 1960s, tolerance had turned into its opposite? How could he justify the claim that pure tolerance in that time and place – or, as one might imagine him thinking, in ours today – could function repressively? The answer is implicit in Marcuse's explanation for the degree of conformity he observed in the actual marketplace of ideas. The problem, as he saw it, became particularly evident when the United States was compared with the Soviet Union. Marcuse was a critic of Soviet Marxism, just as he was a lifelong anti-fascist. Despite his hesitations about Millean liberalism, he was as intent as any liberal to protect individuals from fear of the state and from moral coercion too. In this respect, the Soviet Union and Nazi Germany epitomized what Marcuse opposed. But these societies also exhibited a considerable degree of intellectual and political conformity, a fact that Marcuse took to be symptomatic of all that was wrong with them. In the Soviet and Nazi cases, however, the explanation was obvious. Old-fashioned repression suppressed dissent. In the United States, on the other hand, there was hardly any repression of speech. Anyone could say anything with little fear of legal penalties and with only slightly greater fear of the moral coercion of public opinion. But hardly anybody did. Could it be, then, that in the US, tolerance itself, formal tolerance, worked to do what overt repression did elsewhere? This would be, on the face of it, an unlikely claim. Tolerance is the opposite of repression. But could the two be functionally equivalent? Marcuse would have been the first to appreciate that a regime of tolerance is, by far, a kinder and gentler place than a police state, especially for dissident intellectuals like himself. Even so, it is conceivable that, in some contexts, tolerance does what repression does in others; that it helps to maintain the regime in place. This is precisely what Marcuse did believe, and this was what he meant when he claimed that tolerance had turned into its "opposite," that it had become "repressive."

Of course, it is not literally true that in the United States of the 1960s there was the same *kind* of conformity as in the Soviet Union of that period. In the US, there actually was subversive and dissident speech. "Repressive Tolerance" itself was an example. A similarly "critical" piece on Soviet society, written by a Soviet citizen, would probably not have been tolerated by the Soviet authorities. Marcuse's contention, then, was not that repression and pure tolerance work in the same way, but that in the United States, while almost anything could be said without penalty, and while some subversive things actually were said, what was said, beyond a certain, very narrow range, was effectively *marginalized*. It was out there, as it were, in the marketplace of ideas, but it did not register in public discourse. Marcuse's claim was that, in the America of the 1960s – and, presumably, even more so, in America today – a kind of monopoly power distorted the marketplace of ideas, turning it "into its opposite." In a market in products or services, so long as there is free entry, anyone has the right to go up against a monopoly. But it is very unlikely that anyone could do so successfully. Similarly, in a monopolistic marketplace of ideas, anybody can say anything and some people sometimes will take advantage of their freedom, but it is unlikely that genuinely dissident or subversive views, even if heard, would ever be taken seriously. Whatever falls outside the narrow bounds of acceptable discourse is effectively neutralized, helping the system in place to reproduce itself.

Of course, the mere fact that mainstream, non-marginalized opinions fall within a narrow range proves nothing by itself. It is always possible that this convergence of views is a consequence of a rational consensus.

But, in the case of America in the 1960s, Marcuse thought otherwise. He was motivated to do so, in part, because he was an Hegelian Marxist, committed to a vision of a rational society at odds with the one he observed around him. But he hardly needed this philosophical worldview to draw the conclusion he did. Support for a war that was palpably immoral and for social policies that worked plainly to the detriment of human emancipatory interests was mainstream; opposition, especially radical opposition, was marginal. That something other than a rational consensus accounted for this state of affairs was therefore hard to deny. Non- or extra-rational processes were evidently at work.

In addition, Marcuse, like many other observers of the scene, was struck by the fact that, in America and other formally liberal societies, subversive speech is almost always rendered benign and even coopted or integrated into the order it opposes. To cite a contemporaneous example close to Marcuse's own concerns, the hippy movement, at the outset, directly challenged consumer society and other aspects of respectable, middle-class life. But, within a short time, hippy themes were taken on board by advertisers, the mass media and the fashion industry, and symbols of hippy culture were integrated effectively into the apparatus of mainstream consumerism. In contrast, in the Soviet Union and Eastern Europe, where speech was directly repressed, what was subversive remained subversive; indeed, almost anything that ran counter to the thinking of the regime took on a subversive aspect. When it was repressed, as it typically was, it went underground, awaiting release whenever the boot of repression would be lifted. For Marcuse, the contrast was stark and troubling. In liberal societies, freedom itself seems to dissipate subversiveness even more effectively than repression does in non-liberal regimes. And because it operates internally, at the level of social and political consciousness, there is nothing analogous to the boot of repression to remove. Thus "repressive tolerance" is more insidious and difficult to overcome than outright repression is.

To student radicals at the time, it seemed that Marcuse had revealed an obvious, but long concealed, truth. Read today, however, it is fair to say that Marcuse's account of repressive tolerance was, to the say least, exaggerated, and that pure tolerance is not nearly as effective at maintaining a status quo detrimental to humanity's emancipatory interests as Marcuse made it out to be. But for the radical students of the 1960's, Marcuse hit a nerve because the Vietnam War was a creature of mainstream liberal politics, and the immediate targets of their political struggles were liberal institutions, especially universities. It was therefore natural for them to suspect that liberalism itself was a root cause of what they opposed. Marcuse's essay gave that suspicion theoretical expression, underwriting it with the prestige of post-Hegelian German philosophy.

Of course, Marcuse's own situation was very different. But it is tempting to speculate psychologically in his case too. Perhaps Marcuse recalled from his youth that the German authorities during First World War, like their Allied counterparts, never permitted newspapers to propagate news of atrocities perpetrated by their own side. They feared, with good reason, that doing so would undermine support for the war effort. But in the America of the 1960s, Marcuse could turn on his television set and see American troops doing unspeakable things. It didn't seem to matter, however. It was as if peoples' moral capacities had become numb. Since Marcuse was disinclined to believe that the German authorities of his youth had been wrong to think that overt repression was necessary in their circumstances, he concluded that circumstances must have changed, that repression had become unnecessary or even counterproductive. This was the line of thinking Marcuse pursued. But, of course, in retrospect, it appears that the news broadcasts Marcuse thought ineffective did eventually help to mobilize popular opposition to the war; and, more generally, that Marcuse overstated the phenomenon he set out to explain. Still, the phenomenon was real enough. The marketplace of ideas was not working as it was supposed to work; moral and intellectual capacities were dulled, and "critical thinking" had, at best, only marginal effects. Dissent was tolerated, but also neutralized and even, as Marcuse said, "turned into its opposite" – perhaps not quite to the extent Marcuse portrayed, but to some extent. This phenomenon does call for an explanation. Unfortunately, Marcuse's own explanations were not much more satisfactory than his account of the phenomenon itself. But he did see clearly how important both the phenomenon and its explanations are for Mill's account of tolerance and for liberal positions generally. To see why, we must look, briefly, to the explanations he offered.

If it is granted that, in ideal conditions, the marketplace of ideas makes outcomes better, and also that Marcuse was right in saying that it was not in fact doing so, it can only be that factors not taken into account by Mill were systematically undermining its beneficial effects. The most obvious factor, that formal tolerance exists against a background of economic inequality, did register in "Repressive Tolerance." But Marcuse had little to say about economic inequality or its effects on public discourse. Still, the old saying that there is freedom of the press only for those who own newspapers is relevant to any account of the real world functioning of pure tolerance. If everyone has an equal right to speak, but not everyone can be heard or heard equally, the marketplace of ideas is not a genuinely free market, and what holds for free markets would therefore not automatically hold for it. With the means for disseminating ideas privately owned and concentrated in the hands of those who have an interest in maintaining the status quo, it is only to be expected that ideas opposed to the status quo would be marginalized. Economic inequality would spill over into the marketplace of ideas, undoing its potentially salutary effects.

However, Marcuse's principal reason for thinking that the marketplace of ideas was not functioning as it was supposed to was, again, something one might expect a sensitive representative of high European culture to make of America in the 1960s. Marcuse thought that technological changes, specifically the nature of new media, were partly to blame for repressive tolerance. His idea, more intimated than defended, was that literary media-like newspapers and books – because they require their audience to do something active, to read – encourage intellectual activity and therefore tend to enhance individuals' capacities for critical thinking. But visual media do not. They encourage passivity, to the detriment of critical thought. Thus they undermine the development of individuals' moral and intellectual capacities, diminishing consumer competence in the marketplace of ideas. Needless to say, this claim, though intriguing, is, if true at all, extremely overdrawn. Read today, it seems dated and uninformed about the potentialities of visual media. It is telling too that Marcuse nowhere adequately defended it or even formulated it clearly. Even so, pointing out how consumer competence can be diminished even in formally free conditions does illustrate, again, the importance of competency thresholds for arguments like Marcuse's and Mill's. In the ideal case, freedom of thought and expression can be counted on to enhance individuals' moral and intellectual capacities. But exogenous circumstances, like the introduction of new technologies, that systematically moronize can countervail the otherwise beneficial effects of pure tolerance. They can help to turn tolerance "into its opposite."

To repeat, Marcuse's contention, sound or not, was not intended to oppose the advice Mill or his followers today would give to the elites who control institutions. It was addressed to insurgent groups who found themselves in circumstances in which the rules of the political game, however beneficial they might be in principle, work systematically against the emancipatory interests they are supposed to advance. Thus Marcuse in no way advocated changes in government policies with respect to speech. What he defended was only what some radical students and others were already beginning to do – intentionally disrupting the ordinary workings of the real world marketplace of ideas in order to make their own, otherwise marginalized, voices heard. It can be necessary to do so, Marcuse thought, both to counter the consequences for rational discourse of economic inequality and also, above all, the debilitating effects of technological innovations in the means for disseminating ideas that optimistic nineteenth-century liberals like Mill could not possibly have foreseen.

To his intended audience, Marcuse's case is roughly analogous to the case a typical non-pacifist might make to a pacifist. The non-pacifist, let us suppose, believes, as the pacifist does, that, in ideal conditions, it would never be necessary to resort to violence, that a good society would be a non-violent one. The non-pacifist maintains, however, that, in some cases, it may be necessary to resort to violence, perhaps even that violence is necessary to create the conditions for the possibility of a genuinely non-violent world. On this decisive point, the pacifist would, of course, disagree, insisting that everyone ought to act here and now as if ideal conditions were already in place. But this position would make sense only if there were a moral prohibition against resorts to violence that holds categorically. Since Mill was a utilitarian, for him to hold such a view, he would have to maintain that a categorical proscription of violence maximizes utility overall. There is no reason to think either that Mill could have defended such a claim, or that he would have wanted to, if he could. He was not a pacifist. He did think, though, like most non-pacifists do, that an ideal society would be non-violent. With respect to violence, then, Mill's position was roughly what Marcuse's was with respect to speech and expression.

I would venture that, despite the impression *On Liberty* conveys, Mill held a similar view with respect to speech too; in other words, that he would have agreed in principle with Marcuse. Mill was, after all, more than ready to countenance deviations from pure tolerance for entire categories of human beings who fall below the competency threshold – children, idiots, lunatics and even, as one might expect of a nineteenth-century Englishman, colonial peoples who, in Mill's view, had not yet benefitted from living under institutions that cultivated their moral and intellectual capacities sufficiently to warrant living in a regime of tolerance.[4] In short,

---

[4] In this respect, colonial peoples are, like children, disposed to benefit from paternalism. Therefore, insofar as they are not, by nature, incapable of becoming "civilized," it should be possible to bring them up to the competency threshold by benevolent paternalistic policies. Inasmuch as Mill never claimed that the peoples the European powers dominated were inferior by nature, it must have been his view that colonial peoples, like children, can in principle become "adult members of civilized communities." If this was in fact what Mill believed, he was plainly more progressive

Mill was hardly committed to tolerance, regardless of circumstances. Thus contemporary followers of Mill, who are not dogmatic supporters of the policy on free speech that Mill argued for in a different time and place, would have to agree that Marcuse *could* be right – that a judicious use of intolerance, like a judicious recourse to violence, *could* be justifiable in some circumstances. Whether or not it is turns on no philosophical disagreements of consequence or indeed on any substantive questions of principle. It depends on what the facts of the matter are and therefore on what the likely consequences are of acting in one way or another.

It is easy to be misled on this point. In the 1960s, the student radicals whose disruptive tactics Marcuse's essay defends were accused of "elitism," of being so sure that they were right that they were willing to exclude contrary views. This charge was unfair; the student radicals were not intent on foreclosing debate. They only wanted to get their own views heard. But the fact that this charge could be raised and that it seemed plausible suggests that perhaps Marcuse's position was not in accord with Mill's after all; that Marcuse was less bothered than Mill by the fact of human fallibility. However, this was not so. As remarked, Marcuse had more historical evidence than Mill to assess. Given what had happened in the hundred or so years separating their work, and his own experiences in turbulent times, it is not surprising that Marcuse was less optimistic than Mill was about the beneficial effects of pure tolerance. Even so, Marcuse never questioned Mill's claim for human fallibility, not even implicitly. His support for the disruptive tactics of radical students was motivated by his belief that their actions promised to expand the range of political discussion in ways that would advance human emancipatory interests in that time and place; and, of course, in relevantly similar times and places. In no way did it rest on the conviction that these students were right beyond doubt. Indeed, Marcuse was nearly as inclined as Mill to support a healthy skepticism on all matters, and for much the same reasons.

But where skepticism is concerned, one can always ask – *how skeptical is it reasonable to be?* Thus in Descartes' first *Meditation*, Descartes insisted that, in doing "first philosophy," it is reasonable to doubt everything that cannot be established with certainty. But no skeptic, including

on the question of colonialism than those of his contemporaries, undoubtedly the vast majority, who had no interest in "educating" colonial peoples or in ending colonial domination. It is implied by Mill's view that there should come a time when the colonial powers, having discharged their "civilizing mission," should withdraw from their "responsibilities" as colonial masters – in just the way that, as they mature, parents should come to acknowledge and respect their children's independence.

Descartes, has ever maintained that it would be reasonable to live by this standard, even for brief periods of time. Cartesian skepticism was a strictly contemplative program, undertaken for a particular philosophical purpose. What this example shows is that the reasonableness of one or another kind of skepticism depends on the situation. Marcuse's claim was that it can be unreasonable, in societies like our own, to be as skeptical in practice as dogmatic followers of Mill would be. It was his view that, for all practical purposes, some questions can be regarded as settled; at least to a degree sufficient to warrant deviations from the usual norms of civility on the part of proponents of marginalized positions. For example, the idea that it is right to exterminate entire peoples is wrong beyond any reasonable doubt. Even so, it probably cannot be established with a degree of certainty that would satisfy someone intent on doubting everything. Is it nevertheless salutary to treat this idea with the respect that, in ideal cases, is owed to all ideas? The view of some of Mill's followers today would be *yes;* not because there is any non-negligible chance that it might be true, but because they believe that no harm and some benefit comes from leaving all questions open. Marcuse was more wary. He thought that, in some circumstances, the risks implicit in leaving some (settled) questions open can outweigh the benefits. This was especially true, Marcuse thought, of ideas that threaten to impede humankind's permanent struggle for its own emancipation. In his not unreasonable view, the evidence of recent history supported this conclusion.

But, again, for Marcuse, and perhaps for Mill too, though not for those followers of his who would insist on pure tolerance in all circumstances, there are no unbreakable moral prohibitions on acting in ways that would be wrong in the ideal case. There is only a strong presumption against intolerance. Whether or not to violate this presumption is a strategic question, just as the appropriateness of recourse to violence is a strategic question for non-pacifists who believe that, in ideal conditions, violence too is wrong. In this regard, it is worth reflecting on the fact that in our world, as in the America of the 1960s, Millean policies are part of the civic culture. Mill's case has triumphed so completely that everyone today pays homage to free speech, even as they quarrel over the implications of this conviction. Therefore, on any strategic reflection about what to do, it would have to be taken into account that the presumption against acting in ways that deviate from the prevailing norm of pure tolerance is very powerful. This is, in fact, what the student radicals Marcuse defended soon found out. When they disrupted speeches, attention turned away from the marginalized views that they wanted to air, and focused on free speech issues instead. Their disruptions were therefore almost always counterproductive. Thus, in the America of the 1960s, and in the present time as well, it may almost always be strategically unwise to violate Millean norms of behavior. But, if Marcuse was right, this judgment turns upon an assessment of the likely consequences of doing so, not on a robust and categorical moral prohibition.

Ironically, then, the lesson of Marcuse's essay is of greater theoretical than practical political importance. It is that, in less than ideal conditions, Mill's claim that tolerance is an improver does not always obtain. Instead, tolerance can help to marginalize potentially emancipatory positions, impeding the permanent struggle for human emancipation. In Mill's terms, it can work to the detriment of "the permanent interests of man as a progressive being." Thus even if Marcuse's political judgment was flawed, as I have suggested it was, the lesson he provided serves to remind us of a point that Mill was too inclined to forget – that consequentialists must be flexible in their policy prescriptions. In this respect, Marcuse was perhaps truer to the spirit of Mill's utilitarian birthright and therefore to Mill's official way of defending tolerance than Mill was himself.

5
Rawls

Philosophy aims to resolve puzzlements of a generally conceptual kind that arise out of changes in peoples' understandings of the world and their place in it and, in the case of political philosophy, in transformations of social and political life. The dissolution of feudal society and the rise of the nation state in the seventeenth and eighteenth centuries put the questions of political authority and political obligation at the top of the philosophical agenda. These issues have hardly been settled definitively but their urgency has waned as people generally and philosophers along with them have grown accustomed to the state form of political organization and to an atomized social order. By Mill's time, these topics had already diminished in importance, as issues pertaining to the *limits* of political authority took center stage. Since the mid-nineteenth century, questions about distributive justice have assumed an increasingly paramount importance in social and political philosophy in consequence of a number of related social and political changes – the irreversible entry of the popular masses into the political arena, the rise of the labor movement, and more generally, persistent contestation over the distribution of society's benefits and burdens. Mill's concerns are still, of course, with us – not so much because the idea of limited sovereignty remains controversial, but because the triumph of Mill's vision has been so complete. Nowadays, nearly everyone agrees with Mill's conclusions. The question, for philosophers, is how best to theorize this fundamental commitment of the prevailing political culture. Both of these concerns, the problem of justice and the foundations of liberalism, come together in John Rawls's (1921–) political philosophy.

The Problem of Justice

As remarked (in chapter 1), philosophers, following Aristotle's lead in Book 5 of the *Nicomachean Ethics*, typically divide questions of justice into those that have to do with punishment, *retributive justice,* and those that concern the distribution of benefits and burdens, *distributive justice.* Rawls's theory of justice is a theory of distributive justice. But it is nevertheless instructive, in discussing his views, to make an important affinity between retributive and distributive justice explicit. In both cases, justice requires that *like cases be treated alike.*[1] This is a *formal* principle because it specifies neither what counts as a like case nor what counts as equal treatment. These are place-holder terms, awaiting further elaboration. But the formal principle of justice is not without consequences. With respect to the administration of punishments, it requires that members of the same category of wrong-doers, however identified, be punished in the same way. Anything else would be unfair. A similar thought obtains with respect to the distribution of benefits and burdens. There too, justice is ultimately about fairness. In the theory of distributive justice, a variety of *substantive* principles effectively supply content to the formal principle that joins all invocations of justice together. These include, among others, "to each according to merit," "to each according to need," and "to each according to productive contribution." In general, as Aristotle also made plain, substantive principles of justice that are appropriate in some contexts will almost certainly not be appropriate in others. "To each according to merit," may apply, for example, to the assignment of prizes in competitions. "To each according to need" would almost never be appropriate in this context, though this principle might be relevant, say, to the distribution of food among the hungry, a domain in which "to each according to merit" would plainly not be apt. The issue is complicated because even when there is a consensus about *what* principle applies in a particular domain, there can and often will be contestation over how the relevant principle should be understood and how it should affect individuals' treatment. People might agree, for example, that prizes in competitions should be distributed according to merit, but disagree about what merit is or about how it should be reflected in the assignment of awards. The same holds for all other likely substantive principles except the one we might call *the egalitarian principle,* "to each the same."

[1] What follows in this paragraph and the next draws on Chaim Perelman, *The Idea of Justice and the Problem of Argument* (New York: Humanities Press, 1963).

Whenever this principle applies, the claim is that there is no normatively relevant way to differentiate cases among those who fall under the principle's scope.

Substantive principles of justice can apply to all of humanity or to some subset of it. The egalitarian principle, for example, could express a general egalitarian vision that encompasses all of humankind. Or, as in some monastic or ascetic orders, it could apply only to one particular group. Then, rather than expressing a sense of universal human solidarity, it would function, in the main, to foster a sense of in-group identity and a corresponding sense of difference from the outside world. Modern liberal theories of justice evince a profound sense of universal human solidarity. This understanding was already evident in Mill's thinking. It is fundamental to Rawls's philosophical project.

Questions of justice are morally urgent whenever what Rawls, following Hume, called *the circumstances of justice* apply – that is, whenever generally self-interested people find themselves in a world of *relative scarcity*. The circumstances of justice bear a close resemblance to traditional contractarian accounts of the state of nature. General self-interest is a softer version of Hobbes's claim that human beings are, by nature, diffident, competitive and vainglorious. Relative scarcity was a feature of Hobbes's state of nature and is a mainstay of other traditional contractarian accounts. Relative scarcity is distinguished from *absolute scarcity* and from *abundance*. When a good is relatively scarce, generally self-interested individuals have something to gain by cooperating in its acquisition. In contrast, when a good is absolutely scarce – for example when there is only enough water on a life raft for one of the raft's occupants – there can be no gains from cooperation. In these circumstances, the struggle for water is a "zero-sum" game in which there can only be a winner and a loser. A society in which most of the things generally self-interested people want are absolutely scarce would be a society *beneath* justice, a society too poor for questions of fair distribution to arise. On the other hand, when a good is abundant, as air generally is, when all of that good that anyone is likely to want can be obtained at virtually no social cost, cooperation is also unnecessary and questions of distributive justice also lose their urgency. A society in which most of the things generally self-interested people want are abundant would be a society *beyond* justice. Communism, as Marx conceived it, is a society beyond justice. But, this side of communism, most of the things that people want are relatively scarce. Therefore considerations of justice are nearly always pertinent. This is why Rawls says that justice is "the first virtue" of social institutions in the way that truth is of systems of thought (*Theory of Justice*, hereafter *TJ*, 3). Whenever the circumstances of justice apply, justice is a preeminently urgent normative concern.

In these conditions, fairness matters. We can gain a deeper understanding of what fairness is by imagining competitive situations in which some individuals do better than others. By hypothesis, the losers, being self-interested, dislike the outcome. In their effort to improve their situation, they might therefore seek redress from the other competitors. But what kinds of reasons could they offer in support of their claims? If all they can say is that they regret how they fared, others might empathize with them. But no one would have a normatively compelling reason to undo the outcome they dislike. On the other hand, if the losers can claim that they were somehow "cheated," if they can show that the rules of the competition were violated, then others, if they are reasonable, would have to acknowledge the legitimacy of their complaints. In these circumstances, the losers' charge would be that the competition was unfair. What they would be telling their fellow participants is not just that the outcome is contrary to their own agent-particular desires. They would also be saying that the outcome is contrary to genuinely agent-neutral interests that everyone ought to acknowledge; that it is wrong from the moral point of view.

Fairness, then, is an impartial standard, with moral force, that governs situations in which there is competition for relatively scarce resources. Rawls's aim is to show what fairness requires – not in all cases, but with respect to fundamental social, political and economic arrangements in societies like our own. His thought is that, in assessing institutional arrangements normatively, fairness is a bedrock justifying principle. In just the way that the ultimate defense of a scientific theory is that it is true, the ultimate defense of an institution is that it is just or, insofar as other factors also figure in typical justifying theories, that it is at least not unjust. Rawls calls a society's fundamental, economic, social, and political institutions its *basic structure*. His principal concern, then, is to determine what a just basic structure is. What he has to say about justice therefore does not apply, directly or without substantial modification, to other contexts in which the terms "just" or "unjust" are appropriately used. The idea of a just person falls beyond the scope of his theory. So too would considerations of "local justice," the justice of particular social interactions, and "cosmic" justice, the justice (or lack of it) inherit in the natural order.

Because his focus is on the basic structure, Rawls effectively assumes that justice as fairness pertains to "the whole community" and not to some sub-group of it. Thus, insofar as Rawls's theory is egalitarian, it is egalitarian in the way that Mill's was and that modern liberalism generally is. Its implicit invocations of the principle "to each the same" suppose a sense of universal human solidarity, not in-group difference. But we should not overemphasize the universality of Rawls's vision. For Rawls, "the whole community" designates particular political communities, not all human beings irrespective of their political connections. Rawls's theory of justice applies to the basic structure *of particular societies*. Justice between societies is a different, though related, matter.

Rawls's focus on communities individuated politically is distinctively modern. So too is the assumption underlying his guiding conviction – that a society's basic structure should be just. The idea that persons are equal with respect to what matters fundamentally is very ancient. It was the view, for example, of the Medieval Church, according to which all persons are "equal in the mind of God." But the idea that equality of what matters fundamentally has implications for how basic societal institutions ought to treat individuals is a distinctively modern notion. Medieval Christianity recognized no presumption for equal treatment on the part of basic social, political, or economic institutions. Its implicit understanding of just or fair treatment was, if anything, incompatible with the modern idea. That it would be unfair, say, for lords and serfs to be treated alike was the commonsense view of people in premodern times.

However, Rawls's thinking is not entirely in the vein established by Hobbes, Rousseau, and Locke. After devoting decades to elaborating a theory of justice and developing an account of political legitimacy, Rawls broached the prospect of going beyond the conceptual horizons of those who, centuries earlier, sought to make sense of the emerging state form of political organization. In a masterful coda to his main work, Rawls suggested that what he calls *the law of peoples* should substitute for the traditional, modern conception of sovereignty or supreme authority.[2] Once again, philosophy imitates life. As the world economy becomes increasingly integrated and as extra-national forms of political organization like the European Union develop correspondingly, a challenge, still marginal but nevertheless real, is posed to the old world order of nation states. In practice, however, not a great deal has changed. Thus there is still no deep conceptual crisis centered on the notion of political authority; nothing like the one that motivated the rise of modern political philosophy in the seventeenth and eighteenth centuries. Fundamental questions about the nature of political authority therefore remain far from the center of

---

[2] See *The Law of Peoples; with the Idea of Public Reason Revisited* (Cambridge, Mass.: Harvard University Press, 1999).

attention in contemporary political thought. Rawls's intimations that somehow a law of peoples might supersede the modern understanding of sovereignty reflects this state of affairs. At this point, it is more a programmatic suggestion than a substantive break from the past. In any case, because Rawls's account of the law of peoples is something of an afterthought to his main contributions to modern political philosophy, and because what he says about the law of peoples draws substantially on his earlier work, I will have little more to say about that topic here. I will focus instead on justice and political legitimacy, the twin foci of Rawls's life's work.

Justification

In moral and political philosophy, unlike in science, results can never be established or infirmed by checking them against evidence. That the facts of the matter are morally relevant is plain, as we have seen repeatedly. But evidence can never establish or unseat moral principles by itself. We therefore need some other way to ascertain when a normative theory is correct. Rawls makes explicit a methodology suitable to this purpose, the method of *reflective equilibrium*. It is a method that all of the authors discussed here tacitly adhered to in one way or another. The idea, in short, is that philosophers should repeatedly test their considered intuitions against their theoretical convictions, as often as need be, modifying one or the other as seems appropriate, until they arrive at a satisfactory resolution of all conflicts between them; in other words, until their (revised) intuitions and their (revised) theoretical convictions reach an equilibrium point at which all modifications that can be made have been made.

The method of reflective equilibrium would be a non-starter if there were no reason to be confident that peoples' considered intuitions, including one's own, are generally in accord. If there were no consensus about what fairness is, there would be nothing reliable to test theoretical claims against. It therefore follows that Rawls must think that peoples' intuitions about justice are, in fact, substantially in accord. Rawls's claim, then, is that people in particular societies or, at least in societies relevantly like our own, in liberal societies, share a sense of fairness, and that it is a legitimate philosophical undertaking to articulate that consensus view theoretically. Rawls's aim is to give theoretical expression to *liberal* justice, to what fairness is to people living in generally liberal societies.

This is not the same thing as saying what fairness *is* "under the aspect of eternity." If Rawls's aim were to say what fairness *really* is, he would have to assume more about prevailing intuitions than he actually does. He would have to assume that peoples' intuitions track the truth. This was how Kant thought of moral experience in the first two sections of *The Groundwork of the Metaphysics of Morals*. Kant wanted ultimately to defend morality against skeptical attacks. He thought that the best way to execute this task was, first, to establish what the conditions for the possibility of moral experience are, and only then to try to establish their reality. To this end, he deliberately set skeptical doubts about morality aside, assumed that "the ordinary rational knowledge of morality" was a reliable indicator of what morality is, and then proceeded to "discover" what its *grounding* must be if, in fact, morality is real. It was only at that point that he went on to argue that morality actually is real because these conditions obtain. In *A Theory of Justice*, Rawls expressly identified with the Kantian tradition in moral philosophy (see *TJ*, pp. 251–7). One might therefore suppose that Rawls too thought that prevailing views of justice are not only sufficiently alike for the method of reflective equilibrium to work, but also that these views are at least approximately correct. Had Rawls written nothing after *A Theory of Justice*, even a careful reader might have the impression that this was indeed Rawls's position and therefore that his aim was not only to articulate a particular conception of justice, the one he shares with his fellow citizens, but to say what justice really is. However, in light of Rawls's subsequent work, including his own retrospective comments on some of the key arguments in *A Theory of Justice*, it is plain that Rawls's intent is and perhaps always has been to articulate the sense of justice that people living in modern, liberal societies share. *A Theory of Justice* is about *our* sense of fairness, as his use of the indirect article suggests. Rawls never claimed to have elaborated *the* theory of justice, an account that would hold for all peoples everywhere. In all likelihood, no such theory is possible because notions of fairness and therefore of justice are always historically specific. But however that may be, Rawls's aim with respect to justice is only to explicate what justice is *for us*.

Justification reaches its terminus when there are no further informative or corrective gains to be made from continuing the interactive juxtaposition of considered intuitions and tentative theoretical claims. This is the position that Rawls attempts to reach in deriving principles of justice from an "original position." The original position is a "representational device" for moving intuitions about fairness, shaped by the institutional arrangements of liberal societies, and tentative theoretical views about a just basic structure, motivated by a core commitment to the idea of the moral equality of persons, to an equilibrium point.

Rawls's Principles

Rawls declares that, in arguing for principles of justice from an original position, he is "generalizing" and carrying to "a higher level of abstraction" the contractarianism of Rousseau, Locke and also Kant, the arch-theorist of the moral equality of persons (*TJ*, p. 11). It is worth noting that Rawls did not include Hobbes in this list. Perhaps this is because Hobbes's contractarianism is interest-driven, and Rawls is skeptical of the prospect of grounding a full-fledged theory of justice as fairness on this basis. In any case, Rawls's concern is with fairness directly, irrespective of its connections to self-interest. Rawls's aim is to discover principles for regulating social interactions the fairness of which all reasonable people would be obliged to acknowledge.

A word on terminology is appropriate at this point. What Rawls says, strictly speaking, is that the principles of justice ought to regulate *cooperative* interactions. I have modified Rawls's terminology, changing *cooperative* to *social* because, in chapter 1, I distinguished cooperative ways of coordinating individuals' behaviors from political ways. In those terms, cooperation occurs when individuals *voluntarily* defer from doing what is individually best for the sake of some overriding common objective; political coordination, on the other hand, is always *involuntary*, involving the use or threat of force. By "cooperation," Rawls intends both cooperation and also political coordination, as thus defined. The principles of justice regulate the basic structure, and the basic structure includes political institutions. There should be no misunderstanding of this point: justice as fairness straddles both sides of the voluntary/involuntary divide. Realizing that this is so actually brings Rawls's understanding of justice closer to Hobbes's. For Hobbes, justice was, at root, a matter of reciprocity, of sharing collective burdens fairly. This was the idea implicit in Hobbes's otherwise odd insistence that justice consists in "abiding by covenants made." Similarly, for Rawls, justice is a property of collective endeavors that applies whenever there are gains to be made by coordinating individuals behaviors that impose costs on the individuals involved; whenever, in other words, for the sake of some common good, some individuals must not do what would be individually best. The idea, then, is that whether individuals' sacrifices are voluntary or not, benefits and burdens should be distributed fairly.

Hobbes would have agreed. His differences with Rawls have less to do with what fairness is than with the background conditions under which it matters. For Rawls, fairness matters whenever the circumstances of justice obtain. For fairness to matter for Hobbes, there must also be civil order; the war of all against all must have been laid to rest. But the war of all against all is not in Rawls's purview. Like nearly all other political philosophers of the past two hundred years, Rawls is a statist by assumption, not by explicit concern. To be sure, it is fair to say of him that, like nearly everyone else, he implicitly endorses the generic Hobbesian argument for states – the idea that whatever else, if anything, states are good for, they are indispensable for providing public goods. But, again, like other recent and contemporary political philosophers who are statists for generally Hobbesian reasons, Rawls does not take the question of political authority to be fundamental in the way that Hobbes, Rousseau, and Locke did. For justice to matter, it is enough, for Rawls, that people are generally self-interested, and that they therefore seek to increase their own distributive shares in conditions of relative scarcity. There is therefore no need, in concocting a theory of justice, to focus on the devastating character of a state of nature; especially one marked by the potentially lethal interplay of diffidence and relative equality. There is no need either to make the existence of political authority a precondition for the moral urgency of justice or to worry about a generalized condition of rulessness that threatens to undermine any prospect of a just, well-ordered society. For Rawls, the question of political authority is sufficiently settled – whether or not the state form of political organization is in question, as it implicitly is in *The Law of Peoples*, and as it is not in *A Theory of Justice*. It is therefore unnecessary for Rawls to address issues pertaining to political authority *before* questions of justice arise.

We already know that, like other modern political philosophers, Rawls assumes a presumption for equal treatment on the part of basic political, social, and economic institutions. It is also plain, as Rawls himself has often insisted, that the modern, liberal sense of equality is historically conditioned. It will therefore be instructive to introduce Rawls's principles of justice by reflecting on the historically particular notions of equality they express. There are subtle differences in the way these principles are formulated at different points in *A Theory of Justice* and in subsequent texts, though the basic ideas they articulate are everywhere the same. The versions that follow are therefore composites, intended to capture the common conceptual core that runs through all of Rawls's various formulations.

These principles regulate the distribution of what Rawls calls *primary goods*. Primary goods are means that are generally instrumental for those ends, whatever they might be, that individuals regulated by the principles of justice are likely to hold. Rawls's list of primary goods has changed slightly over the years, much as his formulations of the principles of justice themselves have changed. But, as with the principles of justice, there remains a common core. These include basic rights and liberties, powers and offices, and income and wealth. These goods play a more prominent role in the derivation of Rawls's principles than do others that have been added along the way – a certain level of leisure, for example, and "the bases for self-respect." Primary goods are resources. They are means for whatever might be thought to matter intrinsically, not ends in themselves. The different principles of justice regulate the distribution of different primary goods on the core list.

The first principle – *that basic rights and liberties be distributed equally and at the highest possible level* – bears a plain affinity to the consensus view in liberal political cultures that, in a just society, there must be equality of citizenship. The idea, in short, is that everyone should count equally in the determination of social choices, that there should be equality in courts of law, that legally defined restrictions on liberty should pertain equally to everyone, and so on. This is the idea of equality that Rousseau defended and that, according to the standard historical interpretation, the French Revolution irreversibly implanted into the consciousness of modern peoples. Nowadays, virtually everyone supports this idea, at least in principle. Its practical implementation is another matter. Thus, for a very long time, regimes officially committed to the idea of political equality denied women the right to vote. In the United States, where the idea of equal citizenship is deeply entrenched in the political culture and plainly articulated in its founding documents, most citizens of African ancestry were, in practice, denied the franchise well into the 1960s, their ancestors having been kept as slaves, with full Constitutional support, for most of the country's first century of existence. It took powerful social movements eventually to extend the franchise, first to women, then to most African Americans; to abolish slavery required a Civil War. These and other struggles within liberal societies for equal citizenship were hard fought and protracted. But, in retrospect, it seems as if their ultimate victory was assured by the depth of the commitment to equality of citizenship rights that prevails in modern, liberal political cultures. Thus it seems obvious nowadays that all citizens have a right to vote in consequence of principles everyone in the political culture supports. Even more assuredly, it is plain that the idea of slavery offends everyone's sense of justice.

Rawls's second principle maintains, in part, *that powers and offices be open to all under conditions of equality of opportunity* and, by extension, that equality of opportunity should obtain in all competitive circumstances that fall within the scope of a theory of justice for a society's basic structure. This principle too reflects a consensus in our political culture – in favor of equal opportunity. As with political equality, no one today opposes this ideal. But there is a difference. What political equality involves is not controversial; what equality of opportunity requires is. The idea is *essentially contested* in the sense that, while support for it comes from all over the political spectrum, there is intense disagreement over what equality of opportunity implies. In other words, there is contestation over the idea of equal opportunity itself. All sides want to enlist the concept, as they construe it, for their own purposes. At one extreme, on the political Right, there are supporters of equal opportunity who would effectively collapse the idea into political equality. In their view, equality of opportunity obtains whenever legal impedances in the way of persons competing for powers and offices or other relatively scarce goods are removed. For them, equality of opportunity is tantamount to the absence of official discrimination. During the French Revolution, equal opportunity, so conceived, was a standard in the service of the struggle against aristocratic privilege. The conviction that careers should be open to talents and not dependent on conditions of birth was a powerful ingredient in the successful effort to make Rousseau's notion of equal citizenship a real world political fact. It is ironic that today's right-wing understanding of equal opportunity was once emblematic of what is perhaps the most enduring achievement of the French Revolution – the abolition of the *ancien régime's* system of *estates,* and its replacement by a concept of citizenship coextensive with the nation itself. But it soon became evident that, so long as competitive advantages attach to factors other than citizenship rights, as they plainly do, the removal of legal impedances to competitions is unlikely to do much to give competitors equal chances to obtain the powers and offices and other goods they seek. It therefore became clear to nearly everyone, especially on the Left, that even where political equality is firmly in place, inequalities of wealth and power still substantially affect competitors prospects for success. Thus there arose the idea that equality of opportunity exists only if, in addition to removing legal discriminations, background institutional impedances to competitions for relatively scarce goods are also removed. In *A Theory of Justice*, Rawls submitted this idea to careful scrutiny, eventually adopting a moderate version of the left wing view of equal opportunity. Rawls advocates what he calls *fair* equality of opportunity. Unlike those to his left, he would not have powers and offices and other competitive goods be distributed in such a way that members of all (associational) groups receive a proportional share. But he would insist that there be institutional mechanisms in place to assure that group membership not have an adverse causal effect on individuals' chances of succeeding. Incorporating this idea into the first part of Rawls's second principle, the claim then is *that powers and offices be open to all under conditions of fair equality of opportunity.*

Rawls's view of equal opportunity, like the more extreme view he rejects, and indeed like any view that does not collapse equality of opportunity into political equality, assumes that there is a theoretically defensible way to identify those group memberships that should be neither disabilities nor advantages in competitions for powers and offices and other primary goods. Rawls has virtually nothing to say about this issue. But received understandings and common sense are useful indicators. Therefore, this omission is not very serious. Even in the absence of a worked out view, Rawls can assume, with confidence, and in accord with the considered intuitions of most of his fellow citizens, that the fact that an individual is a man or a woman should not affect his or her prospects for success, and that neither should an individual's racial or ethnic identity. It is also Rawls's view that differences in income and wealth ought not to affect individuals' opportunities. The idea of *fair equality of opportunity* makes these historically conditioned intuitions explicit.

All partisans of equal opportunity, whether of the Left or the Right, believe that ultimately competitions must be equal *for individuals*. Left-wing partisans of equal opportunity, like Rawls, believe that the attainment of this goal requires measures directed specifically at countering the effects of (relevant) group memberships. Right-wing defenders of the idea take issue with this claim. No doubt their differences can be explained, in part, by the fact that, in the real world, the Left and the Right represent the *interests* of different constituencies, and by the further fact that these interests, consciously or not, register in peoples' intuitive judgments and in their corresponding theoretical convictions. But if we abstract these interests away and consider the question disinterestedly, the difference between the Right and the Left on equality of opportunity reduces to a disagreement about the degree to which the removal of legal impedances in competitive contexts eliminates *unfair* – that is, impartially indefensible – hindrances to *individual* competitors. It is by reflecting on this issue that Rawls came to construe equality of opportunity as he did.

The other part of Rawls's second principle, the *Difference Principle*, maintains that *unequal distributions of income and wealth and of other primary goods, not already regulated by the first principle of justice, are justified if and only if they work to the advantage of the least well off* or, more precisely, to *a "representative member" of the least well-off group*

– where, in this context, "group" means class-group. This claim articulates the consensus view that there is a presumption for what might be called *material equality*. Inequalities of income and wealth and perhaps of other primary goods too are allowable and even encouraged according to the consensus view, but they must be justified. This is an understanding that Rawls shares with proponents of rival theories of justice, including his principal opponents, the utilitarians. Utilitarians also acknowledge a presumption for material equality. But they think that this presumption can be overcome if an unequal distribution would maximize total (or average) utility for the whole community. Rawls has a different view of what would overcome the presumption for equal distribution. He thinks unequal distributions must work to the advantage of the least well-off.

However, what material equality is is eminently contestable. What, then, do partisans of material equality want? Unlike in the case of equal opportunity, it is impossible to array different answers to this question along a left–right continuum or, for that matter, to compare them across any dimension whatever. Anyone who acknowledges a presumption for material equality must, however, address this issue because it is incoherent to advocate equal distributions of everything that advocates of material equality might plausibly have in mind. The reason why is that an equal distribution of X, where X is something that might be of concern to a proponent of equal distributions of material things, almost always entails an unequal distribution of Y, some other possible object of concern. For example, to advocate an equal distribution of income is *ipso facto* to advocate an unequal distribution of, say, welfare – because people differ, in this instance at the rate at which they transform income into welfare. Someone with expensive tastes would require more income than someone with cheaper tastes to be at the same welfare level. An equal distribution of income between these individuals would therefore entail an unequal distribution of welfare, and vice versa. Whoever would advocate equal distributions of *anything* material – or even anyone, like Rawls, who only acknowledges a *presumption* for equal distributions of material things – is therefore obliged to say just what they would distribute equally. This is what Rawls does in supplying a list of primary goods. Primary goods are means for realizing any of the particular ends that individuals are likely to make their own. Thus, in Rawls's view, it is ultimately the distribution of (some) resources, not welfare, that matters for justice. In this respect, Rawls and the utilitarians part ways.

The Difference Principle takes issue with utilitarianism in other ways too. Utilitarians want to maximize utility. They are therefore concerned with distributional questions only indirectly; because distributional issues can bear on how much utility there is overall. For the same reason, utilitarians do not care about *whose* utility is maximized, except insofar as the identities of the bearers of utility affect, in turn, how much overall utility there is. The Difference Principle, on the other hand, focuses precisely on *who* benefits. It mandates that inequalities are justified if and only if they benefit particular individuals, those who fall into the category of *the least well-off*. Thus, the Difference Principle *names* persons; utilitarianism does not.

The Original Position

Although it has receded in prominence in Rawls's recent work, Rawls's best known effort to derive the principles of justice is still his argument from "the original position." This argument draws expressly on contractarian strategies for justifying political authority. As remarked, the "original position" is not literally a "state of nature," a world like our own but without *political* institutions. However, the original position does play a role in Rawls's case for the principles of justice that is similar to the role played by the state of nature in traditional, contractarian accounts of political authority and obligation. Very generally, the idea is to imagine a world without justice, and then to show how rational, self-interested individuals can and would concoct principles of justice from this starting-point.

The argument from the original position is a thought-experiment. Individuals are asked to place themselves under an informational constraint, "the veil of ignorance." The veil denies them information about their own particular conditions. Under it, they know nothing about their places in society or their class positions; they do not know what their fortunes are in the distribution of talents and other physical and mental endowments; they know nothing of their psychological dispositions, including their attitudes towards risk; and, most importantly, they do not know what their own conceptions of the good are. Because Rawls also wanted to use this device to think about justice between peoples and across generations, a promise he has left largely unfulfilled, he also stipulated that, under the veil of ignorance, individuals know nothing about the level of development of their own society or even to what generation they belong. The only particular fact that bears on their own situation that they do know is that, for them, the circumstances of justice obtain. This fact must be let through the veil of ignorance in order to motivate the selection of principles. For it is only when the circumstances of justice obtain that individuals have a compelling reason to seek to coordinate their activities on terms that they can all recognize as fair (*TJ*, pp. 136–42).

General information also filters through the veil of ignorance. Thus, according to Rawls, individuals in an original position know, as well as anyone can, what the basic laws of sociology, economics and psychology are, insofar as these laws bear on the selection of principles of justice. They also have as wide a knowledge as is feasible of social, economic, and psychological facts that pertain to the selection of principles. In short, they know everything in general that pertains to their condition, but nothing in particular about themselves. Rawls's thought, then, is that, under these conditions, rational persons would select fair principles; the ones that he defends.

This claim must, of course, be defended. It cannot be ruled out in advance that, from an original position, rational agents might choose different principles. They might, for example, seek to maximize average utility. This was the conclusion of an argument very similar to Rawls's that had previously been developed by John Harsanyi.[3] Rawls's case for the principles he favors amounts to a rejoinder to Harsanyi and constitutes his best case against utilitarianism generally. It should be noted, however, that Rawls's method is deliberately non-utilitarian, even if it is not deliberately biased against utilitarianism. Rawls does not start out with a conception of the good, as utilitarians do. Indeed, under the veil of ignorance, individuals are prevented from doing so because they are denied information about what their own conceptions of the good are. Rawls's method assumes that conceptions of the good are bound to be controversial, and that this fact must be accommodated in any just society, dedicated to maintaining a basic structure that respects the moral equality of persons.

The argument from the original position supposes that people are generally rational in the Hobbesian sense, that they are capable of adopting means to ends. It also assumes, as Hobbes did, that people seek to maximize their own distributive shares. But persons in Rawls's original position do not exactly bargain with one another, as individuals in a Hobbesian state of nature do. The information constraint that they are under precludes this possibility. This is why, appearance to the contrary, the kind of deliberation Rawls imagines is more Rousseauean than Hobbesian in character. For Hobbes, the social contract is the result of interest-driven

---

[3] See John C. Harsanyi, "Cardinal Utility in Welfare Economics and in the Theory of Risk-Taking," *Journal of Political Economy*, vol. 61 (1953).

negotiations. It culminates in the authorization of a sovereign because, in the end, it is in every negotiator's interest that sovereignty be established; because living under a sovereign is better for everyone than remaining in a state of nature, the only feasible alternative. On the other hand, for Rousseau, even if he does not quite say so unambiguously, the social contract is the result of an individual reflection; one that holds for all individuals insofar as they are rational. What justifies Hobbesian sovereignty is mutual advantage; what justifies Rousseauean sovereignty is the moral point of view, the fact that the establishment of sovereignty is impartially better than remaining in a state of nature. This important distinction is obscured in Rawls's account of the argument from the original position. It might therefore seem that Rawls and Hobbes thought of justice in a similar way. But this is not so. The veil of ignorance transforms what would otherwise be a self-interested negotiating process into an impartial deliberation. It permits Rawls to argue for a Rousseauean conclusion from a Hobbesian starting-point. Thus there is a sense in which, in the original position, individuals do negotiate over principles of justice. But because they do not know who they are, they cannot know what outcomes would be advantageous for themselves. They therefore have no choice but to consider alternatives impartially. Because they know everything in general that bears on their negotiations but nothing about what their own interests are, they are like labor-management negotiators wrangling over a collective bargaining agreement in complete cognizance of all the relevant facts affecting the negotiation but not knowing which side they represent. In these circumstances, the negotiators, if they are to serve their own sides well, have no choice but to negotiate a "fair" or, better, an *impartial* outcome – one that is as advantageous as can be to both sides given all the relevant background circumstances. "Justice as fairness" is therefore a form of what Brian Barry has called "justice as impartiality," in contrast to "justice as mutual advantage."[4]

However, the effect of imposing a veil of ignorance is not quite to impose the moral point of view *per se*. It is to introduce a particular understanding of it, a *liberal* understanding. What the veil of ignorance does is to abstract away all factors that bear on the selection of principles of justice that are *arbitrary* from the moral point of view. Thus the reason why individuals' natural endowments and class positions and attitudes towards risk are neutralized by the veil of ignorance is that differences among individuals in these respects have no moral standing;

---

[4] Brian Barry, *Justice as Impartiality* (Oxford and New York: Oxford University Press, 1995).

from an impartial vantage-point, they are arbitrary. But, then, what is not arbitrary? Because Rawls does not address this question directly and because political philosophers influenced by him have approached it in subtly different ways, this question cannot be answered with precision. However, the general drift of an answer, true to Rawls's intentions, is clear enough. The idea is that individuals should be held accountable for the distributional consequences of what they freely choose to do. Transposed into the theory of distributive justice, this is essentially the idea Kant pressed in the second section of *The Groundwork of the Metaphysics of Morals*, where he argued for the equivalence of formulations of the categorical imperative that focus, first, on universalizability (impartiality), then on accountability, and finally on autonomy.[5] If Kant was right, as Rawls believes he was, the moral point of view entails a notion of individual responsibility – for the consequences of autonomous choice. In Rawls's view, this morally compelling requirement ought to be reflected in the size and composition of individuals' holdings, and nothing else should, except for reasons that self-interested, rational individuals can all accept. What the veil of ignorance does, then, is deny individuals information about factors that affect distributional shares in real world economies that do not result from free choices. People do not choose their natural endowments or class positions or their attitudes towards risk; nor do they choose the generation to which they belong or the level

[5] It is customary to identify five distinct formulations of the categorical imperative in the second section of the *Groundwork*. The first two, traditionally designated the Formula of Universal Law ("Act only according to that maxim whereby you can at the same time will that it should become a universal law") and the Formula of the Law of Nature ("Act as if the maxim of your action were to become through your will a universal law of nature") focus on universalizability; the third, the Formula of Humanity as an End In Itself ("Act in such a way that you treat humanity, whether in your own person or in the person of another, always at the same time as an end and never simply as a means"), introduces a strong notion of accountability or responsibility; the two final formulations (or near-formulations, since Kant never quite states them in a way that is analogous to the others), the Formula of Autonomy ("the idea of the will of every rational being as a will that legislates universal law") and the Formula of the Kingdom of Ends ("a systematic union of rational beings through common objective laws; i.e. a kingdom that may be called a kingdom of ends ... inasmuch as these laws have in view, the very relation of such beings to one another as ends and means"), focus on the idea of autonomy. [According to the standard pagination, usually printed in the margins of English language editions of the *Groundwork*, the first two formulations occur at 421, the third at 429, the fourth at 431, and the fifth at 433.] Kant maintained that these distinct formulations are equivalent and therefore that there is ultimately only one categorical imperative.

of development of the society into which they are born. Therefore these factors should not affect their deliberations about principles of justice. But people do make choices. Their choice of principles of justice should recognize this fact as well.

It is because Rawls wants to hold individuals accountable that his principles regulate the distribution of means, primary goods, rather than welfare or anything else that might be considered intrinsically valuable. *Liberal* justice insists on respecting the distributional consequences of individuals' free choices. It therefore cannot concern itself with what matters intrinsically. Doing so would be incompatible with individual, moral accountability. A society committed to implementing a particular distributional pattern of welfare, for example, would not be able to hold persons properly accountable because, in order to implement the favored pattern, it would be necessary to indemnify individuals for the consequences of their free choices. Thus a welfare egalitarian would be obliged to maintain that individuals who freely squander their wealth, to the detriment of their own welfare, should be compensated by everyone else in order to bring their welfare levels back up to the levels everyone else enjoys. But this is just what Kant wanted to proscribe – treating individuals as means only; in this case, means for achieving a particular distribution of welfare. Categorically respecting essential humanity in those who freely squander their wealth requires holding them responsible for what they freely (autonomously) do. In contrast, distributing resources – or, as Rawls would have it, a subset of resources, the primary goods – justly, discharges the requirement that others be treated as ends in themselves. It assures that what individuals do with their holdings is their own responsibility. If they fail to respect essential humanity in themselves, as Kant might say of those who squander their distributive shares, the fault is theirs alone and they must bear the consequences. It is not the responsibility of anyone else to set them right. Indeed, it is everyone else's responsibility to hold them accountable for what they did.

Rawlsian justice has far-reaching egalitarian implications, as we will presently see. But because it is liberal, because it insists on holding individuals accountable for the *distributional* consequences of their own free choices, it can never fully endorse the egalitarian principle "to each the same." This is not the place to gainsay this defining tenet of Rawlsian liberalism. I would point out, however, that the Kantian notion of moral accountability, implicit in the categorical imperative to treat humanity in oneself and others always as an end and never as a means only, merely suggests that individuals' distributive shares ought to reflect individuals' choices about what they do with the resources they control. It does not imply it. There may be other, better, ways to register moral accountability. Thus the Kantian view of individual responsibility that Rawls and liberals after him endorse need not carry over into the theory of distributive justice. That it does, however, is a core conviction of Rawls's and of all the liberals who follow in his wake.

Ironically, then, Rawlsian liberalism introduces a notion of moral *desert* or *entitlement* into the theory of justice, at the same time that Rawls and his followers agree verbally with neo-Lockeans, like Robert Nozick, that their view of justice, unlike his, eschews the very idea.[6] For Nozick, the fact that Rawls's is not an entitlement theory is a reason to fault it; for Rawls, it is a mark in its favor. But both are wrong. Thanks to its purchase on moral accountability, Rawls's is a kind of entitlement theory.

Rawls's method in the argument from the original position is expressly contractarian. The plain implication is that justice, like political authority and political obligation for Hobbes, Rousseau and Locke, is ultimately a human invention, concocted to serve fundamental human interests. Ostensibly, then, what justice requires is not pre-contractual, in the way that Lockean rights claims are. No explicit moral requirements constrain the selection of principles of justice. But because Rawls is committed to holding individuals accountable for the distributional consequences of their own free choices, there is an implicit pre-contractual constraint on justice, after all. Principles that regulate individuals social interactions fairly must respect the consequences of individuals' free choices. Free choices generate morally compelling entitlements to distributive shares.

It is important not to confuse claims for *moral* desert with ordinary, unproblematic desert claims. A student who does consistently A-level work, deserves or is entitled to an A for the course; a runner who comes in first in a race deserves or is entitled to the prize. In these cases, "the rules of the game" specify entitlements to outcomes. In contrast, Locke's theory of property, invokes a very different and more controversial notion of desert or entitlement. According to Locke, whatever is acquired in a rightful way is one's own – not in consequence of any humanly contrived system of rules governing the acquisition and transfer of property, but as a matter of primordial moral right. Property rights therefore do not derive their authority from the consent of those whose behaviors they regulate; their authority is normatively prior to any possible conferral of consent. That is why any institutional arrangements that individuals concoct to serve their own purposes, including the constitution of

---

[6] See Robert Nozick, *Anarchy, State, Utopia* (New York: Basic Books, 1974). On Nozick's way of thinking about justice, see chapter 3 above.

sovereignty, must respect this moral fact, and in no way infringe upon morally primary rights. It is this *moralized* notion of desert, not the commonplace non-moralized notion that everyone uses and accepts, that Rawls wants to avoid. He wants to avoid it for the reason that motivates contractarian political philosophy generally – because, like his contractarian predecessors, Rawls believes that social institutions are, in the final analysis, human concoctions, even when they are not deliberately contrived, and that they are justified to the extent that they can reasonably be held to serve legitimate human ends. Claims for the existence of morally prior constraints on what human beings can rightfully devise pull in the opposite direction. Perhaps the clearest articulation of the contractarian idea is Rousseau's theory of sovereignty, according to which individuals are ultimately the authors of the laws to which they are subject. But despite his deliberate attempt to link justice as fairness to this idea of Rousseau's, Rawls's dedication to holding individuals responsible for the distributional consequences of what they freely choose to do prevents him from doing so or, more exactly, from doing so completely.

Rawls's position is therefore closer to Locke's than is commonly supposed or than Rawls himself believes. Locke would ground political authority in a social contract, but then insist that this contract not infringe upon morally primary rights, especially property rights that generate entitlements to distributive shares. In a similar vein, Rawls theorizes justice contractually, but then insists implicitly that the principles of justice not disturb the entitlements that individuals' free choices generate. Rawls's real disagreement with followers of Locke like Nozick, then, is not about the existence of entitlements, but about their nature and extent. For Rawls, very little of what individuals actually have in real world economies is morally deserved, because morally arbitrary factors, not individuals' free choices, account for nearly all actual holdings. For the neo-Lockeans, on the other hand, because property rights are morally primary, virtually all holdings are morally deserved, even if, as they would have to concede, morally arbitrary factors play an overwhelmingly important role in their generation.

It should be noted, finally, that the implicit Rawlsian view of desert assumes, first, that genuinely free (autonomous) choices are indeed possible and, then, that some of the choices individuals make as economic agents fall in this category, that they are genuinely free choices. The first assumption raises the perennial philosophical problem of free will. Moral and political philosophers have been inclined to set this issue aside or, rather, to leave it to metaphysicians to investigate, assuming that somehow a satisfactory account of free will or at least a satisfactory grounding for the idea of moral responsibility is in principle available. For good or ill, Rawls stands in this tradition. He has nothing to say about free will or the grounds for moral responsibility. But even if we concede that the problem of free will can be rightfully set aside, it remains to show that the kinds of choices that Rawls and liberals after him want to hold individuals accountable for really are relevantly different from those that result from the factors that Rawls considers morally arbitrary. Rawls does not discuss this issue directly either, but it is fair, even so, to impute the following view to him and to liberals after him. Suppose that there are two individuals A and B, who differ in talents, but who are in all other ways similar. They work with the same materials, with the same technologies, for the same amount of time, and so on, but because they differ in talents, A earns more income than B. Then, for Rawls, while it may be consistent with justice that A's income share be larger than B's, while this inequality may even be required by justice if it enhances the distributive share of the least well off, A has no pre-contractual, *moral* entitlement to a larger distributive share. On the other hand, if A and B are alike in talents and all other respects, but A chooses to expend more effort than B, say by working for a longer time, then A *is* morally entitled to a larger share; indeed, to a share that is larger in proportion to the greater effort A expended. This is the intuition Rawls wants to preserve. But it is far from clear that he can do so and still maintain the view of moral accountability that he holds. For the psychological and other factors that bear causally on differential expenditures of effort, on A's ostensibly free choice to work longer than B are, presumably, as morally arbitrary as is the fact that the "natural lottery" distributed talents differently to A and B. After all, what, other than inherited or socially acquired characteristics, might account for A's and B's choices about how much effort to expend? And what did A or B do to deserve their genes or the socialization they underwent? I will not pursue these issues further here, except to observe that these questions appear to be merely rhetorical and that their obvious answers indicate a problem with the idea that free choices generate moral entitlements, the core theoretical conviction that defines liberal views of distributive justice after Rawls.

The Case for the Principles

There are several distinct strains of argument in Rawls's attempt to derive the principles from the original position, and the arguments that

Rawls emphasizes do not quite entail the conclusions he wants to defend. I will call Rawls's principal rationales the "Paretian (or, better, quasi-Paretian) strain," and the "well-ordered society strain," respectively. There is also an argument that Rawls provides but does not emphasize that I will call the "pure procedural justice strain." It is more successful.

The Paretian strain is so called after Vilfredo Pareto (1848–1923), an Italian-Swiss economist and social theorist. Pareto was convinced, on the one hand, of the fundamental soundness of the core welfarist conviction, articulated by the classical utilitarians, that social and political institutions are justified to the extent that they enhance individuals' well-being or welfare, but also convinced of the impossibility of adding welfares together in the way that the classical utilitarians demanded. Pareto was concerned, above all, with the problem of interpersonal utility comparisons. Because he was persuaded by the arguments of Descartes and philosophers after him that direct (non-inferential) knowledge of other minds is impossible, he thought that the utilities of different individuals cannot be expressed in a common unit and therefore that they cannot be combined in the way that utilitarianism supposes.[7] In part too because he was convinced of the soundness of the growing behaviorist trend in the social sciences, Pareto abhorred the "mentalism" of the traditional utilitarian view. He therefore maintained that the only acceptable way to aggregate welfares requires, first, that welfare be represented ordinally (using the ordinal numbers, first, second, third . . .), not cardinally (using the cardinal numbers, 1, 2, 3 . . .), as the utilitarians propose – in other words, that analysts seek to represent information about individuals' *rankings* of alternatives, but not about preference *intensities,* as

[7] According to Descartes, the "I," whose existence is established by the *cogito* argument ("I think, therefore I am"), is a unitary consciousness. This I is, as a matter of fact, intimately associated with a particular body, my own, and somehow there are interactions between material events, involving my body, and my mind. [How this can be so is the "mind–body problem" that was one of Descartes' many legacies to modern philosophy.] But even if, contrary to fact, I could feel pain in some other individual's body, it would still be *my* pain. Therefore, even in principle, I can have no access to a consciousness that is not my own – except, of course, by making inferences from behaviors, based on analogies with my own behavior. Thus if I know that I hold my head in a certain way when I have a headache – in other words, if I can correlate a behavior of mine with a mental state of mine – and if I observe your behaving in the way that I do when I have a headache, I can infer that you have a headache and therefore that your mental state is similar to mine when I have a headache. But I can never know that you are having a headache directly; I can never literally feel your pain.

utilitarianism also requires. Then, Pareto reasoned, we can still say that state of affairs X is better in a welfarist sense than state of affairs Y, if all individuals rank X above Y. We may even be able to extend this thought by maintaining, as economists after Pareto ingeniously did, that X is better in a welfarist sense than Y, even when it is not unanimously preferred, if some of the people, those who prefer X to Y, can compensate the others, those who prefer Y to X, at least enough to bring them back up to their former welfare levels and still be better off.

Of course, Rawls's principles of justice regulate the distribution of primary goods, not welfare. Therefore Rawls cannot argue for principles of justice on strictly Paretian grounds. But he can and does adopt Pareto's idea to his own purpose. His position can therefore be described as quasi-Paretian. Rawls maintains that inequalities of income and wealth that work to everyone's advantage are permissible. If we then deny that individuals in the original position are envious or that their deliberations over principles of justice reflect any other sort of preference for or against particular distributional patterns, we can also say that inequalities that enhance at least one person's share of income or wealth, leaving everything else unchanged, are also permissible. Needless to say, anyone who would use the contractarian method to derive principles of justice cannot assume that individuals in the original position are already committed to implementing particular distributional outcomes. Otherwise, the answer that the contractarian program is intended to provide would be built tendentiously into the problem the contractarian method is invoked to solve. A contractarian must therefore assume that people take no interest in other peoples' distributive shares, except insofar as other peoples' holdings affect their own. For the task at hand, a contractarian must assume that people care only about the payoffs to themselves. On that assumption, *any* distribution that would enhance the share of primary goods of at least one person, in comparison to what their share would be under an equal distribution, without diminishing anyone else's distributive share, would be superior to an equal distribution.

Pareto's idea, modified for Rawls's purpose, like the utilitarian idea it partly captures, is strictly aggregative in content. Whoever would argue in the way Pareto did is concerned, in the first instance, with how much of something, preference satisfaction in Pareto's case, primary goods in Rawls's, there is; not with how it is distributed. The quasi-Paretian strain of Rawls's argument therefore disallows privileging the least well-off or, indeed, privileging any individual or group of individuals because of *who* they are or *where* they stand in the overall distributional pattern. Thus it does not actually support the Difference Principle, except in the sense that it demonstrates that the presumption for equal distribution can be overridden in order to increase the distributive share(s) of some individual(s). But a move away from strictly equal distributions is also entailed by other strains of argument in Rawls's case for the Difference Principle. It is therefore hard to resist the conclusion that, however conspicuous their role in the derivation of principles of justice from an original position, the quasi-Paretian considerations Rawls musters are, at best, superfluous to the position he ultimately wants to defend.

It will be instructive to turn next to the pure procedural justice strain of Rawls's argument. Rawls does say that the original position argument deploys the idea of pure procedural justice in a contractarian context (*TJ*, pp. 84–5). But this idea became obscured as he emphasized other arguments. Nevertheless, Rawls's appeal to pure procedural justice explains his commitment to the Difference Principle better than anything else he says on its behalf. It also puts some other key Rawlsian positions in a clearer light.

Inasmuch as there is no way to check a particular distributional outcome against an ideal template to determine how well it accords with what fairness requires, it is natural to rely on *procedures* that are fair, and then to maintain that whatever outcomes these procedures generate must be fair in turn. Intuitions about the fairness of procedures are, in fact, quite robust, and examples of fair procedures come readily to mind. If the idea can be successfully adapted to Rawls' purpose – in other words, if the principles of justice can articulate the thought behind pure procedural justice – there will be a compelling reason to think that outcomes consistent with that principle are fair – not directly in consequence of their structure, but because their structure is generated by a fair procedure.

Consider a paradigm of pure procedural justice. Imagine that we want to divide a pie fairly among self-interested and rational individuals who each want as much pie as they can obtain, and who are not envious or in any other way concerned with the size of any one else's share except insofar as it affects their own. As is intuitively obvious, a fair procedure, in this case, would be to have one person cut the pie into pieces and then have that person be the last to choose a piece of the pie. This procedure is fair because it permits the individual who will get the last piece, which will also be the smallest piece, given what we have assumed about individuals' interests and capacities, to determine its size, subject only to the condition that the entire pie must be divided among all the participating people. That person would have an incentive to make the last available piece or, what comes to the same thing, the smallest piece as large as possible. The way to do this, of course, would be to divide the pie equally. Thus an equal division would be a fair division *in this instance*. Observe, however, that an equal division maximizes the minimal share. In this case, equality is consistent with the Difference Principle. We can therefore think of *this* equal division as a special case of a *maximin* division, a division that maximizes the minimal share, the idea that the Difference Principle articulates. I will return to this thought presently. For now, what should be noticed is that this conclusion follows from the fairness of the procedure employed in dividing the pie. The fact that a fair division of a the pie is an equal division was discovered, not assumed.

It should be noted too that this equal division will, in all likelihood, produce an unequal distribution of pleasure or desire satisfaction; in other words, an unequal distribution of what might be thought in this case and perhaps also in general to matter intrinsically. Because people differ, because they *process* pieces of pie into pleasure at different *rates,* an equal division of pie will produce an unequal distribution of pleasure. To distribute pleasure equally between Tiny Tim and the pre-Christmas Eve Scrooge, Scrooge would have to get a much larger piece of the pie. If the pie were divided equally, Tiny Tim would be much better off – assuming that Tiny Tim does not feel guilty and that Scrooge does not feel slighted or, more generally, that neither takes any direct interest in the size of the other's distributive share. What this case shows is that, for Rawls and indeed for anyone who thinks that justice is about the distribution of means for obtaining what matters intrinsically, a just or fair distribution of the material things that the principles of justice regulate will almost always entail a different and unpredictable *but not unfair* distribution of what is ultimately of concern.

To gain a deeper understanding of Rawls's case for the principles of justice, it will be instructive to revisit his claim that these principles regulate the distribution of primary goods, where primary goods are generalized means to whatever particular ends agents are likely to hold. In the original position, people do not know what their particular conceptions of the good are. But they do know, roughly, what the range of conceptions of the good in the general population are and they know in general what is instrumental for their realization. Thus even in the original position, where individuals do not know who they are or what they want, they can be confident that it is in their interest to augment their share of primary goods. They can therefore have rational desires without knowing their particular ends.

Rawls's contention, then, is that income and wealth, along with the other primary goods, are instrumental for the realization of the particular conceptions of the good that persons are likely to hold; not for any conception that agents could hold. This is a plausible position. But it is in no way logically necessitated. The world could be such that, for example, income and wealth are not generally beneficial for realizing individuals' plans of life, where plans of life are motivated, in part, by conceptions of the good. Indeed, even in the world as it is, income and wealth are not means for the realization of literally all life plans. Still, the knowledge that income and wealth are instrumental for the realization of most plans of life makes it rational for individuals in the original position to seek to augment their distributive shares of income and wealth. If someone then turns out to have a conception of the good for which income and wealth are not instrumental, this need not embarrass Rawls's claim. But, of course, if many people have such conceptions or, worse still, if many people have conceptions of the good for which income and wealth are somehow detrimental, then income and wealth could not be counted among the primary goods.

To draw up a list of primary goods, it is therefore necessary to make empirical assumptions about human beings's ends and about their desires. If, contrary to what Rawls believes, individuals' conceptions of the good ranged so widely that no plausible list of primary goods could be constructed, Rawls would not be able to proceed as he does. His case for the Difference Principle might still hold, but the Difference Principle itself would be fatally indeterminate with respect to its range of application. People in the original position, under a veil of ignorance, would therefore be unable even to formulate negotiating positions. The informational constraint under which they deliberate would be too severe for the contractarian method to generate any outcome at all. But because the facts are as they are, and because general information does filter through the veil of ignorance, the Difference Principle is determinate and, more importantly, applicable – but only to some of the primary goods on Rawls's list. As we have seen, it is Rawls's view that in societies relevantly like our own – developed, modern liberal societies – some primary goods fall outside the scope of the Difference Principle altogether. Thus the first principle of justice mandates that basic rights and liberties be distributed equally and at the highest level possible. It therefore marks off basic rights and liberties from other primary goods. The Difference Principle does not pertain to them.

It might seem that Rawls's reason for distinguishing basic rights and liberties from other primary goods is just, as I suggested earlier, that he wants the principles of justice to reflect the strong consensus in our political culture in favor of political equality. This is undoubtedly so, but it is not the whole story. More of Rawls's rationale becomes evident if we reflect, again, on the differences between dividing a pie and dividing, for example, income. In the pie-dividing case, a maximin division is equivalent to an equal division because the size of the pie does not change according to how the pie is divided. With income however, insofar as individuals's levels of productivity respond to economic incentives, the division does affect the amount of income to be divided. Where income is concerned, it is therefore possible and even likely that an unequal division will make it possible to improve the distributive share of the least well-off. Then maximin and equality will part ways; and because maximin, not equality, is the idea consistent with the thought behind pure procedural justice, maximin prevails. Another reason, then, for separating basic rights and liberties from the other primary goods is that, for them, the amount to be distributed does not vary with inequalities in their distribution. Distributing basic rights and liberties is like dividing a pie; distributing income is not.

But, then, if, equal distributions, when apt, are only special cases of maximin distributions, why not rely on the Difference Principle alone? More specifically, the Difference Principle, applied to basic rights and liberties, mandates equal distributions at the highest possible level, just as the first principle of justice does. Why, then, enshrine this thought in a separate principle? Why maintain that there are two principles of justice rather than one? The answer to these questions has to do with the special place of citizenship rights in modern political life. But there is another, more technical consideration that underlies Rawls's insistence on articulating his position in the way that he does.

Because the primary goods are irreducibly heterogeneous, whoever would maximize the share of primary goods going to the least well off must somehow solve an indexing problem. How are we to calculate how large an individual's share of primary goods is when holdings vary in their composition of apparently incommensurable items? How are we to compare, for example, a bundle of primary goods in which individual 1 has more income and wealth than individual 2, but fewer of the "bases for self-respect"? By insisting that basic rights and liberties be distributed equally and at the highest possible level, and then maintaining that this requirement be satisfied before the second principle is applied – by insisting, in other words, that the principles be *lexically ordered* and that the first principle precedes the second – Rawls *solves* or, rather, *eliminates* this indexing problem with respect to comparisons of basic rights and liberties against other primary goods. His solution is extreme, but in accord with the modern liberal consensus in favor of political equality. What Rawls maintains is that there can be no trade-offs of basic rights and liberties for income and wealth or indeed for anything else at all. It is Rawls's contention that persons in the original position would come to this realization; and that they would therefore insist on separating the first principle of justice from the second, and on according it lexical priority.

The main non-Paretian case for the Difference Principle in *A Theory of Justice*, the appeal to the idea of a well-ordered society, is consistent with the thought that the pure procedural justice strain of argument articulates. However, it suggests a much weaker conclusion than the one Rawls draws. Arguably too, it even threatens the core commitment to material equality that Rawlsian justice expresses. It is therefore important to reflect on what Rawls has to say about a well-ordered society, not just for its own sake, but also for the light it sheds on egalitarianism. Rawls's reflections on a well-ordered society also anticipate the direction his work would take in the years after *A Theory of Justice* appeared.

What Rawls contends, in brief, is that the Difference Principle is indispensable for sustaining a sense of justice in the individuals regulated by it, and that a sense of justice is necessary, in turn, for maintaining a "well-ordered society" (*TJ*, pp. 453–62). A "well-ordered society" is one that advances the various goods of its members, that is fair to competing conceptions of the good, and that is, at the same time, regulated by a "public conception of justice," one that all of its members acknowledge and support. Rawls holds that what individuals seek in the original position, when they select principles of justice, is principles that can serve as a basis for a well-ordered society. His contention, then, is that they realize with some considerable assurance, given their knowledge of the general facts of human psychology, that a sense of justice can only be sustained when no one is very poorly off. They therefore opt for the Difference Principle, assuring that the worst off are as well off as they can be.

This argument rests on information that penetrates the veil of ignorance. One could be easily misled, however, about precisely what this information is. In the original position, individuals do not know their own attitudes towards risk. However, because they know the general facts of human psychology, they do know something about the array of attitudes towards risk in the general population. They therefore know that, once the veil of ignorance is lifted, they have a good chance of being risk-averse, but also that the chance that they will be risk averse is well below certainty. They will therefore not opt for the Difference Principle on the strength of this consideration. Maximin, the risk-averse strategy underlying the Difference Principle, cannot be defended on the grounds that it fits nearly everyone's psychological profile. The case for maximin follows instead from a different psychological fact in conjunction with a fact about economic life that people in the original position also know. The economic fact is that the mechanisms that regulate real world economies can generate distributions that leave some individuals very badly off. Then psychology teaches that these badly-off individuals are in danger of not developing an appropriate sense of justice. It therefore follows that, because they want a well-ordered society, people in the original position will do whatever they can to assure that this eventuality will not result. The Difference Principle guards against this outcome as well as any principle regulating the distribution of income and wealth can. They will therefore choose it over any of its rivals. In sum, then, it is a universally acknowledged need for order and stability, not information about the distribution of attitudes towards risk within the population, that militates in favor of individuals' settling on a maximin strategy; a strategy that, as it happens, is also ideal for people with risk-averse psychologies.

A problem with this appeal to the idea of a well-ordered society, however, is that it could as well be enlisted in support of a principle that, unlike the Difference Principle, fails altogether to express the commitment to material equality that is constitutive of the modern liberal sense of fairness. For if the idea is only to have a well-ordered society, and if a necessary condition for order is that individuals' resource shares not fall below a certain level, it should be enough to guarantee everyone a minimal share – or, more precisely, to guarantee that the share of primary goods going to those most in danger of failing to develop an adequate sense of justice be *sufficient* to permit these individuals to develop the requisite sensibility. Rawls might therefore have opted for a rule according to which, in any society wealthy enough to provide it, a guaranteed minimum, sufficient to permit a sense of fairness to develop, is assured for everyone. Anyone concerned to implement such a principle would, of course, have to determine what a minimally sufficient resource share is. Had Rawls taken this line, and had his influence over academic political philosophy nevertheless been what it has been, one could imagine right-wing Rawlsians today insisting that it is enough to assure that basic food, clothing, and shelter needs are met, and left-wing Rawlsians maintaining that, in addition, individuals must be supplied with resources sufficient to assure them opportunities to participate fully in their society's political and social life. But however the doctrine of sufficiency is understood, all of its adherents would maintain that once sufficiency is guaranteed for everyone, there is no further reason to be concerned with resource distributions. It would seem, in other words, that Rawls's well-ordered society argument supports the conclusion that everyone must have enough to develop an appropriate sense of justice, and that it then has nothing more to say about the distribution of income and wealth or other primary goods.

This thought has considerable intuitive appeal. If, for example, everyone had an adequate automobile, would it be unfair that some drive Ferraris while others drive Geo Metros? This might, at first, appear to be a rhetorical question. It might appear that there is obviously nothing objectionable about inequalities *above* a certain threshold. One might even conclude, on this basis, that material equality is a misguided ideal; that what its defenders really want, or ought to want, is sufficiency. I would venture, however, that this question is actually quite probative. It is far from obvious when, if at all, an inequality is unobjectionable. Even to begin to address this question, one would have to know a great deal about how social practices and institutional arrangements affect individuals' conditions of life. If some people drive Ferraris while others drive Geo Metros for reasons other than their own idiosyncratic preferences, it may well betoken a failure to respect the moral equality of persons. I will not pursue this question here, since it is not a topic Rawls addresses directly. I would conjecture, though, that, in a direct confrontation, the ideal of equality would best sufficiency; and I would suggest that, even if the issue is not expressly engaged, there are ample resources in *A Theory of Justice* that weigh in in support of this conclusion. Rawls's commitment to material equality is a consequence of his deeper commitment to the moral equality of persons and to the idea that there is a presumption for equal treatment with respect to all parts of a society's basic structure, including its fundamental economic institutions. What Rawls has to say in defense of these commitments and of their implications amounts, indirectly but decisively, to a brief in favor of material equality. In any case, there is no doubt that Rawls would agree that equality, not sufficiency, is the correct moral ideal for liberals. The problem is that his argument for the Difference Principle that appeals to the notion of a well-ordered society appears to suggest the opposite conclusion.

This argument also points towards what would become a central concern of Rawls's in his work after *A Theory of Justice*. It brings issues pertaining to social stability and, more generally, to political legitimacy to the fore. The idea of a well-ordered society, of a society whose institutional arrangements are actively endorsed by those who live under them, is the principal link between "justice as fairness" and "political liberalism."

Political Liberalism

It is important to distinguish positions within political philosophy proper from the underlying moral philosophical views on which they are based. For example, liberalism can be justified by appeal to morally primary rights, as in Locke's case, or on utilitarian grounds, as with Mill, or by a contractarian justifying strategy, as in Rawls's argument from the original position. Because this is so and, more generally, because individuals' fundamental theoretical convictions or, as Rawls would say, their *comprehensive doctrines*[8] are never likely to converge under genuinely free conditions, stability is more at risk than it would be if the basic rules of the game, the "constitution" that governs basic social, political and economic institutions, were somehow supported by principles that everyone endorses or at least, as Thomas Scanlon perspicuously put it, that "no one could reasonably reject."[9] This thought played an important role in causing Rawls to distance himself from the overt identification with contractarianism that he emphasized in *A Theory of Justice*. Increasingly, Rawls became convinced that the theory of justice should not be based on principles that are in any way contentious and therefore inimical to the ideal of a well-ordered society. This conviction led Rawls to develop a specifically *political* liberalism, a political philosophy that is liberal but not dependent on any antecedent, moral philosophical convictions or, more generally, on any of the elements of comprehensive doctrines that can give rise to principled disagreements among reasonable people. In retrospect, the idea of political liberalism was latent in *A Theory of Justice*. In the course of Rawls's work over the next two decades, it became

---

[8]   A *comprehensive doctrine* "includes conceptions of what is of value in human life, and ideals of personal character, as well as ideals of friendship and of familial and associational relationships, and much else that is to inform our conduct and in the limit to our life as a whole. A conception is fully comprehensive if it covers all recognized values and virtues within one rather precisely articulated system; whereas a conception is only partially comprehensive when it comprises a number of, but by no means all, nonpolitical values and virtues and is rather loosely articulated" (*Political Liberalism*, hereafter *PL*, p. 13).

[9]   Thomas Scanlon, "Contractualism and Utilitarianism" in Amartya Sen and Bernard Williams (eds.), *Utilitarianism and Beyond* (Cambridge: Cambridge University Press, 1982), pp. 103–28.

increasingly the focus of his attention. With the publication of *Political Liberalism* in 1993, a redacted version of essays Rawls had published over the preceding decade and a half, political liberalism finally came to full fruition.

By focusing on the idea of a well-ordered society and, relatedly, on *publically* defensible accounts of the principles that regulate social life, political liberalism effectively brought the problem of order or social stability back to the center of modern political philosophy. Ironically, in light of Rawls's many differences from Hobbes, it revived Hobbes's main theoretical and practical concern. The difference, of course, is that Hobbes would achieve stability illiberally – by establishing a sovereign with unlimited powers, capable of instilling order through fear. Rawls seeks order too, but in a way that is consonant with core liberal values; especially with the conviction that individuals ought to be as free as possible from the coercive power of the state. Accordingly, political liberalism seeks to ground order in the enthusiastic support of a society's members for the institutions under which they live and therefore, ultimately, for the principles through which they regulate their own social interactions.

Political liberalism is, in the first instance, a theory of political legitimacy. In this sense, it is an alternative to the accounts of legitimacy found in the work of Hobbes, Rousseau, and Locke. But, as already remarked, in contrast to *The Leviathan* or *The Social Contract* or *The Second Treatise of Government,* the question of political legitimacy is hardly broached in *A Theory of Justice* – in part because the real world transformations that led seventeenth- and eighteenth-century political philosophers to question the foundations of political authority and political obligation had been effectively played out long ago. In the final decades of the twentieth century, neither the nation state nor an atomized civil society any longer elicited the kind of conceptual puzzlement that gave rise to philosophical inquiry centuries earlier. Even so, it was Rawls's view that liberalism was in need of a more satisfactory foundation than the philosophical traditions that had sustained it for the past two centuries provided, at least if stability was, again, to become a central concern. Rawls therefore claimed that the problem with all previous views of political legitimacy was precisely that they were *philosophical.* Paradoxically, then, Rawls reinvigorated the venerable philosophical question of political legitimacy by insisting that the question not be approached philosophically. What he had in mind, however, is as philosophical, according to the usual understanding of the term, as any previous treatment of the topic had been. The difference is that Rawls's account is intended to be neutral with respect to disagreements among comprehensive doctrines. It is in this sense that it is a *political*, not a metaphysical, theory. It is for this reason too that Rawls's reworking of the problem of political legitimacy leaves the old issues of political authority and political obligation to the side, focusing instead on peoples' extant views – that is, on what people already believe, whether they realize it or not.

Thus Rawls's account of political legitimacy is structurally very different from, say, Rousseau's. Rousseau was intent on defending the idea of a just or legitimate state, and he took pains to differentiate this normative concern from questions about peoples' attitudes towards existing institutional arrangements. For Rousseau, issues pertaining to *de facto* and *de jure* legitimacy were utterly distinct. Throughout *Political Liberalism*, however, Rawls conflates these issues, effectively collapsing questions about political stability and other concerns that bear on the prospects for the *de facto* legitimacy of existing political arrangements into a view of *de jure* legitimacy, legitimacy in right. For Rawls, *de jure* legitimacy is assured whenever *reasonable* people believe in the rightness of the institutions under which they live; in other words, whenever the *de facto* legitimacy of existing institutional arrangements is secured *for them*. In reconstructing Rawls's position, it is necessary to follow his lead rather than Rousseau's, and not distinguish *de jure* from *de facto* legitimacy systematically. This is especially so in scrutinizing Rawls's contention that (most) people in societies like our own can be brought to endorse constitutional principles that support public institutions regulated by principles of justice that articulate the modern liberal conception of fairness – for reasons that *they* cannot reasonably reject.

Because it is supposed to follow from an (imputed) consensus that could fail to exist, political liberalism is not a universally applicable political philosophy. Officially, political liberalism is not based on any underlying "metaphysical" truths at all. But although it holds only for people in certain times and places, it is not a relativist doctrine, at least according to one commonly accepted understanding of relativism. Rawls is not committed to the view that there are no "metaphysical" truths of the kind to which political philosophers have traditionally appealed. His claim is only that political philosophy need not and should not appeal to them. But insofar as certain institutional forms and not others are legitimate, their legitimacy is context-dependent. Rawls's view of political legitimacy therefore is relativist in a sense; the legitimacy of a regime is relative to its social and historical circumstances. Rawls therefore cannot say, as Locke or Mill could, that political institutions should be liberal everywhere. His claim is only that support for liberal constitutional principles is possible and desirable in the conditions that obtain in generally liberal societies or, more precisely, in societies in which most people have the core valuational commitments and beliefs that people in modern, liberal societies share. Rawls's contention is that liberalism is right *for us now* because it alone fosters the kind of social stability that modern, liberal people want; stability that is (potentially) uncoerced because it is grounded in prevailing understandings of what fairness requires.

For the sake of social stability, so conceived, it is desirable that people enthusiastically support liberal institutions. Accordingly, political liberalism suggests a political project: to secure the requisite kind of support. To this end, Rawls would build on what he calls an *overlapping consensus* of comprehensive doctrines. An overlapping consensus contrasts with a *modus vivendi,* an agreement to get along in the face of contentious and generally intractable disagreements. A *modus vivendi,* Rawls maintains, is too fragile a basis for a well-ordered society; among other things, it is prone to become undone as the balance of forces within society changes. Far better, therefore, to base support for liberal institutions on convictions actively endorsed throughout the political community. But except for those citizens whose underlying comprehensive doctrines are already liberal, support for liberalism will be, at best, only latent. The task, then, is to make it manifest; to develop backing for a liberal constitutional order by appealing to elements already present in the comprehensive doctrines individuals actually hold. This project will be feasible if and only if support for liberal institutions can be teased out of the comprehensive doctrines people do, in fact, endorse; if, despite their many differences, these doctrines *overlap* around a (potentially) liberal core. Assuming this is the case, the idea, then, is to forge an explicit *overlapping consensus* sufficiently powerful to ground support for liberal constitutional principles. Rawls is confident that the requisite consensus does exist, at least potentially. In consequence of the cultural and political transformations wrought by the Protestant Reformation, the Enlightenment, and the history of liberalism itself many, perhaps most, existing comprehensive doctrines are, in fact, sufficiently *reasonable,* in Rawls's view, for an overlapping consensus of the requi-site sort to emerge.

For Rawls, then, social order, based on voluntary support for existing constitutional arrangements is both a condition for the possibility of liberal regimes and a goal of liberal politics. A constitutional regime backed by an overlapping consensus of reasonable comprehensive doctrines or, as Rawls sometimes says, a *well-ordered society* functions very much like Mill thought tolerance does. Recall that, for Mill, a certain level of tolerance is necessary before tolerance can have beneficial effects. Beyond that threshold, the more tolerance there is, the more beneficial tolerance becomes; beneath it, tolerance is not an improver at all. Similarly, a consensus in support of liberal constitutional arrangements presupposes a threshold level of social order, based on support for the regime in place, when that regime is already generally liberal. Then there can be well-functioning liberal institutions that, in turn, foster the sensibilities required for a well-ordered, liberal society. Thus liberal institutions reinforce the conditions for their own possibility. Put differently, to have a well-ordered liberal society, it is necessary, first, that society already be somewhat liberal and well-ordered. If it is not, it must be made so. Unlike Hobbes, then, Rawls is not an advocate of stability for its own sake. Rawls values the stability of *liberal* regimes, not stability in general. Rawlsian liberals living in non-liberal circumstances might therefore be rebels or even revolutionaries. Genuine Hobbesians could never be. They are anti-revolutionaries to the core.

There is, however, a respect in which both Rawls and Hobbes, because they emphasize stability, do agree politically: they would both *depoliticize* the body politic to enhance social unity. But because Rawls, like Locke and Mill, is a democrat as well as a liberal, he is obliged to balance the imperative to depoliticize with the need to maintain government of, by and for the people. Like Locke and Mill, Rawls must therefore reconcile these competing claims. Political liberalism is suited to this task, perhaps even more than Lockean or Millean liberalism are, because it has a well-developed, practical model to follow – the constitutional system that has developed over the years in the flagship liberal democracies, above all, in the United States.

Both Locke and Mill recognized that representative government helps to mitigate social conflict and therefore to advance social unity. Rawls would agree. But the political liberal project supposes, even so, that channeling potentially destabilizing social divisions into the framework of party politics and legislative assemblies is not enough to insure the kind of stability liberals want. It is necessary, in addition, to remove the most divisive issues from the sphere of collective decision making altogether. Of course, there is a limit to how much potential divisiveness can be neutralized in this way. In an era in which the entry of the *demos*, the popular masses, into the political arena has become an incontrovertible fact, political legitimacy itself would be in jeopardy if popular governance were too severely curtailed. It is therefore crucial to strike the right balance. This is the genius of the American model. It effectively removes many potentially divisive political disagreements from the legislative arena, turning them into legal disputes about the meaning of a Constitution that nearly everyone agrees ought to regulate public life. There is, of course, a place for public deliberation and collective choice in liberal democracies whose constitutional arrangements accord with this conception. But it is not a large place. It is fair to say that, in Rawls's view, the American way of balancing the conflicting claims of liberalism and democracy is about right. Political liberalism generalizes this idea. It seeks to consign potentially divisive concerns to a kind of principled, constitutional predetermination. Thus the fear of the sovereign's police that Hobbes sought to instill gives way, in Rawls's vision, to a system that insures order by according dominion to law itself. Thus Rawls's account of a well-ordered liberal society implies that the sphere of public deliberation and collective choice be circumscribed, just as Locke's and Mill's attempts to reconcile liberalism and democracy did. But for anyone who values a well-ordered liberal society, this detriment to democracy is not entirely to be regretted. Democracy's loss is social unity's gain. For the political liberal, then, the task of forming a well-ordered society, governed by a sense of justice, falls more to constitutional constraints than to the potentially destabilizing perturbations of democratic politics.

But for this plan to work, the underlying constitutional arrangements that sustain a well-ordered liberal society must enjoy the active support of its subjects.The problem, then, is plain. Rawls wants the *de facto* legitimacy of liberal institutions to be based upon the fact that these institutions really are legitimate; that they are legitimate *de jure*. But, at the same time, he insists that, in a generally free society, many different comprehensive doctrines will have adherents, and that some of these comprehensive doctrines will be non- or even anti-liberal. In these circumstances, what can a *liberal* partisan of social stability do? The only possible answer it seems is that the requisite consensus, insofar as it is not already manifest, must be forged – not through coercion, but through rational persuasion. Is this possible? The conviction that motivates the political liberal project is that it is. If it is not, then the political liberal's confidence in the prospect of developing and sustaining a well-ordered society will fail. For it is not enough to show that legitimate authority is conceivable. Rawls must also demonstrate that the concept is applicable – in our time and place.

Rawls's strategy, then, is this: begin with extant and ostensibly opposing comprehensive doctrines, some of which may appear to be illiberal; find higher-order commitments that proponents of all of these views endorse; and then, as far as possible, derive a consensus supporting liberal constitutional arrangements on the basis of these higher-order commitments. The foundational commitments that Rawls identifies are, in fact, uncontentious – the idea that persons are morally equal in possessing capacities for a sense of justice and for a conception of the good, and that people have capacities for judgment, thought, and inference. But even in *Political Liberalism*, where the notion of an overlapping consensus is extensively developed, the claim that a consensus on individuals' moral powers and rational capacities entails support for fairness to competing conceptions of the good and all that follows from it is more asserted than demonstrated. Rawls nowhere *shows* how an overlapping consensus can be forged. What he does instead is adduce inconclusive considerations in support of the claim that a particular subset of extant positions, those he calls "reasonable," can be dialectically shaped into a consensus of the requisite sort. Insofar as "reasonable" is defined independently, so that it is not true by definition that reasonable comprehensive doctrines support liberal constitutional principles (at least implicitly), this conviction is an empirical speculation, not an incontrovertible fact. It is more of a promissory note than an established conclusion. For political liberalism, however, it an article of faith. Rawls believes that in modern, liberal societies, many, perhaps most, comprehensive doctrines are, in fact, reasonable. Implicitly, though, Rawls is committed to the view that, if he is wrong on this point, liberal institutions might still be able to survive through fear or indifference on the part of the citizenry. But a well-ordered, liberal society of the kind he envisions would remain an elusive ideal.

Throughout *Political Liberalism*, Rawls takes full advantage of the idea of the reasonable. To be included in an overlapping consensus, comprehensive doctrines must be reasonable. To be good citizens of liberal polities, individuals must be reasonable. In short, reasonableness is indispensable for a well-ordered society. But "reasonable" is, at best, a vague term, borrowed, not surprisingly, from jurisprudence and especially from the American tradition of Constitutional interpretation, where it is a widely applied standard. The idea is especially vague when it is used to describe comprehensive doctrines.[10] In Rawls's hands, it is also ambiguous, des-

10 Even Rawls agrees that it is "deliberately loose." This characterization follows his most extensive gloss on the idea, which goes as follows: "Reasonable comprehensive doctrines . . . have three main features. One is that a reasonable doctrine is an exercise of theoretical reason: it covers the major religious, philosophical , and moral aspects of human life in a more or less consistent and coherent manner. It organizes and characterizes recognized values so that they are compatible with one another and express an intelligible view of the world. Each doctrine will do this in ways that distinguish it from other doctrines, for example, by giving certain values a particular

ignating more than one sense at the same time. On the one hand, a comprehensive doctrine is reasonable if it can be modified or at least redescribed in a way that makes cooperation with others who hold different views possible on free and equal terms. "Reasonable" in this sense means "flexible" or "cooperative." A reasonable comprehensive doctrine, then, is one that encourages flexible, cooperative attitudes on the part of individuals who adhere to it. Comprehensive doctrines that value tolerance expressly are plainly reasonable in this sense. But so too, Rawls thinks, are all comprehensive doctrines that foster the sense of reciprocity that motivates justice as fairness; the idea that one is obligated to do one's fair share in collective endeavors. On the other hand, a comprehensive doctrine is reasonable if it is plausible, given the uncertainties that inevitably afflict human deliberations, what Rawls calls "the burdens of judgment." Rawls holds that disagreements with respect to fundamental religious or moral issues are reasonable in this sense, so long as their existence cannot be explained by willful or inadvertent blindness or blatant irrationality. Indeed, it is only *blatant* irrationality that disqualifies comprehensive doctrines from inclusion in the reasonable category. Thus Rawls is eager, in practice, to welcome comprehensive doctrines that rest on beliefs that fail to meet ordinary standards of rational belief acceptance, "faith based" positions especially. It might seem counter-intuitive to count irrational beliefs as reasonable. But Rawls's thought seems to be that it is right to do so, given the uncertainties and "burdens" that inevitably attend the exercise of human beings' rational capabilities – lack of evidence, difficulties in the way of prioritizing values, and the sheer intractability of questions of ultimate concern, along with lack of time and the pressures of day-by-day existence. Rawls insists that reasonable disagreements, so understood, are permanent and ineradicable features of modern societies. The expectation that fundamental moral, philosophical and religious differences will eventually disappear is therefore unreasonable (in the sense that contrasts with "plausible"). To be sure, Rawls nowhere demonstrates that extant comprehensive doctrines, religious or otherwise, are reasonable even in this attenuated sense. He only assumes that most of them are.

primacy and weight. In singling out which values to count as especially significant and how to balance them when they conflict, a reasonable comprehensive doctrine is also an exercise of practical reason. . . . Finally, a third feature is that while a reasonable comprehensive doctrine is not necessarily fixed and unchanging, it normally belongs to, or draws upon, a tradition of thought and doctrine. Although stable over time, and not subject to sudden and unexplained changes, it tends to evolve slowly in the light of what, from its point of view, it sees as good and sufficient conditions" (*PL*, p. 59).

But, of course, what is reasonable in light of the burdens of judgment, even on the most expansive understanding of the idea, need not also be reasonable in the sense of flexible or cooperative, and vice versa. Rawls effectively blurs the line between these senses of "reasonable" by saying that a view is held reasonably only if its proponents recognize the hopelessness of trying to convert everybody to it. The idea, it seems, is that people will moderate their claims for the sake of social cooperation whenever they acknowledge the futility of defeating conflicting or incommensurable comprehensive doctrines non-coercively – through the force of argument or, where arguments fail, through extra-rational forms of persuasion that are not illiberal. The contrast, apparently, is with scientific communities in which a consensus around basic theoretical orientations is a fair expectation, at least for those "hard" sciences that are theoretically mature and relatively insulated from political and religious pressures. Rawls's conviction, then, is that fundamental moral, philosophical and religious differences can never be surmounted, unlike fundamental scientific differences which, when they occur, are temporary phenomena that the progress of science will eventually resolve (*PL*, p. 55). Therefore, if individuals are to be accorded the equal respect they are due, the comprehensive doctrines they support, because they are so central to their concerns, must be accorded equal respect and therefore treated fairly. In practice, this entails that public institutions be *neutral* with respect to competing claims.

If the issue in question were *de facto* legitimacy, in Rousseau's sense, Rawls's account would be exaggerated, at best. Liberal societies are no longer riven by the threat of religious or civil war. If anything, indifference about comprehensive doctrines, not fanatical adherence, has become the norm. But Rawls's claims in behalf of an overlapping consensus of reasonable comprehensive doctrines pertain to the problem of *de jure* legitimacy, and therefore to the issue of *de facto* legitimacy only indirectly. Unlike Hobbes, Rawls's concern is not with what is necessary for civil peace. It is with what is required to justify or legitimate the use of public coercive force. His answer to this venerable question is familiar enough: what legitimates coercion is, ultimately, the consent of those on whom it is deployed.

Rawls does not quite couch his account of political legitimacy in these terms. To do so would strain the distinction he wants to draw between political and philosophical liberalism, inasmuch as "consent" is a term of art in the contractarian tradition, a tradition reasonable people can and have rejected. But we should recall that, throughout modern political philosophy, "consent" seldom, if ever, literally means consent. It is a place-holder term, standing in for whatever individuals *do* that confers legitimacy upon political arrangements. Different philosophers conceive consent in different ways. In all its uses, though, the idea presupposes that institutional arrangements are, in the end, human concoctions, justified to the extent that they advance fundamental human interests. I have suggested that all modern political philosophers, not just contractarians, agree on this point (see chapter 4). Contractarians have their own purchase on how it is that institutional arrangements can be shown to advance fundamental human interests; utilitarians and rights theorists have theirs. What is key for contractarians is that the legitimacy-conferring property, consent, is something individuals *do* or rather something individuals can be said to have done, by way of rational reconstruction. Like other contractarians, Rawls has his own distinctive understanding of the idea. The notion of consent that political liberalism invokes, albeit without using the word, is (implicit) support for constitutional principles, grounded in (reasonable) individuals' core valuational commitments. In Rawls's view, this support is forthcoming, in principle, when and insofar as the constitution itself *actively respects* the moral dignity and equality of persons by according their core valuational commitments equal respect – specifically, by treating competing conceptions of the good and therefore rival comprehensive doctrines fairly. Even if Rawls would be reluctant to identify with this description, his idea, however original it may be, is ultimately only a variant of the core intuition motivating contractarian political philosophy generally.

In the final analysis, then, political liberalism falls within the contractarian mold. Rawls may insist that political philosophy ought to distance itself from contentious philosophical positions, and he may maintain that political liberalism is political precisely because it does so. But, in the end, the Rawls of *Political Liberalism* is a contractarian, just as the Rawls of *A Theory of Justice* claimed to be and genuinely was. What mainly distinguishes Rawls's view of political legitimacy from those of his contractarian predecessors is only that he is more ecumenical than they were. Instead of looking to philosophical doctrines that could be reasonably rejected in light of the burdens of judgment, he would appeal instead to principles that no one can reasonably reject. Rawls's innovation, then, is his claim that such consent is forthcoming, at least in principle, from all reasonable persons – that is, from the vast majority of the citizens of liberal regimes.

6

Marx

Karl Marx's (1818–83) work stands apart from the story of modern political philosophy. Marx was a critic of the individualism that has shaped political theory from Hobbes through Rawls; and Marx's attitude towards the state was, in some respects, out of line with the Hobbesian view of its timeless necessity, a conviction nearly all modern political philosophers share. Above all, Marx's radical political vision, his notion of what is humanly possible, and his politics, his sense of how to get from where we now are to that point, differed profoundly from that of even such progressive liberal thinkers as Mill and Rawls. But Marx's thought is nevertheless relevant to modern political philosophy, not just because of its role in the political history of the past two centuries, but for philosophical reasons as well. It is appropriate, therefore, to conclude these encounters with modern political philosophy with Marx – for the perspective his ideas cast on the thought of the authors already discussed, and also for the timeliness of some of his distinctive theoretical contributions. This last contention may seem unlikely, given the disrepute into which the "ism" associated with Marx's name has fallen in recent years. It is nevertheless apt.

With the arguable exception of some of his early work, none of Marx's writings on political matters are directly philosophical in the strictest sense of the term. But a good deal of what Marx had to say about politics has important implications for many of the central concerns of modern political philosophy. The discussion here will focus specifically on three such issues: those that cluster around the concept of *alienation;* those that have to do with Marx's views on the connection between the *state* and *class struggle;* and those that pertain to Marx's *theory of history.* Of these topics, the first differs substantially from the other two, largely because alienation was a central concern of Marx's only in the early 1840s, when he was still a very young man. Few of Marx's writings from this period were known until well after the Russian Revolution (1917), and none were widely read until the 1950s. This aspect of Marx's thinking therefore had hardly anything to do with the "Marxism" that emerged after Marx's death in the 1880's. For the past half century, though, the young Marx has been an object of intense scrutiny. The reason why is clear: from the time that Marx*ism* emerged as a "comprehensive doctrine" almost until the collapse of Communism in 1989, theoreticians and militants of very different stripes wanted to appropriate the designation "Marxist" for themselves. There was therefore a perennial and unresolved debate about what "Marxism" is. By the end of the 1950s, Marx's early work played a crucial role in that essentially political contestation. Thus Marxist "humanists," for whom the young Marx was the true Marx, vied with defenders of Marxist orthodoxy, who were disposed to relegate the young Marx to virtual oblivion. This debate was never strictly academic, even when it raged within academic institutions. Its main participants were, in varying ways and to varying degrees, politically engaged. Therefore even the most scholarly work on the young Marx was politicized to a degree that is probably unprecedented in the history of Western thought.

But that was then, and this is now. Today, the "ism" associated with Marx's name appears to have suffered an historical defeat. What will emerge from the wreckage of one hundred years of this "ism" remains unclear. What is plain, however, is that, for the time being, the Marxist corpus, including Marx's early writings, can be read in a way that was not possible before. It is plain too that the various sides of the old debate overstated their positions, for reasons that were more political than philosophical. Nevertheless, it is clear that the concept of "alienation" that Marx developed in his early writings is not entirely of a piece with ideas evident in Marx's mature thinking. Even Marx himself proclaimed in *The German Ideology* (1845) that he had "settled accounts" with his "erstwhile philosophical conscience." It is wise, of course, not to exaggerate the extent to which Marx broke with his own past. But, in the end, one cannot deny the fundamental discontinuity internal to Marx's own intellectual development. The old debate on the young Marx has now subsided. But it is well to recognize, even so, that the side that emphasized discontinuities was more right than wrong. What follows here reflects this judgment.

The Young Marx

The young Marx was a Young Hegelian, a member of a philosophical
and political movement comprised of a number of outstanding individuals who, along with Marx himself, would go on to become leading intellectual figures in Germany – Bruno Bauer, Heinrich Heine, and, above
all, Ludwig Feuerbach. Feuerbach was the undisputed leader of the group;
to such an extent that it would only be a slight exaggeration to say that
Marx in this period was his intellectual disciple.

The world of the Young Hegelians is remote and strange, but some
sense of it can be obtained by reflecting on their own understanding of
their philosophical and historical mission. To be sure, the Young Hegelians
were hardly of one mind on anything, including their own place in the
history of philosophy. Even so, at a very high level of generality, it is fair
to concoct a composite account. It is essentially the story told by Marx
himself in the 1843 "Introduction" to *Towards a Critique of Hegel's
Philosophy of Right* and resumed didactically, years later, by Friederich
Engels in *Ludwig Feuerbach and the Outcome of Classical German Philosophy* (1888). The story goes as follows. Philosophy, understood as a
way of concocting rationally compelling theories intended to make sense
of the world and of human beings' experience of it, began in ancient
Greece in the fourth century BC and culminated in Germany in the work
of Immanuel Kant. With Kant, it became clear, finally, that what philosophy had been about all along was, at least in part, developing and
then defending a certain notion of freedom, the idea that emerged in
Rousseau's political philosophy. But Kantian philosophy was wrought
with internal tensions, the resolution of which became the task of "classical German philosophy." That project was completed by Hegel, for
whom freedom was an essentially historical notion, embodied in institutional arrangements. It fell to Hegel too to ascertain the real structure of
what is and therefore, since, for him, the Real is the Rational, of human
knowledge of it. This structure is dialectical – a process of *becoming* in
which what is, an *affirmation* or *thesis,* develops its own *negation* or
antithesis with which it is in internal opposition or *contradiction* until its
two contradictory moments are incorporated into a higher unity, a *synthesis* or *supersession (Aufhebung)*. But, the story goes, Hegel's philosophy, because it was idealist, was incapable by itself of realizing freedom.
That task was taken up by the Young Hegelians, including Marx; *materialists* bent on making lived experience Rational, as Hegel had revealed
it to be in principle, but not (yet) in fact. Thus the Young Hegelians saw

themselves as the heirs of the materialist and Hegelian traditions of Western thought and, as such, as the emancipators of humankind. They struggled to put these various strains of theory and practice together, partly succeeding with Feuerbach's "critique" of religious experience in *The Essence of Christianity* (1841). But it fell to Marx, standing above the rest and eventually in opposition to the other Young Hegelians, to develop a properly materialist and dialectical purchase on the world. How he accomplished this feat is, to this day, a matter of dispute. According to Marx himself in the *Theses on Feuerbach* (1845), he did so by developing a notion of *praxis*, of goal directed material activity in which the subject and object of knowledge mutually and interactively constitute one another. It is this rather obscure notion that the Marxist humanists made their own. But also, in contemporaneous writings such as *The German Ideology,* Marx claimed to have done precisely what orthodox Marxists claim he did – inaugurate a new science, the science of history.

Marx also came to believe that the task of changing the world fell to the proletariat, to those who, in the words of *The Communist Manifesto*, had "nothing to lose but their chains." Thus, for him, it was the mission of the proletariat, whether through its revolutionary *praxis* or guided by a correct, revolutionary theory informed by a science of history, to realize the aims of classical German philosophy and thereby the goals of philosophy itself. Reason, which Kant had already identified with freedom, implied revolution; and for that implication to be made actual, "the arm of criticism" had to pass, as Marx proclaimed in the 1843 "Introduction," into "the criticism of arms." Then, after a socialist revolution, with humanity fully emancipated, the immanent goal of a twenty-five hundred year project would finally be achieved. Philosophy would come to an end. Like so much else in humanity's pre-history, it would be "superseded" in communism.

This bold and, to contemporary eyes, peculiar narrative, according to which philosophy *ends* in a social revolution that liberates humankind, does indeed have conceptual roots in post-Kantian German philosophy and, especially, in the work of Hegel. Fortunately, however, it will be unnecessary here to recount more than the main contours of its history. Nevertheless, some background is indispensable, if only because the concept of alienation is hardly self-explanatory. Without reference to its origins, the Young Hegelians' amalgam of naive political optimism and recondite philosophical theorizing would be incomprehensible.

It is crucial to note that Feuerbach, along with the other Young Hegelians, was, first of all something that Kant himself, according to his own repeated declarations, emphatically was not. Feuerbach was a *philosophical anthropologist*. In his view, all outstanding philosophical questions, whether theoretical or practical, are ultimately questions about essential humanity – that is, about human nature understood in a (vaguely) metaphysical rather than in a straightforwardly psychological or empirical way. Philosophy, after Kant, had taken a transcendental turn; it had become "criticism" in the sense of Kant's *Critiques*. Its aim was to establish "the conditions for the possibility" of one or another form of experience. For Feuerbach, then, because he was both a successor of Kant and a philosophical anthropologist, the point of philosophy or rather of the critical program into which philosophy had been transformed after Kant was to reveal the *human meaning* behind the various, apparently heterogeneous ways that experience presents itself. In this sense, a philosophical anthropology is a general theory of everything; an account of what everything ultimately *means*. And, in the end, everything ultimately means the same thing because everything has a *human* meaning. For the Young Hegelians, then, as for Hegel himself, the real is ultimately One. It is a unity in a process of becoming. The goal of philosophy is to grasp this one real essence as it *becomes* itself. The difference is that, for the Young Hegelians, what is ultimately real is understood anthropologically; it is the human essence.

  This view was controversial in its time and place, but not for its obscurity or for any of a host of other reasons that a contemporary reader might suppose. Virtually all intellectual life in Germany in the early 1840s identified with Hegel's philosophy. Hardly anyone opposed Hegelism in the name of a rival philosophical vision. Instead, exponents of widely disparate theoretical and political positions wrapped themselves in the mantle of Hegel's thought. Thus it was a consensus view that Hegel was not just one philosopher among others, and not even the latest major entrant in an unfolding line of great philosophers. Rather, by all accounts, Hegel was the last philosopher, the one who had finally got everything, or nearly everything, as right as could be while still remaining within the ambit of the philosophical project. The next step, for the Young Hegelians, was to leave that ambit altogether – to move *beyond* philosophy by making the Real actual, not just at the level of thought, as Hegel had already succeeded in doing, but in practice too.

  This was why philosophy was destined to come to an end under communism. In communist societies, life would somehow be transparent; the gap between appearance and reality that made philosophy necessary would cease to exist. Thus the Young Hegelians, including Marx for as long as he remained in their camp, looked forward to the replacement of phil-

osophy by a more direct form of self-understanding and cognitive relation to the world. The Young Hegelians saw themselves as agents of this
epochal transformation. It was their burden to take philosophy or, rather,
criticism as far as it could go – by setting the Hegelian dialectic on a
materialist course. Their mission was to *correct* Hegel by liberating the
dialectic, the rational kernel of Hegelian philosophy, from its outer, idealist shell. To realize this objective would be to abolish philosophy by
removing its reason for being. It was, after all, the experience of opacity
that made philosophy necessary, and that had sustained it for nearly
twenty-five hundred years. By revealing the human meaning underlying
all forms of experience, criticism would explode this condition forever.
There would then be nothing more to do, for those who see the world as
it really is, except to change experience itself, to collapse the difference
between the actual and the real by revolutionizing the actual. It would be
difficult to imagine a more politically charged philosophical enterprise.
At stake, was nothing less than the final and unequivocal realization of
the Idea of freedom.

Philosophy of History

The widespread belief that Hegel's philosophy was as sound as any philosophy could be carried over to Hegel's philosophy of history, where
the debate between the Young Hegelians and their Right Hegelian rivals
was not over Hegel's philosophy of history itself, but over its political
implications. The Right Hegelians believed that the *Rechtstaat* Hegel had
theorized, the state based on universal principles of Right (*Recht*), already existed in Prussia. They therefore maintained that Reason entailed
respect for the institutional arrangements in place. In contrast, the Young
Hegelians saw the Prussian state as the highest and therefore the final
embodiment of unfreedom, awaiting a revolution that would at last make
the actual correspond to the Real. By their own account, the Young
Hegelians were revolutionaries because they were Hegelians; because they
thought that Hegel's philosophy of history implied the need to revolu-
tionize the social and political institutions under which they lived.

The Right Hegelians were, for the most part, Protestant theologians;
a fact that partly explains why Feuerbach's masterwork, *The Essence
of Christianity*, focused on Protestant theology. The Young Hegelians
did battle with their rivals on the enemy's own terrain. But given their
militant atheism, there is a certain irony in the fact that the Young
Hegelians, like their Right Hegelian opponents, adhered so zealously to

Hegel's account of human history. For, despite its secular content, the roots of Hegel's philosophy of history lie within Christian thought. Philosophies of history of the kind Hegel deployed are all, in a sense, theodicies, justifications of God's ways or, in Hegel's own case, of the ways of some secular functional equivalent of God. It is instructive, in fact, to look back to St. Augustine's *City of God*, composed after 410 AD, in the aftermath of the sacking of Rome by the Goths, for a prototype. Augustine sought to make sense of human history – or, at least, of that part of it through which the Roman Empire was passing – retrospectively, from the standpoint of history's *telos* or *end*, a vantage-point that he, like Hegel, thought he could assume because it was already nearly at hand. Augustine's telling of the story of human history or, rather, of the swathe of it that mattered for his theology, implied an account of history's structure and direction. Thus Augustine "explained" history itself in addition to proffering various explanations for particular historical events. The key structuring moments in his account of human history came, of course, from Christian theology. They include the Creation, the Fall, the Resurrection, and the Final Judgment; and it is from the standpoint of the Final Judgment, literally the end of human history as well as its *telos*, that Augustine set out to make sense of what had come before. Hegel's philosophy of history recounts a very different story, that of the career of Freedom. But the idea that history as such can be explained by telling a story from the vantage-point of its end, and the corresponding idea that what it is to make sense of history is to discern its real structure and direction, were Augustinian. That a philosophy of history of this sort arose in a Christian context is, on reflection, unsurprising. A world religion like Christianity that grounds its legitimacy on what it takes to be an historical event – in this case, the redemption of the human race through Christ's suffering and resurrection – calls for a sweeping historical narrative into which that event can be inserted, and from which it derives its meaning. Augustine rose to the task of concocting an appropriate story. Nearly a millennium and a half later, Hegel followed in his path.

Vantage-points are, of course, relative to the particular positions individuals occupy. But for philosophers of history of the Augustinian–Hegelian type, the narrative that explains human history itself is *objective*. It is relative to no particular position or, more precisely, to no arbitrarily assumed perspective. Augustine's and Hegel's idea, then, is that there is a definitive vantage-point from which the story of history can be told – the vantage-point provided by history's *end*. From that non-arbitrary position, the story that unfolds renders the past intelligible, and makes the real structure and directionality of history evident. But because this perspective is only one point of view, it excludes everything that falls outside its horizon. It therefore excludes nearly everything that happened in the past – not just for pragmatic reasons, because there is not time enough to recount it all, but because most of what happened is irrelevant from the perspective from which the story of history is told. There are entire peoples, then, whose pasts fall outside the scope of human history. Had Augustine been aware of the existence of civilizations beyond the ken of Rome's empire – in China, say, or in sub-Saharan Africa – he would have had to conclude that the Chinese and the sub-Saharan Africans were peoples without a history. They have no histories because their pasts play no role in the *objectively true* story he tells. Hegel's view of the world was, of course, more cosmopolitan. It could hardly have been otherwise, since, as a modern, he had access to knowledge of the earth and its inhabitants that Augustine did not, and since geographical separation mattered much less in the eighteenth and nineteenth centuries than it did in the fifth. Still the story of the career of the Idea of freedom excludes nearly everything that has happened in humanity's past – and, indeed, literally everything that ever happened outside the Eurasian landmass. For Hegel too, many of the world's inhabitants belong to peoples without histories.

The idea that history itself has an explanation is foreign to mainstream historical writing. History is a non-theoretical discipline. It proceeds on the assumption that virtually anything that has already happened can count as an historical *explanandum*, an object of historical explanation, and that virtually any way of making sense of an historical explanandum counts as an historical explanation. But even if every historical event, no matter how it is identified, can in principle be explained, it still makes no sense, in the mainstream view, to say that history itself can be explained. Not even a trivial explanation, produced by joining all particular historical explanations together, is possible because, in order to concoct such a conjunction in a way that would explain history as such, there would have to be a theoretically well motivated way to divide the past into discrete, mutually exclusive parts; and that is exactly what it is impossible to do in the absence of a theory that constrains what counts as an historical explanandum. Philosophies of history of the Augustinian–Hegelian type therefore stand apart from contemporary understandings of history. In his analyses of revolutionary episodes of contemporaneous European (especially French) history, Marx showed himself to be an historian of the first rank, according to the usual understandings of what historical writing involves. Even so, he never abandoned the idea of a theory of history. In fact, he systematically integrated the historical explanations he advanced into his own distinctive account of history's structure and direction. To do so, however, he had first to transform the Augustinian–Hegelian idea of what a theory of history is. We will find that Marx's own theory of history, as it emerges in his mature writings, differs substantially from the theory he assumed in his early works.

The Criticism of Religion

Feuerbach's central contention was that the principle Christian theological doctrine, that God makes Man, represents in an "inverted" form the essential human truth that Man makes God. In other words, for Feuerbach, the idea of God is an "externalization" or "objectification" or, as we might say today, a *projection* of essential human traits. God is an *alienated* (literally, separated) expression of essential humanity in which the human essence stands apart from its real subject. But the idea of God is also utterly insubstantial inasmuch as there is nothing *material* or mind-independent about this "object" onto which essential humanity is projected. Thus the God-idea and the various notions that cluster around it, many of which Feuerbach reconstructed and then interpreted in *The Essence of Christianity*, provide an especially perspicuous access to essential humanity. They reveal the human essence without any material admixture whatsoever. Therefore, to fully grasp the God idea, to discern the human meaning that it represents, is to gain an unadulterated purchase on what human beings essentially are.

Because they were still in the sway of Hegel's philosophy of history, the Young Hegelians believed that the theology of the Right Hegelians, being an expression of religious experience in the "final" stage of human history, represented the "highest" expression of religious consciousness. It represented the human essence in its most alienated form. This is why, for them, the theology of the Right Hegelians was the philosopher's stone, the key to a correct philosophical anthropology. For Feuerbach, everything ultimately means the same thing; everything has a human meaning. But the royal road to uncovering this meaning, in its specificity, is through the criticism of religion in its highest, most alienated, form. It is crucial, moreover, that this meaning be grasped in its specificity. Only then will awareness of it work its emancipatory effects.

In many respects, Feuerbach's critical program anticipated Freudian psychoanalysis, and may even have served as a model for it. For Freud, psychoanalysis, a theory of unconscious mental life, explains many phenomena. But the "royal road" to this theory lies through only some of the phenomena that it helps to explain. Thus it was by analyzing the utterances of patients undergoing psychoanalysis, psychiatric patients who presented symptoms of clinical interest, that Freud developed and, throughout his life, revised psychoanalytic theory. Once the theory was constructed however, it could be applied elsewhere – to the analysis of literary texts, for example, or to jokes or slips of the tongue and other non-clinical aspects of daily life. Thus Freud constructed a general theory, explanatorily pertinent to a wide range of phenomena, on the basis of a kind of evidence that provides privileged access to the structure and dynamics of unconscious mental life. It is therefore fair to say that, for Freud, psychoanalytic therapy is to a general theory of the unconscious what the criticism of religion is to Feuerbach's general theory of everything, his philosophical anthropology.

Despite some rhetorically inspired but intemperate claims of Marx's at the beginning of *The German Ideology*, neither Feuerbach nor any other Young Hegelian, including Marx himself before 1845, believed that discerning the human meaning behind the various forms of lived experience would directly change the world. What criticism does, for those who take it to heart, is change the way the world is apprehended. Criticism brings about a change of standpoint, a "taking consciousness" – not dissimilar, ironically, to the conversion experience promoted in the Lutheran tradition the Young Hegelians inveighed against. In the case of religion, because there is, as it were, no there there, this taking consciousness is directly liberating. The criticism of religion emancipates whoever takes it to heart from the thrall of religious experience. In this respect too, an analogy with psychoanalysis or, rather, with psychoanalytic therapy is evident. For Freud, when patients attain a full-fledged understanding of the connection between their particular symptoms and the general theory of the unconscious, an understanding that is affective as well as cognitive, there is a change of perspective, a *taking consciousness,* that is, in a sense, *emancipatory.* This is why the insight psychoanalysis provides is therapeutic. It liberates patients from the underlying causes of the symptoms they present.

For Feuerbach's general theory of everything to apply generally, for it to explain forms of experience that, unlike religion, have a genuinely materialist (mind-independent) dimension, and for it to emancipate humankind in these material domains, taking consciousness alone is plainly not enough. The material world, not just its representations in thought, must be transformed as Reason requires. As Marx said in the famous eleventh *Thesis on Feuerbach*, "the philosophers have so far only understood the world; the point, however, is to change it." Changing the world is indispensable for seeing it aright. But it was also Marx's view that the kind of understanding criticism fosters is useful, perhaps even indispensable, for changing the world. Before the world can be made right, therefore, its human meaning must be discerned. Feuerbach showed the way. After him, the task was to extend the range of application of the critical program by revealing the human meaning behind *other* aspects of human experience.

It was with this thought in mind that Marx declared, at the beginning of the 1843 "Introduction," that "the criticism of religion" is essentially complete. It had been completed by Feuerbach. Thanks to Feuerbach, a sound philosophical anthropology awaited deployment in other domains. Thus it had become feasible, finally, to turn to the criticism of the real world conditions that generate human suffering; conditions that make religion, the "opium of the people," necessary. Marx's famous expression is telling, and not at all dismissive, as it is often assumed to be. Feuerbach's point, with which Marx agreed, was not that religious claims are literally false – that went without saying – but that they represent a certain human reality in an alienated form. For Marx, this reality includes human affect as well as human knowledge and volition, as anyone schooled, as Marx was, in the Romantic tradition in German thought would insist. Thus religious suffering is an expression of real suffering, but also a relief from it. With a true philosophical anthropology at hand, however, it is possible to move beyond this opiate to a genuine cure. The next step in the critical program, then, is a critique of the material conditions that makes religion necessary, a critique of the law and the state as they come together in the *Rechtstaat*, described and defended by Hegel in *The Philosophy of Right*.

The Critical Program

The term Right (*Recht*) is easily translated into the Romance languages (*droit*, *diritto*, etc.), but it has no exact English equivalent, except perhaps the awkward expression "public law and government." A *Rechtstaat* is a state based on universal principles institutionally embodied, on the idea of *Recht*. It is a regime in which all are equal in the political sphere; in which, therefore, according to the well-known quip, rich and poor, being equally subject to the law, are equally unfree to sleep under the bridges. In short, the *Rechtstaat* represents Rousseau's notion of equal citizenship in institutional form. Marx in 1843 maintained that it is these institutions that are the real, material causes of the suffering that religion expresses and also relieves in its own spurious and therefore ultimately ineffective way. This is why, with the criticism of religion completed, Hegel's *Philosophy of Right* should be taken on next. For it is in that work, Marx believed, that the fullest and most developed account of the institutions that comprise the *Rechtstaat* can be found. In other words, in Marx's view, Hegel got Right (*Recht*) right – in roughly the way that Feuerbach believed that the Right Hegelians got religion right. To *criticize* Hegel's *Philosophy of Right* in the way that Marx proposed is therefore not to fault it, as the term "criticism" usually connotes, nor is it to advance a different, ostensibly better philosophy of Right. Rather, Marx's aim was to do for *The Philosophy of Right* what Feuerbach had done for Right Hegelian theology – to reveal the human meaning that the *Rechtstaat*, like everything else, expresses. His aim was to "translate" what Hegel described into the philosophical anthropology Feuerbach had discovered.

Needless to say, neither Marx nor Feuerbach nor any other Young Hegelian had taken the "linguistic turn" of twentieth-century analytical philosophy. The Young Hegelians were concerned with ideas, thoughts and feelings and, in Marx's case, institutional forms, not linguistic expressions. But this difference aside, it is fair to depict Feuerbachian criticism as a translation program; one in which descriptively adequate representations of forms of experience are translated into Feuerbach's philosophical anthropology. The translations of the Young Hegelians differed, however, from ordinary translations in a crucial respect. To translate, say, German into English is only to establish equivalences between German and English words or expressions. The translation leaves the German and English languages intact. But there is a sense in which the translations the Young Hegelians advanced aimed to *eliminate* the "language" translated into the "language" of Feuerbach. The criticism of religion provided the model. Once the human meaning of Christian doctrine was revealed, Christianity itself was dissolved into the anthropological truths its theology expressed. Christian theology was, as philosophers today might say, *reduced* away – into Feuerbach's philosophical anthropology. In these terms, the critical program is a reduction program; one that establishes equivalences for the sake of eliminating forms of experience or, more precisely, eliminating their illusory and freedom diminishing dimensions. This, again, is why the Young Hegelians took their explanations of particular phenomena to be emancipatory. And this too is why there is a problem in extending the critical program beyond its original field of application. Even if Hegel's philosophy of Right can be successfully reduced into Feuerbach's philosophical anthropology, the institutions Hegel described, unlike the "objects" of religious experience, because they are real (material), do not disappear when their human meaning is revealed. What Hegel described in *The Philosophy of Right* must ultimately be revolutionized in practice. Only then will humanity be free from the *Rechtstaat's* thrall.

Therefore, even if Feuerbach's philosophical anthropology really were a true general theory of everything, it cannot be applied to everything in the way that Feuerbach's own example suggests. It was this thought or rather its implications, once he had thought them through, that led Marx, eventually, to leave the Young Hegelian fold. But the idea was already implicit in Marx's writings before his self-declared break from Feuerbach's circle. In *On the Jewish Question*, for example, a response to Bruno Bauer's reflections on Jewish emancipation after the French Revolution, written in the same year as the 1843 "Introduction," Marx reflected further on the Rousseauean–Hegelian – and, by the early nineteenth century, also liberal – notion of political equality. Because this text focuses on the political aspirations of the French revolutionaries, it is appropriate to examine Marx's reflections from this standpoint.

One of Marx's principal concerns in *On the Jewish Question*, as in the 1843 "Introduction," was to defend *human* as distinct from strictly *political* emancipation. As a liberal, Bauer was a proponent of political emancipation. He wanted, for Germany, what the French Revolution had established in France – a regime based on the principle of equal citizenship rights for all. Equal citizenship would, in Bauer's view, solve the "Jewish Question," the problem of the subordination of the Jews in Christian societies, because where gentiles and Jews are equal as citizens, sectarian affiliations would cease to matter politically. Being a Jew would then be a matter of private conscience only. The Jewish Question would therefore lose its significance because being a Jew or, for that matter, a Christian would no longer be politically consequential. Thus, the problem of subordination would be overcome. In defending human emancipation against Bauer's advocacy of political emancipation only, Marx was therefore obliged to confront the legacy of the French Revolution. Like all progressive thinkers of his time, he believed that the Revolution represented a great leap forward in human history. But he was also aware, more than a half century after the event, that the French Revolution was, at best, "incomplete." The French Revolutionaries had hardly eliminated all human causes of human misery, even where, as in France, they were, on the whole, successful. They had not established "heaven on earth" or, as Feuerbach might have said, restored the vision of heaven to its rightful earthly place. It is therefore not enough, Marx insisted, to bring Germany to the present level of France. Jewish emancipation requires more than political equality; it requires the radical transformation of the entire social structure that sustains Judaism, and Christianity too, and the consequent liberation of humankind itself. Contrary to Bauer's views, the Jewish Question will never be solved simply by conferring citizenship rights on Jews. To make the Jews free, it is necessary to alter the material conditions that make religious consciousness of any sort both necessary and possible. As was implicit in Feuerbach's critique of Protestant theology and as Marx all but said outright in the 1843 "Introduction," humankind will not be fully free until both Judaism and Christianity and, by implication, other forms of religiosity too disappear altogether from human life, not just from the political sphere.

In *On the Jewish Question*, Marx was already groping towards an idea that would dominate his mature thinking – that the way to gain a proper purchase on human freedom, in both theory and practice, is by focusing on the sphere of production, distribution, and exchange; in short, on the economy, as the emerging science of political economy was coming to conceive it. The French Revolution established Rousseauean citizenship in only one aspect of human life, the political sphere. By 1843, Marx was already becoming convinced that the domain of *Recht*, of public law and government, even if it is the material base of religious consciousness in the stage of human history through which the world was passing, was ultimately of only secondary importance. The *Rechtstaat* was not the fundamental problem. Thus, two years before *The German Ideology* and the *Theses on Feuerbach*, Marx was straining against the strictures of Feurbach's thought. While he was still ready to concede that everything ultimately refers back to the alienation of Man from His Essence, and while he was still prepared to believe that taking consciousness of human alienation is an indispensable stage in the realization of the Idea of Freedom, he already maintained, wittingly or not, that not all forms of experience are of equal importance in the struggle for freedom. Already in 1843, Marx began to insist that, with political emancipation, unfreedom – construed in the Rousseauean way, as *heteronomy* – was effectively displaced from the political sphere into civil society and, above all, into the economic arena. A year later, in the 1844 *Paris Manuscripts*, Marx even implied that, in being so displaced, unfreedom actually intensified. Thus Marx thought that despite "political emancipation" in France and elsewhere, humanity was still unfree; indeed, that in the most politically advanced countries – where, not unrelatedly, proletarianization was also most advanced – humanity awaited emancipation more than ever. Paradoxically, though, in consequence of its political backwardness, a condition emphasized repeatedly in the 1843 "Introduction," a German revolution can definitively liberate humankind. Because there are no institutions worth maintaining in Germany, the Germans can leapfrog over the French Revolutionary stage; they can affect a full-fledged transformation of all aspects of their lives. And because German philosophy had already advanced beyond the horizon of 1789, because it had arrived at a correct, though still philosophical, understanding of freedom, the German revolutionaries, Marx maintained, would know what institutions to put in place. Therefore, when the time is ripe for the transition from criticism to revolutionary practice, it will be possible, in German conditions, to skip the stage of political emancipation, and to realize in practice what had already been achieved in thought, a thoroughgoing liberation of all of humankind. Contrary to Bauer's liberal hopes, Jewish emancipation depends, ultimately, on nothing less than full human emancipation – in other words, on the impending German Revolution. No imitation, decades later, of the Revolution in France will suffice.

There was an additional factor that led Marx to focus on the economic sphere. It had to do with Marx's own emerging philosophical anthropology. For Marx, even more than for Feuerbach, becoming fully human, self-realizing, was less a matter of *being* than of *doing*. In this respect, the young Marx was very much an Aristotelian, and an opponent of the utilitarians. For the utilitarians, though perhaps not unequivocally for Mill (see chapter 4), what matters intrinsically is well-being; and well-being, however variously it is understood, is always a state of being – perhaps even a state of consciousness, like pleasure. In contrast, the human being of Marx's philosophical anthropology is a *doer*; it is *functionings*, not states of being, that matter intrinsically. Thus it emerged, unmistakably by 1845, in *The German Ideology*, but already implicitly in *On the Jewish Question* and in the 1844 *Paris Manuscripts*, that human beings are essentially productive animals.

In this respect, despite his focus on functionings, Marx parted ways with Aristotle too. For Aristotle, it was contemplative, not practical, functionings that mattered preeminently. Because he deemed rationality to be a distinctly human trait, Aristotle deemed Man to be essentially a rational animal. Marx's emphasis was different. For him, what it is to be distinctively human is to engage in creative, productive activity or, as we might say today, in "meaningful work." Human beings are, by nature, *producers*. Thus it is political economy, the science of production (along with distribution and exchange) that, more than any other representation of human experience, reflects essential humanity. If the critical program is to fulfill its explanatory mission, it must therefore turn to this sphere.

Alienated Labor

This was the task that Marx undertook in the 1844 *Paris Manuscripts*, a text that reveals both the extent of Marx's commitment to Feuerbachian criticism but also, thanks to the explanatory preeminence Marx accorded political economy, his emerging differences with Feuerbach and the other Young Hegelians. It is in the *Paris Manuscripts* too, in the section on "Alienated Labor" that concludes the first manuscript, that Marx presented his most direct account of the concept of alienation – as the term applies to labor, the activity that Marx was coming increasingly to identify with essential human or, as he called it there, *generic activity*. The text is difficult to decipher, especially in translation. For one thing, two German words used throughout the section on "Alienated Labor," *Entfremdung* (estrangement) and *Entäusserung* (externalization), are commonly translated as "alienation." This is regrettable, but excusable, inasmuch as Marx used these words interchangeably, failing to distinguish systematically the rather different ideas they express. Marx also spoke in that text of four distinct aspects of alienated labor. There is, first of all, alienation from the *product of labor*. In Marx's account, the worker who makes a product fills the role that Man making God played in *The Essence of Christianity*. In the act of producing, the worker externalizes essential human traits, *objectifying* essential humanity. Then there is alienation from the *process of labor*. Generic activity, the doing that is essentially human, becomes foreign or estranged to the doer, the human producer. There is also alienation from *"species-being,"* an obscure notion of Feuerbach's meaning, roughly, awareness of one's own essential humanity, of being a member of the human "species." Finally, there is alienation from one's *fellow human beings* – in other words, from essential humanity in others, from the human community. In Feuerbach's view and also in Marx's, consciousness of species-being in oneself and others is essential to being human. The goal of the critical project, again, was to arrive at an emancipatory understanding of the human condition or, at least, of that part of it that is a consequence of human activity. In Feuerbach's case, the realization that the essence of Christianity is ultimately the human essence eliminates Christianity. Marx imported the Feuerbachian notion of "reducing" experience away into his own critical explanations in political economy. But, in this context, even more than when his focus was Hegel's *Philosophy of Right*, it is not clear what a theoretical reduction implies. For products of labor, even if they are "objectifications" of essential humanity, are also, undeniably, material things. Taking consciousness of their human meaning will not free any-one from their domination. It will not make persons any less subject to the "laws" of political economy. But it is precisely these laws, because they are not willed by those they regulate, that render persons unfree. In what sense, then, is taking consciousness of political economy's human meaning emancipating? It was perhaps because there is no satisfactory answer to this question that Marx's eventual break with Feuerbach was as far-reaching as it turned out to be. In any case, for the critical program to be deployed in this domain, there must be a body of "discourse" that correctly "mirrors" economic life; something that plays the role that the theology of the Right Hegelians played for Feuerbach or that Hegel's *Philosophy of Right* played for Marx the year before he drew up the *Paris Manuscripts*. That "mirroring" role was filled by those whom we today call the classical political economists – above all, by Adam Smith. It was Marx's view in 1844 that Smith got political economy right. Marx therefore had no intention of faulting Smith's economics. It was his aim instead to submit it to an eliminative translation program; specifically, to reduce it to Feuerbach's philosophical anthropology. Thus, in the *Paris Manuscripts*, Marx provided a "critique" of political economy in the Feuerbachian, not the ordinary, sense of the term.

In this respect, the contrast between the young and the mature Marx is as stark as could be. From the 1850s on, Marx devoted himself to the "critique" of political economy in precisely the ordinary sense of the term. In his work anticipating the three volumes of *Capital*, in *Capital* itself, and then in the three lengthy tomes published posthumously under the title *Theories of Surplus Value*, Marx set out to fault and then to transform classical political economy, to construct a better, alternative economic science. It is noteworthy too, for a reason that will emerge presently, that, as this critique unfolded, Marx's view of the respective merits of the political economists changed. It came to be David Ricardo, not Adam Smith, who was the preeminent "bourgeois" economist in Marx's view, and it was Ricardo's work, accordingly, that Marx was mainly concerned to address critically. But, then, one would not expect a very young man, working in the Young Hegelian fold, living in Germany and then, briefly, in France, but not yet in England, to be thoroughly versed in the literature of the English political economists. Marx's ac-quaintance with Ricardo's work in 1844 was still slight. But as the first of the *Paris Manuscripts* attests, Marx did know Smith's work well. And in 1844 he was determined to subject it to a Feuerbachian critique. Thus, if we allow the anachronistic but nevertheless appropriate use of "dis-course" to stand for what Marx, following Feuerbach, somehow conceived of non-linguistically, the explanatory strategy undertaken in the *Paris Manuscripts* can be represented in the following way:

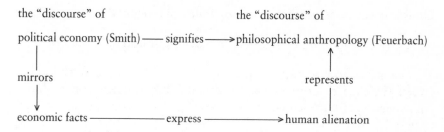

That this general picture obtains was, of course, a tenet of Young Hegelian thought. Feuerbach's philosophical anthropology, representing human alienation, is a general theory of everything, and therefore of descriptively adequate representations of economic facts. Marx's aim, then, was not to establish this position, but to implement it; to show how Smith could be "translated" into Feuerbach. To continue the analogy with psychoanalysis, Marx was in the position of a psychoanalyst, already committed to psychoanalytic theory, helping a patient understand how that theory explains the condition for which the patient is undergoing psychoanalytic treatment.

Because Marx never published the *Paris Manuscripts* and therefore never redacted them carefully, and because, in those manuscripts, Marx was inclined to lapse into an exuberant Hegelian style, philosophizing more by playing on words than by constructing arguments, it requires substantial work on the reader's part to reconstruct his critique of political economy in a cogent way. In that spirit, I would propose that, in the section on "Alienated Labor" and then, less directly, throughout the third of the *Paris Manuscripts*, Marx effectively concocted a lexicon or translation manual intended literally to establish equivalences of meaning between political economic terms and philosophical anthropological terms.

His warrant for doing so was a straightforward play on words. At the beginning of the section on "Alienated Labor," having already recounted Smith's work earlier in the first manuscript, Marx declared that his own account of political economy would begin with an "economic fact," the impoverishment of the worker as the worker creates wealth. What Marx had in mind, it seems, was the so-called Iron Law of Wages, a doctrine of the classical political economists, according to which workers' wages tend to fall to a subsistence level, and also the conviction, equally uncontroversial in the economic theory of the time, that the worker's labor is the source of wealth. Thus Marx proclaimed the following equivalences:

labor of the worker = means for maintaining individual life
labor of the worker = manifestation of species-being

On this basis, he then established the following identity:

means for maintaining individual life = manifestation of species-being

This identification or, rather, equivocation establishes a connection between the two discourses that warrants the construction of more
equivalences, as represented in the following translation manual or "dic-
tionary":[1]

Economy (Smith)	Philosophical Anthropology (Feuerbach)
product	object
labor	species-being (generic activity)
means of subsistence	means of life
capital	estranged being (*fremdes Wesen*)
worker	Man
exchange value	value (dignity: *Würde*)
exchange	community
wealth	*Sinnlichkeit* (sensuousness, the perceptible world)

Ultimately, what this translation manual suggests is an inversion of the
ideal relation between the actual and the real. The way the world appears is the opposite of the way it really is. Means are ends and ends are
means. For example, exchange value, the terms on which products of
labor exchange, is the form of appearance of "dignity" (*Würde*), the name
Kant and his successors gave to what Rousseau had in mind when he
deemed essential humanity *priceless*. And because capital, a thing, a product of human activity, is a *fremdes Wesen*, an estranged being that rules
human beings through its own "laws," the ideal person/thing relation is
inverted too. This is why, as Rousseau announced in *The Social Contract*, "man is born free, and everywhere he is in chains."

---

[1]   This "critical lexicon" is taken, in modified form, from a very useful essay by
Jacques Rancière, called "Le Concept de Critique et la Critique de l'Economie Politique
des *Manuscrits* de 1844 au *Capital*" in Louis Althusser, Etienne Balibar, et al., *Lire le
Capital*, vol. 1 (Paris: Maspero, 1967), pp. 99f. Unfortunately, this essay was not
included in the English version of *Reading Capital*, trans. Ben Brewster (London:
New Left Books, 1970). There is, however, an English translation published is in the
journal *Theoretical Practice*, no. 1 and 2 (1971). The account offered here of Marx's
program in the *Paris Manuscripts* draws substantially on Rancière's essay.

In a world of alienated labor, autonomy is lost. So far from being the masters of their own fates, persons are the "slaves," in Rousseau's sense, of the economic order they have created. What rules humankind is not literally another human being. But in the inverted world human beings have contrived, capital *is* a person; a being separate from the human beings who made it and whom it rules. What determines individuals' wills is an impersonal and unintended consequence of a host of individuals' activities, structured by the exchange relations that increasingly govern human interactions. Within this framework, individuals may choose rationally and deliberately. Indeed, individually rational choices constitute, unintentionally but inexorably, the estranged Being, capital, to whose laws individuals are bound. It is, therefore, the system itself that is irrational and beyond deliberate control; not its victims. But it is nevertheless through their *praxis*, their own practical world-building, world-transforming activity – the activity that creates *Sinnlichkeit*, the sensuous, perceptible world – that human beings enslave themselves. Only a (literally) revolutionary praxis, one that deliberately inverts the inverted world order that humankind has concocted for itself, can free them. This, in the end, is what Reason requires. By deliberately undoing the means/ends, person/thing relations emblematic of the regime of alienated labor, the real can finally become actual. Then Reason will be in control and autonomy, rational self-determination, will finally be realized. The human race will be free at last – not just in the political arena, but in all facets of life.

Marx in Transition

It is therefore in the *Paris Manuscripts* that we find Marx's first use of the notion of praxis, the key to his critique (in the ordinary, not the Feuerbachian sense) of Feuerbach in the *Theses on Feuerbach* and *The German Ideology*. It was in these texts, written just a year after the *Paris Manuscripts*, that Marx self-consciously set out "to settle accounts with his erstwhile philosophical conscience." But his settling of accounts was anything but complete. These works are transitional not only because, in them, Marx remained an Hegelian and therefore, despite himself, still in the grip of his "erstwhile philosophical conscience," but also because it was only after these texts that Marx's attention turned away from philosophy to political economy, history, and social theory. Once a break with Feuerbach was declared, however, Marx did abandon the critical program Feuerbach had contrived, taking up the explanatory strategies of modern science in its stead. The theoretical orientation of his work therefore shifted profoundly. Nevertheless, the general political and normative convictions evident in Marx's early writings survived into his later work. Marx never abandoned his overarching concern with human emancipation, and never altered his view of what it involves. In short, Marx broke with Feuerbach, but not with Rousseau. To the end of his life, he remained as much a partisan of autonomy as Rousseau was. It would therefore be fair to say that Marx remained true to the vision that motivated the Young Hegelian project. But in almost every other aspect of his theoretical work, he did eventually break as decisively as he claimed he did from the philosophical circle within which he came of age politically and intellectually. This break, however, was not yet fully accomplished in 1845, despite Marx's claims to the contrary. Thus, in his writings of that period, Marx's efforts to distance himself from Feuerbach were still couched, tellingly, in Hegelian terms and motivated by Hegelian concerns. Marx lauded Feuerbach's materialism and identified expressly with it. But he castigated Feuerbach for being insufficiently "dialectical" – for failing properly to appropriate the philosophical legacy of Hegel.

These themes were developed most directly in the *Theses on Feuerbach*. The "materialism" Marx defended there, Feuerbach's materialism, was a metaphysical position about the real substantial nature of things.[2] It is a position that only makes sense from within the tradition of thought that was the intellectual legacy of René Descartes's "invention" of modern philosophy in the seventeenth century, the tradition that ran from Descartes through Kant and then to Hegel. Descartes maintained that everything that is is either mental (non-spatial) or material (mind-independent) in its substantial nature. For a variety of reasons, including the need, recognized expressly by Descartes, to understand how mind and matter interact, most philosophers after Descartes abandoned his metaphysical dualism, the idea that there are two radically distinct kinds of being, mind and matter, adopting instead a monistic metaphysics, according to which everything that is is comprised of the same substance. Thus there were materialists, who regarded ostensibly mental phenomena as forms of appearance of matter, and idealists, for whom everything, including physical objects, were ultimately ideal or mental in nature. For a number of historically contingent reasons, it was part of the com-

---

[2] *Substance* was a category Descartes and his successors took over from their medieval predecessors. A substance is a category of being. As such, according to the received understandings, it is radically distinct from other substances.

mon sense of European political culture for nearly two hundred years that materialism implied or at least suggested both atheism and revolutionary politics, and that idealism supported theism and opposition to revolutionary change.[3] Classical German philosophy, from Kant through Hegel, was expressly idealist, as was the theology of the Right Hegelians. The Young Hegelians were materialists. Thus they identified with the atheism and the revolutionary politics of their materialist forebearers, especially in France before the French Revolution. Marx's complaint against them was that, in purporting to reconstruct Hegelian philosophy on a materialist basis, Feuerbach and his followers, including himself while he was still a disciple of Feuerbach's, effectively failed to take over from Hegel a proper sense of the interactive or "dialectical" relation between the subject and object of knowledge. This is the principal claim advanced and developed in the *Theses on Feuerbach*. The idea is implicit too in the first section of *The German Ideology*, where Feuerbach was also ostensibly the target.

In a word, throughout the *Theses on Feuerbach*, Marx insisted that Feuerbach was a Cartesian without knowing it, a follower of Descartes. For Descartes, the central epistemological problem was to grasp how the knowing subject, the "I" (the existence of which Descartes believed he had established with his celebrated *cogito* argument, summarized in the formula "I think, therefore I am") could come to know what is the case in the "external world." Ultimately, Descartes concluded that knowledge of the external world is possible only because an omnipotent, omniscient, and perfectly truthful God guarantees the veracity of certain of the I's ideas, those Descartes called "clear and distinct." Descartes' general view of the problem of knowledge remained in force, in one or another form, until Kant. Against it, Kant argued that to develop a theory of knowledge that could defeat skepticism, philosophers must take into account the knowing subject's contribution to knowledge. They must explain how the knowing subject, Descartes' I, supplies structure to what is "given" to it. This is what Kant set out to do. But to his successors, Kant's successes in this endeavor came at too great a cost. Kant made things-in- themselves, the reality that grounds appearance but that is not part of it, unknowable in principle. It was to defend the possibility of knowledge in this domain too, knowledge of the Real, that Hegel went

---

[3] This view persisted well into the twentieth century, in at least some quarters, thanks to the influence of one of the founding texts of official Soviet (and later Chinese) Marxist–Leninist philosophy, V. I. Lenin's *Materialism and Empirio-Criticism* (1905).

on to argue that things-in-themselves become comprehensible when it is understood that the subject and the object of knowledge constitute each other through their mutual interactivity. Schematically, these views of the relation between the subject and object of knowledge can be depicted as follows:

Descartes: Subject of knowledge   Object of knowledge
Kant: Subject of knowledge ———————→ Object of knowledge
Hegel: Subject of knowledge ←————————→ Object of knowledge

For Descartes, the subject and object of knowledge are radically distinct; for Kant, the knowing subject (partly) constitutes the object of knowledge; for Hegel, the subject and object of knowledge constitute one another in a process of becoming that culminates, in the end (which is also the end of history), in the establishment (or recovery) of an essential unity that overcomes the alienation (separation) of the one from the other.

Because he was persuaded that Hegel's view of the relation between the subject and the object of knowledge was sound, Marx sought to combine Feuerbach's materialism with Hegel's insistence on the interactive relation of the knower and the known. As already indicated, the concept he invoked for this purpose was *praxis*. In the first instance, *praxis* is just the Greek word for "practice." But, for philosophers after Aristotle, the term has a more specific connotation. Aristotle distinguished *praxis* from *poesis*. Aristotle's concern, again, was with what is distinctively human. Many animals are capable of *poesis,* of goal-directed activities. A lion, for example, can find its way to its prey. But, according to Aristotle, only human beings are capable of *praxis*, of purposeful activity undertaken for the sake of realizing an ideal. Following Feuerbach, Marx identified *praxis*, so conceived, with "practical sensuous activity" – the material (mind-independent) constitution of the perceptible "external world" (*Sinnlichkeit*). In consequence of the mutual interactivity of the subject and object of knowledge, this activity constitutes the knowing subject as well.

Marx's main charge in the *Theses on Feuerbach* was that Feuerbach failed to grasp the full implications of the essentially dialectical structure of the real. Specifically, he failed to realize that the human essence itself changes because it is continually created by praxis, just as the perceptible world is. Instead, Feuerbach conceived of the human essence as a timeless presence that human beings either externalize, as history unfolds, or incorporate, after history ends. It is this ahistorical view of essential humanity that Marx had in mind, for example, in the ninth *Thesis*, when he derogated Feuerbach's "perceptual materialism." In contrast, the materialism Marx endorsed accords primacy to the human collectivity, to what Rousseau called "the whole community." It is this collective subject, interacting with the external world, which constitutes both the individual and the human essence, and which is itself always in a process of *becoming*. In the tenth *Thesis*, Marx faulted the ahistoricity of Feuerbach's critical program, even when it is applied, as Marx himself had applied it, to civil society. Then, finally, from a standpoint that accords the concept of praxis its due, Marx declared, in the eleventh *Thesis*, that the goal of the philosophical project of interpretation can only be realized by changing the world the philosophers seek to understand. Thus the *Theses on Feuerbach* elaborate, from an Hegelian perspective, the thought implicit in the narrative sketched in the still Feurbachian 1843 "Introduction," according to which the culmination of the project of classical German philosophy requires nothing less than a genuine social revolution, a transformation of the social world, deliberately undertaken for the sake of an ideal.

However, in the kinds of explanations he provided, the Marx of *The German Ideology* did indeed break with his Feuerbachian past. When Marx was still a Feuerbachian critic, he supposed that to explain is to interpret, to uncover meanings or significances. In the natural sciences, however, the idea that phenomena have meanings had been abandoned long ago. In that domain, to explain a phenomenon is to subsume it under its relevant causal determinations. It is not a goal of the natural sciences to discover what phenomena mean. That would be a futile objective, in any case, since, on the modern view, there are no meanings to discover. The world science investigates just *is*; it means nothing or at least nothing that science can discern, even in principle. Thus the main explanatory goal of the natural sciences has long been to discover the causal structure of the world in which phenomena occur; to identify what Aristotle called "efficient causes," in contrast to the "final causes" of ancient and medieval science and of Hegel's philosophy of history. To be sure, because human action is intentional, interpretation is still an appropriate explanatory objective in historical writing and in other so-called human sciences. But it may also be the case, even for the phenomena that historians and social scientists investigate, that there exist causal relations awaiting discovery. We will see that Marx's mature theory of history makes precisely this claim; that it identifies real causal determinations.

The first intimations of that theory are evident in *The German Ideology*. There we find the beginnings of an account of history's structure and direction that is not teleological. Thus Marx set out an account of history's real *natural kind* divisions, identifying structural discontinuities within human history that have, in his view, genuine theoretical significance. Natural kind divisions contrast with convenient classifications. Classifications that do not represent theoretically meaningful natural kind divisions include, for example, in the theory of evolution, the Age of Mammals or the Age of Dinosaurs, and, in US History, the Age of Lincoln or the Progressive Era. These classifications represent investigators' interests, not real differences underwritten by theoretical claims. In contrast, "the capitalist mode of production" and the various pre-capitalist economic structures Marx identified in *The German Ideology* – "the feudal mode of production," for example, or "the ancient mode of production" or the "Asiatic mode" – do purport to be theoretically meaningful natural kind divisions.

This point is of some importance for understanding the limitations of the young Marx's reflections on alienation. According to Smith, the division of labor is the key to enhancing labor productivity. Thus it was an ever increasing division of labor that accounted for growth in "the wealth of nations," the phenomenon he was mainly concerned to explain. Therefore, in the *Paris Manuscripts*, where Marx assumed that Smith got political economy right, and where he took increasing wealth to signify a diminution of essential humanity, Marx maintained, implicitly, that it is the division of labor itself that explains human alienation and that is therefore responsible for intensifying human unfreedom. He could hardly have concluded otherwise. Smith did not have a developed concept of capitalism, and therefore neither did Marx. A concept of capitalism as a distinct mode of production and natural kind division of human history does appear, however, in *The German Ideology*.

But because the concept was unavailable to Marx a year earlier, it is unclear what a society without alienated labor would be like for the Marx of the *Paris Manuscripts*. Presumably, it would be a society without a developed division of labor. But, then, if Smith was right about the causes of the wealth of nations, a society where individuals were genuinely free (autonomous) in the economic sphere would be a society that is deficient with respect to wealth, to *Sinnlichkeit*. This is hardly a satisfactory view, as Marx himself must have realized. Perhaps this thought helped to motivate Marx, in *The German Ideology* and then in his later writings, to conceptualize an alternative to the world he sought to change. The first step in this process was to name the enemy – capitalism. The next step was to begin to envision an alternative to it. Beginning with *The German Ideology*, Marx conceived that alternative as a distinct *mode of produc-*

tion. In line with the usage of some of the more radical early nineteenth century French socialists, Marx called it *communism.*

Marx's development of the concept mode of production amounted to a conceptual breakthrough. Even so, his reflections on the communist mode of production in *The German Ideology* continue to show Feuerbach's influence. Thus his sketch of life in communist society reveals that, like Feuerbach, Marx still thought of essential humanity as a unified capacity, awaiting realization. As human beings self-actualize under communism, they become ever more able to do all kinds of things – to hunt in the morning, fish in the afternoon, raise cattle in the evening, and criticize at night. Needless to say, this is an unlikely view of human potentialities, made plausible only because the bucolic activities Marx mentions, with the possible exception of "criticism," do not require extensive training. Could anyone seriously contemplate human beings solving complex differential equations in the morning, fixing jet engines in the afternoon, filling cavities in the evening, and then performing as concert pianists at night! To self-realize in any one of these areas, it is necessary to dedicate a considerable portion of one's time and energy to cultivating the requisite capacities, to the detriment of other activities one might pursue. There is, however, a weaker claim that Marx may also have had in mind. It seems to have been Marx's view that freedom is diminished in a world in which people identify themselves with their economic tasks, where they are hunters, say, rather than people who hunt. Undifferentiated, self-realized human beings hunt because they freely choose to do so; hunters hunt because that is what hunters do. Then the claim would be that, under communism, there would only be freely chosen activities; people would perform tasks, but no one would have an occupation. But even if having an occupation does diminish freedom, an unlikely contention, this too is an implausible claim because self-realization typically involves *self-identification* with some activities to the exclusion of others. In general, one cannot self-realize through work without, as it were, making one's work one's own. Marx's idea seems to have been that fully self-realized human beings would be able to do more or less whatever they freely choose to do. Arguably, this is an attractive picture, but it is almost certainly utopian in the derogatory sense of the term. It is an impossible objective. Self-realization involves focusing efforts and identifying with them; not developing in all ways at once.

It is not surprising, therefore, that, after *The German Ideology*, Marx let this aspect of his philosophical anthropology lapse, without ever quite expressly repudiating it. Still, Marx's *German Ideology* reflections on communism express a viable message. The vision of communism that Marx sketched there contrasts in the extreme with the world of alienated labor that he had depicted the year before. The communism of *The German Ideology* is a world of maximal freedom (autonomy), while the world of alienated labor is a world of maximal unfreedom (heteronomy). This idea is retained in Marx's mature theory of history, and in the idea of communism that it underwrites.

It should be observed, finally, that Marx's sense of what is humanly possible differs radically from Hobbes's. For Marx, a world of maximal freedom (autonomy), so far from being a war of all against all, is a maximally harmonious regime in which, as Marx would say in *The Communist Manifesto*, "the condition for the free development of each is the free development of all." It is, in short, Rousseau's just state, generalized to encompass all aspects of social and economic life. This idea is already implicit in *The German Ideology*, though it is presented there in a utopian form. But it is not itself a utopian idea, as Marx's reflections on the state and on history make clear.

The State

Almost everything Marx wrote bore in one way or another on the state, especially in the last three decades of his life when his principal concern was to develop a theory of the capitalist mode of production and of its "laws of motion." For our purposes, however, it will suffice to focus on some of Marx's claims in *The Communist Manifesto* (co-authored with Friedrich Engels), where the general outline of a distinctively Marxist political theory, consonant with Marx's mature views on history and with his developing understanding of political economy, is established.

In *The Communist Manifesto*, Marx and Engels defined the state according to what it does, not according to how it operates. Throughout history, they claimed, the state organizes the *economically* dominant class into a *ruling* class – overcoming internal divisions that would otherwise render it unable to dominate subordinate classes and to sustain the mode of production from which it benefits; while, at the same time, encouraging internal divisions within subordinate classes. The state does so through historically specific institutions. Thus it is a tenet of Marx's political theory that the nature of the state, its institutional form, varies according to the kind of economic system or mode of production it superintends. There is a distinctively capitalist state; and, although Marx had very little to say directly about it, there is also a distinctive form of the state appropriate for the social order that will supersede capitalism, socialism – the "first phase" of communism, the final mode of production.

In *The State and Revolution,* a visionary and free-spirited text written just before the Bolshevik Revolution brought him to power, Vladimir Lenin, drawing on a number of Marx's texts, including the *Communist Manifesto,* maintained that all states are "dictatorships."[4] This claim is plainly false if "dictatorship," is understood to designate a form of government in which an individual or group of individuals rules at is own discretion, without the "checks and balances" of parliamentary or judicial institutions. But this is not what Lenin had in mind. Thus Marx described representative democracy, ostensibly dictatorship's opposite, as the characteristic form of the class dictatorship of the bourgeoisie. And Marx called the Paris Commune of 1871, a short-lived and brutally repressed experiment in direct democracy, the closest historical approximation to the dictatorship of the proletariat. The rationale for Marx's usage becomes apparent, however, when we realize that what Marx and Engels had in mind in calling states "dictatorships" was the *state* in Rousseau's sense of the term, the sense that contrasts with *government.* The state is the political entity itself, not the institutional apparatus through which it conducts its affairs. Their contention, then, was that, in the final analysis, state power rests on force; not on laws or customs, and certainly not on the will of the governed. In other words, Marx and Engels thought of state power, everywhere and in all its forms, as rule based on extra-legal and extra-consensual violence, just as dictatorial governments are. Marx's and Engels' terminology was deviant and misleading; indeed, dangerously so, in view of what would be made of "the dictatorship of the proletariat" after the Bolshevik Revolution. But the point behind this designation is standard throughout modern political philosophy. The idea that force is the foundation of the state has been the dominant view since Hobbes. Where Marx diverged from the mainstream was not in holding that states are dictatorships, but in claiming that states are *class* dictatorships; specifically, dictatorships of the economically dominant class or class coalition.

There is therefore a sense in which Marx's central theoretical claim amounts to an emendation of the interest-based, Hobbesian case for states, at least if Hobbes's argument is understood to have descriptive, not normative, force. For Hobbes, individuals in a state of nature are incapable of coordinating their behaviors in ways that accord with their interests. By doing what is individually best, they unintentionally generate radically

[4] V. I. Lenin, *The State and Revolution, Collected Works,* vol. 25 (Moscow: Progress Publishers, 1954).

sub-optimal outcomes; they improve themselves to ruin in a generalized "war of all against all." The solution to this problem is the institution of sovereignty, of a power sufficiently mighty to coordinate individuals' behaviors through the use or threat of force. Sovereignty or, what comes to the same thing, the state form of political organization therefore solves a Prisoners' Dilemma problem that exists because the payoff structure individuals confront in the state's absence is such that, by maximizing their own utility, they find themselves worse off than they might otherwise be. The state solves this problem by constraining individuals' maximizing behavior. It changes the payoff structure individuals confront, making it irrational for self-interested individuals always to do what would be individually best in a state of nature. Subjects of a sovereign must instead adjust their behaviors to accord with the sovereign's commands. They must maximize their own utility against a background of laws, coercively enforced. Hobbes thought that this constraint makes everyone (or nearly everyone) better off.

Marx took over this view of the state's role in advancing interests, but in a way that echoes Rousseau's claim, in *The Second Discourse*, that the (*de facto*) state is a trick foisted on the poor by the rich. His position follows from his contention that state power is always the power of a social class or coalition of classes. Again, it will be instructive to compare it with Hobbes's. For Hobbes, the point of departure for thinking about political institutions was the atomic individual. For Marx, the fundamental unit of society, for purposes of political theory, was social classes. In Marx's view, then, there is no general, inter-individual coordination problem for the state to solve. There is a class coordination problem. However, unlike Hobbes's atomic individuals, classes are not mired in a war of all against all. To be sure, their interests are antagonistic. But a war of all against all presupposes relative equality and, in consequence of the economic structure in place, classes are too unequal. Among the classes whose interests stand opposed, some (usually one) are powerful enough to dominate the rest. In particular, some (usually one) are in a position to take unfair advantage, to *exploit*, all the others. Strictly speaking, then, the inter-class coordination problem does not require a direct, political solution, analogous to the institution of sovereignty in Hobbes's state of nature. Class relations are coordinated by the economic structure or mode of production itself. But, for the economic structure to be in place and to reproduce itself, there is an intra-class or, more precisely, an intra-ruling class coordination problem, similar to the one Hobbes identified for subjects generally, that must be solved. Among the exploiters, individuals and coalitions of individuals have conflicting interests. But they also have a common interest, analogous to the interest in peace that individuals in a Hobbesian state of nature share. Everyone in the economically dominant class has an interest in maintaining the system of exploitation itself, for it is only in virtue of this system that they are economically dominant. The state is the means through which they succeed in having this interest realized. It is what allows the economically dominant class to overcome its own internal coordination problem, its (potential) *intra*-class "war of all against all," the better to wage "war," class war, against those it dominates economically. The state, in short, is the means by which the exploiters organize their own class dictatorship. It is, as Marx and Engels said in *The Communist Manifesto*, the "executive committee" of the entire ruling class.

Needless to say, subordinate classes also face coordination problems. These problems are exacerbated by the class dictatorship that enforces their subordination in any of a variety of ways. Marx and Engels had little to say about this phenomenon in *The Communist Manifesto* itself, except to reflect on it very generally and abstractly. But it was a perennial theme in many of the very subtle analyses of actual political events that Marx would go on to write. By the 1860s, when he helped to found the First International, a confederation of European and North American working-class political organizations, Marx had come to believe that, under capitalism, working-class political parties are indispensable for countering the state's role in decapacitating the working class, just as he believed them to be indispensable for the conquest of state power itself. But working-class parties, even revolutionary parties, can only do so much. It is only *after* the conquest of state power that the coordination problems of the working class can finally be definitively solved. More generally, it is a tenet of Marx's political theory that it is only by organizing its own "class dictatorship" that a previously subordinate class is able, finally, to act coherently in its own interest.

The dictatorship of the proletariat, then, is a state in which the working class, the proletariat, holds state power. In its original meaning, therefore, "the dictatorship of the proletariat" has nothing to do with dictatorial forms of government or one-party rule or with wholesale transgressions of human rights. Indeed, as remarked, the model for the dictatorship of the proletariat, in Marx's own thinking, was the radically democratized social order that emerged in the Paris Commune. Nevertheless, workers' power is at odds with Hegel's notion of a *Rechtstaat* and its liberal equivalents. The idea of a proletarian class dictatorship implies restrictions on the rights of former exploiters and other social strata whose interests are detrimental to workers' interests. A proletarian class dictatorship is therefore not a state form in which all persons are genuinely equal before the law. The reason why is perfectly general. If it is true that states are always class dictatorships, then genuinely equal citizenship is impossible so long as states exist. This was Marx's view in his early, Feuerbachian period too. In his early writings, however, Marx formulated this thought in a way that accorded with the philosophical preoccupations of the Young Hegelians; in other words, with positions he later abandoned. In *The Communist Manifesto* and then in his sustained reflections on actual political events, he framed his thinking in a way that is consistent with the various bodies of theory he was in the course of developing. But his contention throughout all of his work was that in class divided societies pretensions of equality are always, in the final analysis, shams. Liberal representative democracies, class dictatorships of the bourgeoisie, proclaim equality, the better to organize the domination of the many by the few. Proletarian class dictatorships are no more true to the Hegelian ideal; they are only more transparent. They proclaim inequality, to the advantage of the many and to the detriment of the few, in order to superintend the transition to a classless society in which genuine equality for all is finally achievable. Paradoxically, then, for Marx, a *Rechtstaat* is a utopian dream, an unrealizable ideal. The moment it becomes possible, it is no longer necessary. As Marx famously put it, the state that succeeds the capitalist state "withers away." It does so for want of a sufficient reason for being.

The dictatorship of the proletariat was conceived as a transitional political form, one that superintends the transition from capitalism to communism, a society without a state. It is a state that, through its educative effects as well as through its use of state power, progressively undermines the conditions that make it both necessary and possible. Beyond this very general description, however, Marx had little to say about the dictatorship of the proletariat. His accounts of it are scattered throughout his later, political writings, especially in his reflections on the failed Paris Commune. They consist largely of speculations about its institutional forms. This focus is well chosen inasmuch as different institutional forms are appropriate for different class dictatorships. But it can be misleading. Proletarian class rule does not strictly require a particular set of institutional arrangements. Thus of the measures proposed in *The Communist Manifesto*, some, like the establishment of a progressive income tax and the centralization of the means of communication and transport in the hands of the state, seem obvious or, at least, benign to contemporary readers. Others, like the abolition of private property in land and the "gradual abolition of all the distinction between town and country by a more equitable distribution of the population over the country" seem dangerously utopian. But, whatever their merits, these measures were put forth as a program for the German revolution that would erupt in 1848. Marx and Engels never thought of them as anything other than demands appropriate for their particular time and place. In other times and places, different measures might be correspondingly apt. The same is true of Marx's other, post-Commune recommendations on institutional forms.

Nevertheless, there are some general implications for state institutions when the working class controls the state. Since the proletariat has no interest in maintaining itself as a class, since its interest instead is to abolish class divisions altogether, state institutions in a proletarian class dictatorship will ideally be of such a nature as not to reproduce themselves indefinitely, in contrast with all other forms of state power. Their principle instead will be to seek to undo progressively the conditions that make them necessary. Hobbes would have considered the very idea of a state that seeks to undo the conditions for its own necessity unthinkable, and so too would the overwhelming majority of modern political philosophers whose views fall within the Hobbesian statist tradition. But Rousseau would not. To be sure, Rousseau wrote of the just state as if it were an eternal form. But it follows from his account of *de jure* political authority that state institutions are necessary only insofar as individuals remain recalcitrant to rational self-determination. There is therefore, implicitly, a Rousseauean notion of statelessness too, at least if we suppose, as Rousseau did, that recalcitrance will diminish as "opinion" is shaped by just institutional arrangements. Through its laws and through the active and direct participation of its citizens in law-making, the state educates its citizenry – to the point that it makes itself superfluous. We can therefore say what Rousseau himself never quite said: that the state of *The Social Contract*, like the dictatorship of the proletariat, would "wither away," that it would undo the conditions for its own necessity. Allowing for the very different theoretical contexts within which the ideas were contrived, it would even be fair to say that the dictatorship of the proletariat, as Marx conceived it, *is* Rousseau's just state. More precisely, the dictatorship of the proletariat is the state of *The Social Contract*, conditioned by a conviction that Marx retained from his Young Hegelian past, the idea that political institutions be understood in their historical specificity, and guided by the discovery, proclaimed at the beginning of *The Communist Manifesto*, that human history is a "history of class struggles."

In view of the many affinities joining the political theories of Rousseau and Marx, it will be well, before turning to Marx's views on history itself, to acknowledge that his account of the state – or, more precisely, of the state that oversees the transition to communism – is flawed in just the way that Rousseau's vision of the just state was. In short, both Rousseau and Marx saw humanity's possible future too clearly, underestimating the difficulties in the way of getting from here to there – from a state of nature (with or without *de facto* legitimate states) to the just state in Rousseau's case, or from capitalist civilization to communism in Marx's. Rousseau failed to appreciate the full extent of the difficulties in the way of overcoming human recalcitrance, of putting reason in control. Similarly, Marx failed to appreciate the extent to which life in class societies, especially during the capitalist era, turned humankind away from its solidary and egalitarian vocation, rendering cooperative solutions to coordination problems, internally organized ventures in general will coordination, difficult to attain. Both were therefore unduly dismissive of the kinds of protections that liberals sought to defend; both seriously underestimated the normative importance of restrictions on state power. To put this point somewhat differently, both Rousseau and Marx were concerned, very nearly to the exclusion of all else, with what had to be done in order to arrive at a destination they both thought humanly possible and normatively compelling. Both were therefore too quick to dismiss the pessimistic concern, the fear of impending tyranny, that has motivated liberalism since its inception. Both were therefore loathe to focus on the all important question of what is *not* to be done, the paramount issue for Locke, Mill and Rawls and indeed for liberals generally.

Arguably, this is a difficulty with the Rousseauan–Marxian strain of political theory that can be remedied without detriment to the core of Rousseau's and Marx's common political vision. But it is a difficulty that must be addressed somehow. If it is not, the consequences can be tragic, as the history of illiberal regimes in the twentieth century attests. Some of these horrors were committed by men and women who took themselves, in all sincerity, to be followers of Marx. But however history finally judges the official Marxisms of the twentieth century, it is plain that it would be recklessly unfair to blame the *gulag* on Marx's political theory or on Rousseau's. Still, it must be acknowledged that neither Marx nor Rousseau did nearly enough to address the concerns that the liberals have made central to their own understanding of political morality. In retrospect, it therefore seems clear that Marx's political theory calls out for liberal supplementation.

Nowadays it has become a dogma of the prevailing political culture that *any* visionary political philosophy, not just Marx's, inevitably leads to disaster. The idea that Marx's notion of what is humanly possible and historically feasible might somehow be joined to a liberal political program is therefore likely to invite skepticism. I would hazard, though, that this reaction is wrong, and also that it debilitates both political philosophy and political life. However, I will not attempt to defend this conviction here, except insofar as the ensuing discussion of Marx's theory of history speaks to the issue. In the end, the question of the plausibility of Marx's vision cannot be resolved by philosophical arguments alone. One would have to reflect too on the course of real history to speculate reasonably about whether, on balance, it is worth attempting to implement anything like what Marx thought humankind could attain and, if so, how to go about attaining it. The history of world Communism, in and out of power, from the 1917 Bolshevik Revolution through the fall of the Soviet Union in 1991, though plainly relevant, hardly provides decisive evidence, if only because the kind of Marxism to which the Communist parties of the world adhered had so little to do with the political theory of *The Communist Manifesto* or, for that matter, of *The State and Revolution*. If and when a radical politics motivated by the values that mobilized so many for so long under the banner of Marxism revives, it will be necessary, in order not to repeat the old mistakes, to subject this long and complicated history to careful scrutiny. Obviously this is a task that, in its entirety, extends beyond the range of political philosophy. It involves economic theory, historical analysis, and social science; in short, all the fields that Marx himself contributed to incisively. In this larger endeavor, though, the philosophical study of Marx's political philosophy will have a role to play. Throughout the twentieth century, Marx's political theory was perhaps the least well understood side of his thinking. Many important affinities joining Marx's positions to the liberal tradition have therefore gone unnoticed.[5] Marx himself was loathe to acknowledge these connections. He wanted to draw a line of demarcation between socialist and liberal politics. Without passing judgment on whether or not this political stance was, on balance, misguided or wise, I would venture that it partly explains the disfavor into which Marx's political thought has fallen in recent years, even in the eyes of those who not long ago saw Marxism as the repository of all truth. It may also partly explain why so many truly egregious mistakes and even crimes were committed in Marx's name.

---

[5] I elaborate on this claim in *Arguing for Socialism: Theoretical Considerations*, (London: Routledge & Kegan Paul, 1984), 2nd edn. (London: Verso, 1988), ch. 6; *The End of the State* (London: Verso, 1987); *The General Will: Rousseau, Marx, Communism* (Cambridge: Cambridge University Press, 1993), chs. 5–9; and in *Rethinking Liberal Equality: From a "Utopian" Point of View* (Ithaca, NY: Cornell University Press, 1998), chapter 5.

History

Marx's theory of history, *historical materialism,* aims to account for history's structure and direction by identifying a real causal process internal to human history, an *endogenous* process, that supplies history with a determinate trajectory or, strictly speaking, that would do so in the absence of countervailing exogenous causes. It is important to acknowledge this potential limitation on historical materialism's explanatory power. It is one thing to identify an endogenous causal process and something else to maintain that it actually explains the phenomena it would explain if nothing else were involved. For example, biologists may discover that all organisms are, so to speak, genetically programmed to die, but, within particular populations, deaths may in some or even in all cases be caused by factors other than the execution of this program. Perhaps an environmental toxin kills off all members of the population before old age and death set in, as they otherwise would. Then the fact that the organisms are programmed to die would probably explain *something.* It might explain the nature of the organisms' life stages, for example. But it would not explain why some or all of the organisms died. Similarly, there is good reason to think that Marx's theory of history explains *something* of why history has taken the course that it has; why capitalism, once introduced, has been so successful and what its possible futures may be. But Marx was probably wrong to maintain, as he claimed in the "Preface" to the 1859 *Critique of Political Economy,* that it explains actual epochal historical transformations. With respect to that explanandum, contingent and exogenous factors are very likely more important.

Historical materialism purports to identify real natural kind divisions within human history and to explain movement from one natural kind division to another. This is a very strong ambition. In chemistry, for example, the periodic table of elements provides an account of the natural kind divisions of matter. In specifying what the *elements* are, it identifies all the ways that matter can be; it provides a map of possibilities. But the periodic table is only a map. It makes no claim about movement from one element to another. Historical materialism does. Not only does it propose an account of possible modes of production or economic structures, a map describing all the ways economies can be; it also predicts movement, of an irreversible and progressive kind, from one point on the map to another. As in chemistry, however, it requires a body of theory even to conceptualize the possibilities. That there is, say, a capitalist mode of production is no more self-evident, no more a part of pre-theoretical "common sense," than the existence of oxygen was before Priestley isolated it in 1774. That "capitalism" designates a certain reality may seem unexceptionable to people nowadays. But this fact is due, in part, to the effects of Marx's theorizing on the larger intellectual culture, not to the obviousness of the concept.

However, it was widely acknowledged by the end of the eighteenth century that a "great transformation" in European, especially British, society was taking place, and that economic changes were central to the changes in progress. There was considerable disagreement, however, about how to characterize these changes and about how to account for them. Major technological transformations in manufacturing, the so-called Industrial Revolution, clearly had a great deal to do with the emerging social order, a fact not lost on contemporary thinkers. So too did changes in the organization of production, especially the increasing division of labor. We have seen how Adam Smith, in particular, thought the division of labor crucial, and how this idea of his was taken over by Marx in his youthful reflections on alienation. The idea that changes in real property relations, in control and revenue rights over productive resources, are key to understanding the great transformation then taking place was an idea that was distinctively Marx's. Of course, no new idea comes out of nowhere. There were others, before Marx, for whom property relations were of prime importance. French socialists, along with their English counterparts, those whom Marx called "utopian socialists," had already made forms of property central to their thinking about ideal social arrangements. The utopian socialists despised private property, upholding various forms of social ownership in its stead. Their indictment of private property regimes was palpable, and of a piece with Marx's fervent reproach against the emerging status quo in the 1844 *Paris Manuscripts*. Marx followed their lead. This is why, in "Three Sources and Component Parts of Marxism" (1913), Lenin identified French socialism, along with British political economy and German philosophy, as one of the roots from which Marx's thought sprang.

But even the utopian socialists did not quite grasp how *economic structures* or *modes of production* constitute distinct, historically specific, ways of organizing human societies. They named what they opposed *capitalism;* and they called what they proposed *socialism*. But, in Marx's view, they had, at best, a very inadequate understanding of these economic forms. They can hardly be blamed for this shortcoming, however. The idea of an economic structure or mode of production is unintuitive. Thus, it would be difficult to imagine someone for whom the concept of capitalism was not already available thinking, say, that fifteenth-century Italian city states and late twentieth-century Japan fall under the same theoretical designation. But this is just what Marx's theory of history implies. Marx contended that the modes of production he first identified in *The German Ideology* – feudalism, capitalism, and socialism, among others – are real, natural kind divisions of human history, and that understanding their internal functioning is indispensable for grasping the course of history itself.

An *economic structure* or *mode of production* is a set of real property relations, where "property," again, designates a bundle of control and revenue rights over productive resources. In pre-capitalist societies, there is private ownership of persons and also of things. Chattel slavery, of the sort that existed in the American South before the Civil War, is a clear example of ownership of other persons. Ownership of other persons existed too, in a less severe form, under feudalism – where lords had property rights in (some of) their serfs' labor. Under capitalism, there is private ownership of external things, but not of other persons. In communist societies, as Marx envisioned them, neither other persons nor external productive resources are privately owned – though, presumably, personal property would still exist. The abolition of private property in major external productive resources is also a distinguishing feature of any likely *socialism*, communism's "first phase."

Marx used the terms *production relations* or *social relations of production* to designate real property relations, effective control and/or revenue rights over productive assets. *Production relations* are distinguished from *productive forces* or *forces of production*. Marx used these terms to designate technology in the broadest sense, that by means of which human beings engage in productive activities. Thus means of production like tools and instruments, the organization of the production process, and also knowledge, insofar as it figures in production, are included among the productive forces. An *economic structure* or *mode of production* may then be defined as a set of production relations. The chief explanatory claim of Marx's theory of history, its first Master Thesis, is that *the level of development of productive forces* explains *the nature of the economic structure*.[6]

---

[6] What follows draws substantially on the seminal work of G. A. Cohen in *Karl Marx's Theory of History: A Defense* (Oxford and Princeton: Oxford University Press and Princeton University Press, 1978). Cohen calls the claim just stated the Primacy Thesis. In the Appendix to this chapter, I offer a brief reconstruction of Cohen's case for the Primacy Thesis, and some critical assessments of it.

Explains in this context means "*functionally* explains." Functional explanations are genuine causal explanations, unlike the teleological explanations advanced in Hegel's philosophy of history. Where X explains Y functionally, X and Y causally affect one another. There is, to be sure, an explanatory asymmetry, but, in a genuine functional explanation, X and Y do causally interact. Consider, for example, the causal connection between a furnace and the ambient temperature in a room heated by that furnace and regulated by a thermostat. Thanks to the workings of the thermostat, the ambient temperature in the room causally affects the operation of the furnace, and the operation of the furnace causally affects the ambient temperature in the room. But it is the function of the furnace to regulate the room temperature; it is not the function of the room temperature to regulate the operation of the furnace. The same relation holds in the theory of evolution by natural selection. Natural selection is an optimizing "mechanism." It purports to explain why, for example, giraffes have long necks. Within the population of giraffe ancestors, those individuals who had longer necks, thanks to random variations in neck size, did better than individuals with shorter necks. They were more successful at obtaining nourishment from leaves that grow on tall trees, and therefore had a better chance of surviving to reproductive age. Thus they produced more offspring, and so their descendants, rather than the descendants of shorter-necked giraffes, came to be prevalent in later giraffe generations. If this explanation is correct, there is a causal interaction between the long necks of giraffes and the trees whose leaves giraffes eat. But there is, again, an explanatory asymmetry. The function of giraffes' long necks is to obtain the leaves that grow on tall trees; it is not the function of the trees and their leaves to lengthen giraffes' necks.

Because the theory of evolution by natural selection is so well supported by evidence, functional explanations are well established in the biological sciences. They are more controversial in the social sciences, where they are sometimes offered with reckless abandon. For social scientists of all intellectual tendencies, including some who identify with the intellectual tradition inaugurated by Marx, it is inordinately tempting to infer from the fact that because X benefits Y that X stands in a functional relation to Y. Since it is so easy to confound benefits with genuine functional relations, it is often worth demanding of those who would proffer functional explanations, that they provide an account of the mechanism(s) through which the functional relations they purport to have discovered are achieved – in other words, that they identify what plays a role analogous to thermostats or to natural selection. Marx fell short on this account; he had very little, if anything, to say about *how* forces of production explain relations of production but not vice versa. This shortcoming does not automatically render his theory false, especially if, in each case of an epochal historical transformation, a plausible causal story can be told that explains why one mode of production succeeded another. But the absence of a developed account of the mechanisms through which there is movement along the map of historical possibilities is a concern. In this respect, historical materialism is in roughly the situation that the theory of evolution was in before Darwin discovered natural selection. Before this mechanism was understood, people could truthfully say that giraffes have long necks *because* it helps them obtain food. But they either had no idea how this functional relation was achieved or else they had a false idea; they believed, for example, that God designed giraffes' necks for this purpose.

There is a second Master Thesis of historical materialism: that *economic structures or "modes of production" explain legal and political "superstructures" and also ways of thinking or "forms of consciousness."* The idea, in other words, is that the economic structure or *base* explains non-economic phenomena. Again, the relevant sense of "explains" is *functionally explains*. The contention, then, is that the legal and political superstructure, the state and its laws, and also forms of consciousness help to *stabilize* and *reproduce* the economic "base." Thus they stand in a functional relation to the economic base. In this sense, the economic base explains superstructural phenomena. The state and its laws and also forms of consciousness are as they are because the economic base needs them to be just that way in order to sustain and reproduce itself.

G. A. Cohen has pointed out, contrary to the orthodox Marxist view and very likely to Marx's own understanding as well, that there is no compelling reason to interpret what Marx said about the relation between superstructural phenomena and the economic base in an "inclusive" way.[7] To sustain the claim that forces (functionally) explain relations of production, it is not necessary to maintain that there are economic explanations for all non-economic phenomena. That claim is not only unnecessary; it is almost certainly false. It is possible, of course, that anything can be explained by reference to its role in stabilizing and reproducing the economic base. But is it even remotely plausible, for example, that there is an economic explanation for why Kant formulated the cat-

---

[7] See G. A. Cohen, "Restricted and Inclusive Historical Materialism," reprinted in G. A. Cohen, *History, Labour and Freedom: Themes from Marx* (Oxford: Oxford University Press, 1988).

egorical imperative in five versions rather than, say, in two or seven? Is there an economic reason why September has thirty days while October has thirty-one? In all likelihood, there is not. Thus while it is possible that anything is susceptible to an economic explanation, it is plainly not the case that literally everything actually is.

Cohen's suggestion is that historical materialists need only hold that economic structures functionally explain those non-economic phenomena that have effects on social relations of production and therefore on the endogenous historical dynamic that historical materialism identifies. Cohen calls this view *restricted* historical materialism, in contrast to the *inclusive* historical materialism of orthodox Marxism and of Marx himself. For inclusive historical materialists, Marx's theory of history is comprised of two distinct claims, each asserting a functional relation – forces of production (technology, broadly conceived) functionally explain relations or production (real property relations), and then these relations (or, rather, sets of production relations) functionally explain the legal and political superstructure (the law and the state) and forms of consciousness. For restricted historical materialists, however, the two Master Theses of historical materialism are intimately joined. What counts as "superstructural" in the sense of the second Master Thesis cannot be specified independently of the first Master Thesis. Non-economic phenomena are superstructural if and only if they affect the endogenous dynamic process that moves history along. Because many aspects of political life have nothing to do with the connection between forces and relations of production, they fall outside the scope of Marx's theory of history altogether. Similarly much, indeed most, of humankind's intellectual, artistic, religious, and scientific history also falls outside historical materialism's purview. Restricted historical materialism is not a theory of everything historical. It is therefore much weaker in its explanatory pretensions than inclusive historical materialism is. But it is also much more plausible, and much less vulnerable to facile refutation. It would not challenge restricted historical materialism, as it would inclusive historical materialism, if it should turn out that, for example, the US Constitution requires a two-thirds (rather than, say, a three-fourths) majority in both houses of Congress (rather than in only one) to override a Presidential veto for reasons that are strictly political and that therefore have nothing to do with the underlying economic base, or that the doctrinal differences between, say, Presbyterians and Methodists are explicable for theological, not economic, reasons. Unless these phenomena somehow impinge on the underlying historical materialist dynamic, they have nothing to do with historical materialism's second Master Thesis, and historical materialism, accordingly, has nothing to offer in the way of explanations for them.

Even so, in conjunction with the historical materialist view of history's structure and direction, restricted historical materialism has important implications for political philosophy. Above all, it underwrites the claim that the state form of political organization is not, as Hobbes believed, an eternal human necessity. It is instead a creature of a "moment" in human history, spanning roughly the period from the emergence and consolidation of the capitalist mode of production to the dawn of the end of class divisions under communism. In its time, the state is indispensable for satisfying urgent human interests. In atomized, market societies, it is necessary for order, as Hobbes believed. With the end of capitalism, it is required for moving people along to a point where communism becomes feasible. But, if the socialist state, the dictatorship of the proletariat, does its job well, people will eventually be able to do without states altogether. As productive forces develop and as appropriate economic and political changes take place, either automatically or as a result of deliberate state policies, the need to which the state responds will pass. This is why, under communism, there will be no state at all.

Marx's Politics

On the face of it, Marx's contention that statelessness is feasible contradicts the statism endemic to modern political philosophy. But there is a sense in which it is also consistent with it. Hobbes maintained that the state is a trans-historical human necessity thanks to what he took to be ineluctable facts about human nature and the human condition. Marx agreed, in effect, with Hobbes's argument; it was Hobbes's premise that he would qualify. In Marx's view, the facts of human nature and the human condition that make states necessary are not beyond transformation. As the forces of production develop, the human condition can change to a point where the factors that make states necessary no longer obtain. Then, at the end of the trajectory historical materialism describes, the anarchists' ideal, regimes in which individuals' behaviors are coordinated in accord with their interests *but without coercion,* finally appears on the historical agenda.

Restricted historical materialism, in conjunction with the claim that economic structures rise and fall to track ever increasing levels of technological development, also explains the centrality Marx accorded class struggle in his account of the state, in contrast to the untrammeled individualism emblematic of mainstream political theory. To be sure, orthodox interpretations of Marx's view of the relation of base and superstructure claimed too much for class analysis, in part because the historical materialism of orthodox Marxism, inclusive historical materialism, implied the pertinence of class analysis to all questions bearing on political and "ideological" affairs. If, however, restricted historical materialism takes the place of its more encompassing rival, class analysis is strictly prescribed only for what affects the underlying historical materialist dynamic; otherwise, its explanatory pertinence is an open question. The degree to which restricted historical materialism deflates historical materialism's explanatory range is therefore quite extensive. But even restricted historical materialism leaves Marx committed to a very powerful claim. It implies the relevance of economic explanations for justifying theories of political institutions or, at least, for those aspects of justifying theories that pertain to institutional arrangements that stabilize or reproduce the existing economic system in the case of capitalist states, or that work to undo the conditions for their own possibility in the states of socialist societies.

In contrast, mainstream political philosophy proceeds in almost complete obliviousness to class relations and class struggles. Especially in its liberal form, it is concerned with what Marx would consider superstructural phenomena, to the exclusion of nearly everything else. Underlying (class) power relations that purportedly explain why the law and the state are as they are therefore fall outside its range of concern. This is a theoretical difference with important practical implications. It is what turns liberalism away from political orientations that would radically alter underlying class relations. It leads even the most progressive liberal thinkers, like Mill or Rawls, to address social problems by engineering away society's ills, rather than by revolutionizing society itself. The idea that changes of the kind necessary to advance what Mill called "the permanent interests of man as a progressive being" might have to be radical and comprehensive, that they might have to transform social relations of production fundamentally, is foreign to the liberal way of thinking. If Marx view was generally sound, liberalism is bereft of a satisfactory account of the forms and limits of political arrangements. It is therefore incapable of motivating a politics adequate to the task of changing life radically for the better.

The idea that the economic base must be socialist and eventually communist if human beings are to make the social world as good as it can be was one of Marx's signal contributions to political theory. So too was the idea, implicit in this larger conviction, that the agents of change must, in the end, be the bearers of new social relations, not existing elites, no matter how enlightened or benevolent they may be. This understanding is central to Marx's notion of communism, and of the politics necessary to establish and sustain it. I will conclude by focusing, very briefly, on two problematic aspects of Marx's view.

The first follows from the fact that Marx's politics is similar to Rousseau's, though, unlike Rousseau's, it is generalized beyond the political sphere and conditioned by the understanding of what is materially possible that historical materialism provides. In just the way that Rousseau's *de jure* state is feasible if and only if its citizens transform themselves to the point that they are able, as the theory prescribes, to place themselves "under the supreme direction of the general will," Marx's communism is feasible if and only if persons develop their capacities for internally coordinated self-governance to the fullest possible extent. Like Rousseau's citizens, communist men and women are the authors and directors of the institutions that affect their lives. But genuinely communal and autonomous agents of this kind do not yet exist. If they are ever to exist, they must be created. Because social engineering is inadequate to this task, would-be communists must create themselves. Individuals and groups who would make the communist ideal real must, like Rousseauean citizens, transform themselves, through their praxis, to the point that they genuinely become the communist men and women communism requires. Thus, for Marx, the movement is what matters most. As declared in the third of the *Theses on Feuerbach*, it is what "educates the educators." This process of self- and world-transformation is more important than theoretical speculations about what is materially and humanly possible. As the third *Thesis* continues, "the coincidence of the changing of circumstances and of human activity or self-changing can be conceived and rationally understood only as revolutionary practice." In other words, it is ultimately the self-activity of those who would remake society for the better that determines the content of the ideal, not the speculations of philosophers intent on "interpreting the world." Is this a defensible strategy? The idea that human beings can transform themselves radically goes against the grain of modern political philosophy. It is fundamentally non-Hobbesian. But as Rousseau's example attests, Marx's thought is not without precedent in the tradition. In any case, on this issue, appeals to authority are unavailing. The adequacy of the Rousseauean–Marxian hope for changing humankind is ultimately an empirical question that only real historical events can settle.

A more problematic claim implicit in Marx's politics has to do with *who* the agent of this self-transforming and world-transforming process is. Already in the 1843 "Introduction," Marx vested this historical mission with the (then nascent) proletariat, with those workers who are, as Marx put it, *in* civil society, but not *of it,* the direct producers of the emerging industrial order. This thought survived Marx's break with Feuerbach and came to full fruition in the development of his mature social and economic theory. But the proletariat, as Marx conceived it, no longer exists, if it ever did. In consequence of the political and social transformations of nineteenth- and twentieth-century capitalist societies, and in no small part thanks to the successes of the labor movement itself, the direct producers are no longer society's principal victims. They do not stand, in the words of the labor song "Solidarity Forever," "outcast and starving midst the wonders. . . . [they] have made." Quite the contrary. Modern liberal democracies have, to some considerable degree, succeeded in *integrating* the working class into the capitalist order. Thus, contrary to the proclamation that concludes *The Communist Manifesto,* the vast majority of direct producers have a good deal more than their chains to lose. Needless to say, many of the world's inhabitants, especially in the so-called "developing countries," live in wretched conditions. They are indeed "outcast and starving." But they do not exactly constitute a proletariat in Marx's sense, for they are not *in* civil society in the right way; they are not bearers of communist social relations. Can Marx's vision of communism survive the absence of a proletariat? This is perhaps the most serious question confronting anyone who would attempt to assess the relevance of Marx's thought today.

The jury is out on this question; out for an indefinite term. In startling contrast to what was the case only a few decades ago, Marx's work is nowadays all but ignored. Will the pendulum swing back? I think it will because the real world problems that Marx addressed, like the hopes he articulated, remain as urgent as they ever were. But the Marx who will have a role to play in the political philosophy of the future will almost certainly not be the Marx whose specter haunted twentieth century liberalism. At this point, no one can say with assurance what a revival of the intellectual and political tendency Marx epitomized will be like or what role the study of Marx's own work will play in it. I would only register the opinion that political philosophers ignore this magisterial thinker at their peril, and that they would do well, once again, to make some of his more radical ideals and aspirations their own.

Appendix: The Primacy Thesis[8]

Following Cohen's lead, let us call historical materialism's first Master Thesis, *that the level of development of the forces of production (functionally) explains the social relations of production,* the **Primacy Thesis.** Then Marx's case for the Primacy Thesis breaks down into a number of subordinate claims, from which the Primacy Thesis follows:

(A) **The Compatibility Thesis:** Given levels of *productive forces* are compatible with only certain types of *economic structures* or *modes of production;* in other words, with certain kinds of *production relations;*

(B) **The Development Thesis:** The productive forces tend to develop throughout human history;

(C) **The Contradiction Thesis:** Given the reciprocal limits that exist between forces and relations of production (Thesis A) and the tendency of the productive forces to develop (Thesis B), with sufficient time, the productive forces will develop to a point where they are no longer compatible with the relations of production under which they had previously developed;

(D) **The Capacity Thesis:** Because there is an objective human interest in transforming the relations of production in order to restore compatibility with the productive forces, the very same interest that purportedly makes Thesis B correct, the capacity for bringing that change about will eventually come into being. In particular, a social *class* will emerge with the capacity to bring about the requisite transformation;

(E) **The Transformation Thesis:** When forces and relations of production are incompatible, as they will eventually become as long as development proceeds in class divided societies, the relations will change in a way that restores compatibility between forces and relations of production. It is, in other words, the set of production relations that will change; the productive forces will not regress.

(F) **The Optimality Thesis:** When the productions relations change, they will be replaced by production relations that are functionally optimal for the use and further development of the productive forces.

---

[8] The point of reference for what follows is G. A. Cohen's reconstruction of Marx's theory in *Karl Marx's Theory of History: A Defense.* For a fuller elaboration of what follows and also of some of the preceding remarks on historical materialism, see Erik Olin Wright, Andrew Levine, Elliott Sober, *Reconstructing Marxism* (London: Verso, 1992). Terms in *italics* have been explained above, in the main body of the text.

(F) is, effectively, what the Primacy Thesis claims. The modes of production identified in *The German Ideology* are optimal sets of production relations for particular levels of development of productive forces. It should be noted, however, that Cohen's reconstruction of historical materialism acknowledges fewer modes of production or economic structures than Marx did. For Cohen, the Primacy Thesis explains the transition from "primitive communism," a classless society with only barely developed means of production, to pre-capitalist class societies, to capitalism, to post-capitalism (socialism). Thus Cohen assimilates the Asiatic mode of production, the ancient mode of production, the feudal mode of production, and all the rest into the single category of pre-capitalist class society.

The Optimality Thesis makes clear that the sense of "explains" intended in the Primacy Thesis is indeed *functionally explains*. The claim is that, at its inception, a set of production relations is optimal for furthering the development of productive forces; in other words, that at the level of development already attained, the economic structure put in place by the appropriate class agent is as good as can be for furthering future development. Then, as development proceeds under the aegis of this economic structure, structural instabilities, "contradictions," emerge. The formerly optimal set of production relations increasingly *fetters* further development. At that point, a radical transformation of production relations occurs, a *social revolution*. A new economic structure, optimal for further development, replaces the economic structure that had become a fetter.

Communism, the last economic structure, is therefore the *end* of history, but not in the Hegelian sense. It is not history's *telos*. Communism is the end of history in the sense that it is an economic structure suitable to massively developed productive forces. In contrast to class divided societies that presuppose relative scarcity, communism presupposes *abundance* – not in the (clearly impossible) sense that everyone can have everything they could possibly want without expending any effort at all, but in the sense that everyone can have all (or nearly all) of what they actually do want or, rather, of what they would want if they were truly the authors of their own desires, without expending more effort than they freely choose to spend. To the end of his life, Marx believed that people are, at root, productive animals. He was therefore confident that communist men and women will want to expend effort, even in conditions of abundance. But they will only want to produce in a "meaningful," unalienated way. Of course, there is a sense in which this is just what people in all times and places want, whether they realize it or not. But it is an impossible aspiration as long as scarcity structures human life. Under communism, because scarcity no longer obtains, unalienated labor will replace burdensome toil completely. As Marx and Engels insisted in *The Communist Manifesto*, it is the historical mission of capitalism to bring the level of development of productive forces to the point that socialism and then communism are materially possible. When that level of development is reached, the urgent human need to develop productive forces will wane. Communism will therefore not be undone by further development. This is why it is the final economic structure.

It is also the most rational economic structure; the one most in accord with genuine human interests. In this way too, something of the old Hegelian idea of the end of history is retrieved in Marx's mature theory. At the terminus of the historical materialist sequence of economic structures, the social order is at last fully rational. But it requires a long and brutal history of class struggles to arrive at that happy destination. This history is indispensable for creating capitalism and then for developing productive forces under its auspices. The price humanity must pay for a regime of uncoerced cooperation among genuinely autonomous agents is therefore very high. In maintaining that alienation is an unavoidable stage in the process of history's unfolding, in making the Rational real, Hegel articulated a similar thought through the prism of German idealist philosophy. Thus there is a sense in which Marx did place Hegel's philosophy on a sound, materialist basis, after all. He reconstructed it in terms that are unexceptionable by mainstream explanatory standards, turning a brilliant but obscure intuition into a defensible theoretical claim.

Marx was not consistently clear on the issue, but it is fair to say, even so, that, in addition to being an *inclusive* historical materialist, he was also a *strong* historical materialist. Strong historical materialism purports to provide an account of epochal historical transformations, of transitions from one economic structure or mode or production to another. For a strong historical materialist, it is contradictions between forces and relations of production that explain epochal change. But because Marx advanced a variety of distinct, though overlapping, theoretical positions, the strong historical materialist explanation is not the only account of transitions from one economic structure to another that can legitimately be called "Marxist." Even in his own historical writings, Marx was more inclined to focus directly on class relations and class struggles than on underlying structural contradictions between forces and relations of production. It is therefore possible to concoct a "Marxist" explanation for, say, the emergence of capitalism that has more to do with the peculiarities of the class struggle in early modern Europe than with the fettering of productive forces. This possibility suggests that the Primacy Thesis's explanatory force may be more limited than first appears.

As remarked, it might turn out that the Primacy Thesis is true in the sense that the endogenous developmental process it identifies is real, but that it does not explain actual historical transformations because exogenous factors typically intervene. Then the historical materialist account of epochal change *would* hold in the absence of countervailing causes but, as a matter of fact, countervailing causes always do swamp the historical materialist dynamic. This is one way that the Primacy Thesis might not, in fact, explain epochal historical transformations. There is, however, another, more significant sense in which it might fail to do all that Marx thought it did. Thus one might hold that all the Primacy Thesis does is provide an account of what is *materially possible* in the way of epochal historical change, of what is on the historical agenda. Such a theory might be called *weak* historical materialism. Weak historical materialism, like strong historical materialism, maintains that economic structures, sets of production relations, track increasing levels of development of productive forces. It therefore demonstrates what economic structures are compatible with given levels of technological development. Arguably too, in consequence of the Development and Transformation Theses, it shows that regression along the historical materialist trajectory is impossible; that, barring an exogenous catastrophe that sets the course of human civilization on a retrograde track, movement from one to another economic structure can only be in one direction. Beyond this, however, it makes no further claim. Thus weak historical materialism provides an account (a) of necessary (material) conditions for epochal historical transformations; (b) of the direction of change; and (c) of the means through which change is achieved (social revolutions organized by sufficiently capacitated social classes). It does not provide an account (d) of *sufficient* conditions for change. Therefore weak historical materialism does not predict what *would* happen in the absence of other factors. It only shows what *could* happen. Strong historical materialism, on the other hand, provides an account of (a), (b), (c) *and* (d). Typically too, strong historical materialists *also* maintain that these sufficient conditions actually do explain the emergence of new economic structures; that exogenous factors did not, in fact, swamp the endogenous historical materialist dynamic.

Weak historical materialism turns Marx's theory of history from an organism development theory, an account of history's necessary stages, into a theory of possible historical trajectories. It does so by denying that the Capacity Thesis is generally true. This seems right. Why, after all, should class agents capable of effecting epochal historical changes appear whenever and wherever they are needed? But if agents capable of transforming relations of production are not always forthcoming, production relations that are optimal for further development may not be established. The road map of historical development can then have forks and detours; junctures in which more than one option is materially possible and in which outcomes that are suboptimal with respect to "unfettering" can result.

For a strong historical materialist, on the other hand, there is a fixed trajectory that history must run through. For a strong historical materialist, even creatures quite different from human beings, inhabitants, say, of distant planets, would pass through the same succession of economic structures – provided only that these beings are rational in the Hobbesian sense (capable of adopting means to ends), that they live in conditions of relative scarcity, and that overcoming scarcity is a compelling interest of theirs. For a weak historical materialist, on the other hand, capitalism could have failed to emerge even on earth. Thus weak historical materialism resembles current views about the origin of life, of self-replicating organisms. Life *could* emerge wherever the material – presumably, chemical – conditions for it exist. But the actual emergence of life may require something in addition; perhaps an unlikely configuration of geo-thermal events. Then life could have never developed, even though all the material conditions for it were in place. On a weak historical materialist view, much the same is true of capitalism. A weak historical materialist could hold that capitalism emerged when and where it did thanks to an historically contingent concatenation of geographical, economic, and political circumstances – perhaps including the particular pattern of town–countryside relations in Western Europe, the infusion of gold and silver from the New World, the demise of some political regimes, the rise of others, and so on. These conditions might never have appeared. Thus capitalism might never have developed. Even Marx seems to have countenanced this possibility in some of his scattered remarks on the so-called Asiatic mode of production. It was his view that capitalism could not emerge endogenously, say, in China, not even in thousands of years, despite the fact that for very many years and certainly at the time of capitalism's emergence in Europe, productive forces in China were more technologically developed and more "fettered" than anywhere else on earth. The problem was that political and social circumstances blocked the emergence of a class agent capable of transforming the prevailing mode of production. In contrast to Europe, China therefore faced a prospect of indefinite economic stagnation.

Another similarity with current thinking about the origin of life also suggests itself. It is probable that once living organisms do emerge, they will never do so again, not only because sufficient conditions for life have a low probability of occurring, but also because living beings systematically devour the conditions necessary for life to develop. Thus all living things will be descendants of the first living organism(s). Similarly, once capitalism appears once, it is likely that it will never do so again, at least not in territories that are in contact with capitalist societies. For capitalism also devours. It imposes itself aggressively on pre-capitalist societies, typically inserting them into a subordinate role in a world capitalist system. Or else, less frequently, it inspires imitation, as in Japan during the Meiji Restoration, where the ruling class deliberately established capitalist social relations. At most, then, strong historical materialism only explains the emergence of capitalism once. Weak historical materialism explains even less. It only explains how and when capitalism is materially possible, and how and when it can be surpassed.

But, for all its diminished explanatory force, weak historical materialism, like restricted historical materialism with which it is easily joined, is still a powerful and highly plausible theory. I would therefore submit that Marx ought to have been a weak, restricted historical materialist; not a strong, inclusive historical materialist. Marx *overstated* what is, at root, a sound theoretical insight: that, in the end, human beings' collective productive capacities establish the nature and limits of their political and social institutions which affect, in turn, their collective lives generally – to some important degree, though not entirely as Marx and most Marxists after him believed. Political philosophers would do well to take this contention to heart and to examine its implications with care.

Conclusion

It is an article of faith, for Marxists, that, under communism, "the governance of men" will give way to "the administration of things"; in other words, that not only the state but politics itself will "wither away" as systemic conflicts of interest wane, leaving only technical, administrative problems in their stead. An observer of life on earth at the dawn of the new millennium might conclude that, ironically, at least part of this prophecy has already been fulfilled, contrary to all expectations, under the aegis of the capitalist "mode of production." The state survives, of course; but political life does seem to be withering away. Not since modern political philosophy began in the seventeenth century has there been a time in which political contestation has been so attenuated. Elites throughout the world, but especially in the established liberal democracies, declare that there is no alternative to the globalized, neo-liberal economic regime that is extending its grasp over the entire planet, and that there is no better form of political organization than liberal democracy, especially its American version. In terms reminiscent of headier times, it has even been proclaimed that, with "the new world order" that has succeeded the Cold War, humanity has reached "the end of history."[1] Some counter-indications are beginning to appear; the emerging global system of finance and trade encounters increasing resistance. But in much the way that, according to Rousseau, "the true founder of civil society" was the individual who marked off a plot of land, said "this is mine," and found others "foolish enough to believe him," most people nowadays are foolish enough to believe elite opinion. Thus it has become part of the politi-

[1] Francis Fukuyama, *The End of History and the Last Man* (New York: Free Press, 1992).

cal common sense of our time that, wherever liberal democratic institutions are in place, there is no political task left but to administer the existing regime.

A diminished political life is deadly for political philosophy. Each of the authors treated here was an advocate of a political ideal, formed in robust competition with alternative visions. With politics in decline, there is nothing left but to refine old ideals, or at least the one old ideal left standing. This is, in fact, what has happened. The best political philosophy today aims at getting liberalism right. Rawls's "political liberalism" is a case in point. We have seen how, substantively, *Political Liberalism* is of a piece with *A Theory of Justice*, Rawls's work of a quarter century ago. But as Rawls's focus has turned away from the theory of justice to the problem of political legitimacy, it has emerged that the goal of Rawlsian liberalism, as it has evolved over the years, is to take ideas implicit in American constitutional jurisprudence and develop them into a general political theory. Because actually existing liberal democracy falls so far short of its promise, this objective motivates a powerful reforming project. But, even in comparison with the more contentious, social democratic or New Deal–Great Society thrust of *A Theory of Justice*, *Political Liberalism* hardly represents the kind of bold political intervention that propelled modern political philosophy along since its inception. Perhaps it is unfair to fault it on this account; after all, its claim just is that the American model or some close facsimile is the right ideal. But even those who are persuaded of this by Rawls might still wonder where political philosophy might go after the theory of the regime in place is made true to its own best principles? The palpable exhaustion of real world political life and its inevitable consequence, a corresponding depletion of political ideas, makes this seem a rhetorical question.

There is reason to think, though, that the desultory state of affairs through which we are now passing is only temporary, an unhappy consequence of a confluence of circumstances including, above all, the collapse of Communism and the end of the Cold War. Now there is no alternative to the regime in place; not even a deeply flawed one. In some respects, these signal events have made life better for the world's peoples. If nothing else, our planet is now a safer place than it once was, and liberal freedoms are now more universally distributed than they formerly were. But these changes in the political landscape have also turned out to have their down side. They have exacerbated the sense of hopelessness and passivity that has become the hallmark of political life at the beginning of the twenty-first century.

We should not forget, though, that modern political philosophy arose and developed in part thanks to changing real world social and political circumstances, and that transformations in these domains continue apace as productive capacities expand and the world economic system evolves. These changes cannot help but register, eventually, in the larger political culture, and therefore ultimately in political philosophy too. I suggested at the outset that the great transformations that motivated Hobbes, Locke, and Rousseau and that continue to give modern political philosophy its shape consisted, mainly, in the rise of the nation state and the atomization of social life. Paradoxically, the very processes that have brought real world politics and its philosophical representations to a virtual standstill are transforming these conditions. In an increasingly global economic order dominated by a single superpower, the nation state form of political organization is sure to become increasingly undone; a process that is already underway, albeit more slowly than is sometimes claimed. Already this changed fact on the ground has had some resonance in political philosophy – for example, in Rawls's latest work, where the venerable and distinctively modern notion of sovereignty has given way, ever so slightly, to a "law of peoples." The increasing interdependence of the world's peoples is bound too, eventually, to create new social solidarities, challenging the pervasive individualism that has shaped political thinking for so long. Thus it is fair to say that the political philosophy of the past, including the recent past, cannot, as is, serve for an indefinite future. Increasingly, conceptual puzzlements as vexing as those that gave rise to modern political philosophy centuries ago are sure to arise, and to call for a fresh philosophical response.

This is not to say that modern political philosophy, as we know it, is about to expire or to turn into something else altogether. Its master thinkers were philosophers of such profundity and insight that aspects of their work are bound to remain timely, despite their historical particularities and limitations. Their political philosophies are replete with resources upon which to build. It is fair to speculate then, that the political philosophy of the future will not so much break away from its past as evolve out of it, in response to new puzzlements and unanticipated theoretical and practical exigencies. I have suggested that some old ideas, including some that have fallen into desuetude, like Marx's notion of communism, may find a new prominence as the forces of production expand, creating new opportunities for freer and more communal forms of social organization. I have also suggested that ideas that now seem timely, like those pro-capitalist notions of Lockean provenance that appear to capture the course of emerging social, political and economic trends, may fade. But, in truth, no one can say what the political philosophy of the future will be like. I would only suggest that, in retrospect, the present era, with its increasingly urgent and unresolved ecological, social, and economic problems will seem more like a turning-point in an ever-unfolding historical drama than the beginning of the end of human history. If so, political philosophy has a lively future ahead, and the ideas of the philosophers whose work has been recounted here will play an important, if unpredictable, role in determining its shape and form.

Still, there are concerns that they do not address or that they address inadequately that can no longer be set aside; environmental problems, for example, or the issues that arise in contemporary work on feminist and multicultural themes. The reason for their silence on these topics is plain: all of them, Rawls partly excepted, lived before events and political movements brought these issues to the fore, at least in their current form. Before the 1970s, there was hardly any environmental movement at all. The massive entry of women into the paid labor force is also a recent phenomenon, as is the not unrelated emergence of contemporary feminism. So too is the increasing mobility of the world's population, brought on by increasingly unequal levels of economic development, and improved means of transport and communication. The end of the colonial system and the disintegration of the old multinational empires, including, most recently, the Soviet Union have also fueled multicultural concerns. These far-reaching changes in political life have already begun to register in political philosophy. They will surely figure prominently in the political philosophy that will emerge in the decades to come.

But, then, it is all the more crucial to retain the advances registered in the work of our six authors. This is not always the case today. In some contemporary, academic discussions, feminist and multicultural claims especially are represented in terms of a "politics of difference," in which imputed or chosen "identities" are accorded preeminence over universal human values. Each of the authors discussed here would cavil at this approach – even Rawls, whose political liberalism could be misconstrued as a species of relativism, akin to the relativisms that underlie some contemporary theories of "difference." They would be right to resist the fashion. Philosophers sympathetic to identity politics have done a service in conveying the news that the tradition has neglected some increasingly important social and political transformations. But the point has been made, even if it may be necessary to repeat it for an indefinite future. No doubt, much will change in consequence. In the end, though, it seems unlikely that anything fundamental will have to give way. Our authors' political philosophies are hardly closed systems inhospitable to new perspectives and insights. Quite the contrary, they provide the best tools available for making sense of what is genuinely important and new in political life. Thus I would venture that the messengers are wrong, at least when they press their case by claiming that the tradition is beyond repair – wedded, as it is, to notions of truth, objectivity, and universality that are now somehow superseded. In fact, it is because of these commitments that the tradition is sound. It is the proponents of relativism and difference who have taken an unpardonable detour.

The idea that political life can be made sense of in ways that accord with the norms of rationality emblematic of the modern period is one of the principal legacies of modern political philosophy; so too is a sense of the essential unity of the human race. It is important that these understandings be retained, even as the range of issues that engage political philosophers expands. As we have seen, political philosophy tracks political life. But it is also a generally progressive enterprise. It advances understanding. I would hazard that, for now and for an indefinite future, its way forward is on the shoulders of the giants of its past.

Index